AF424653

IDENTITY ALCHEMY

Turning Pain Into Gold

Rocío Pérez, IMBA & Dr. David Wheeler

Identity Alchemy: Turning Pain Into Gold

For permissions, please contact the publisher:
Rocío Pérez
Founder & CEO
Victor Publishing, LLC
info@victorpublishing.net
+1 (303) 587-8367

First Edition
ISBN: 979-8-9940736-0-5

Created, Developed, and Edited by the Authors
Cover Design by Maite Sanjurjo, Founder, TopMind
Layout by Dr. David Wheeler

Disclaimer

This book is intended for informational purposes only and does not constitute legal, medical, or psychological advice. The content is based on the authors' personal experiences, research, and opinions. Both authors are curious coaches and neither author is a licensed psychologist. Readers are encouraged to consult appropriate professionals for guidance tailored to their specific circumstances.

The strategies and information shared in this book are general in nature and vary in suitability for different individuals. While every effort has been made to ensure the accuracy and reliability of the information presented, the authors disclaim all liability or responsibility for errors, omissions, or any adverse effects, damages, or consequences resulting from the application of this information.

The events and details shared in this book are portrayed to the best of Pérez's memory. Some names and identifying details have been changed to protect the privacy of individuals involved.

This book contains discussions of trauma, abuse, and other sensitive topics that may be triggering for some readers. Reader discretion is advised.

The authors assume no responsibility for any outcomes resulting from the reader's choice to engage with this book. As the reader, you acknowledge that you assume any risks associated with engaging with this book.

Mention of any specific product, service, or organization in this book is independent of any endorsement or recommendation by the authors.

Contents

ABOUT THE AUTHORS

MY HEALING JOURNEY

MY CLIENTS' JOURNEYS

IN CLOSING

Endorsements

"This work belongs in the hands of every clinician, educator, parent, and leader who wants to understand how true healing happens— from the inside out."

— Dr. Arlen Meyers, President and CEO
Society of Physician Entrepreneurs

"More than just storytelling, Rocío Pérez and Dr. David Wheeler offer readers a transformative roadmap for turning life's most challenging moments into opportunities for growth and hope."

— Liz Elting, Billion-Dollar Company Co-Founder, WSJ Bestselling
Author, CEO, Philanthropist, Elizabeth Elting Foundation

"There are timely and practical resources for therapists to reclaim their inner strength, enabling them to help accelerate the healing process of their clients."

— Dr. Ardeshir Mehran, Human Work Studio

"If you're ready to examine emotional wounds that might be blocking your success and do the real work of transformation, this book will meet you there."

— Dr. Rebecca Corbin, President & CEO, NACCE

"This book is a beacon for anyone ready to rise from the ashes of their past. It reminds us that no story is too broken to be rewritten, and every life holds the power to shine with strength, clarity, and meaning."

— Scott Bemis, Retired Denver Business Journal Publisher
and Founder & CEO, Bemis Business Partners

"Her story is more than a personal memoir; it is a mirror for survivors and a resource for those who support them. She reminds us that healing is as much about the body as it is about the mind, and that recovery opens the door to new interactions, supportive communities, and authentic love."

— Gayatree Dipchan, Trauma Expert

"There is no quick fix when we do inner work, but Pérez and Wheeler provide a way that we can not only free ourselves, but also empower our wider community."

— Paul Rosenthal, Former Special Education
Teacher and Colorado State Legislator

"Reading Identity Alchemy felt like sitting across from a friend, listening as they shared their journey through fire and their return, shimmering with truth. This is so much more than raw storytelling; it's an invitation into the depths of Rocío's journey with a beautiful blend of honesty, tenderness, and fierce courage. Rocío's words remind us that the treasure is already inside us—this book simply helps us find it."

— Celia Herrera, Founder of URBN Brands

"Every trial is a refining flame, every setback a step toward brilliance. Her words give us courage to endure and the vision to emerge luminous."

— David Favela, The Latino StartUp

"Understanding how your body reacts to trauma is something new to me and I have seen emotional benefits to physical healing and now with this book, I believe I have found another way to understand what my body and mind has been through and how to continue to live fully and happily."

— Eduardo Rivera, Fire Captain/Paramedic (Retired)

"There are parts of life most of us would delete if we could. Rocío flips that on its head. Identity Alchemy shows how even the hardest stories can give us strength, and her lived wisdom proves we are built for more than just surviving."

— Camille Garick, Executive Director, expandi TV

"This isn't just a read; it's an invitation to heal, to rise, and to reclaim the masterpiece within yourself."

— Dr. Jamal Bowen, President & Founder |
Empowering Community Entrepreneurs

"Their words echo what I've witnessed in others and experienced myself: that the journey through pain, when held with care and intention, can reveal profound strength and beauty."

— Myrtle Gallow, Creator of the Finish Line Workshop

"This deeply personal narrative intertwined with perspective and actionable next steps is a must for anyone who wants to bring 100% of their best self forward but may not have an immediate how to just yet."

— Senofer Mendoza, Mendoza Ventures

"It's not just about overcoming, it's about rewiring identity at the root, with intention, courage, and tools that actually work. This is a guide for those serious about rewriting their story from a place of strength."

— David Abel, Strategic Brand Architect

"How refreshing it is to imagine a community where this book is being read widely in religious study groups, and spiritual book clubs of all denominations. How self-empowering it would be for persons who might not ever consider making a professional appointment now being engaged in congregational groupings."

— The Reverend Judith Hokhmah, Universal Foundation for
Better Living, Transcendent Spiritual Life Coach, Lecturer

"This book is not only a testament to resilience but also a vital tool for leaders, educators, and advocates committed to true healing."

— Ashley Chesney, Executive Director, Set Free Monterey Bay

"This powerful work equips leaders with the insight and courage to become trauma-informed, fostering trust, empathy, and lasting transformation."

— José L. Montalván, a Marine Corps officer with a 30-year
`military career that includes combat and deployments

"I hope you see this book as an opportunity to be honest with yourself, to continue along your path of healing, and, above all, to learn to care for the most important person in your life: you."

— Shantal Sevilla, Customer Development Leader, Hershey Mexico

"When veterans reclaim their strength, wisdom, and wholeness, they don't just change their own lives; they uplift families, communities, and entire generations."

— Raul "Danny" Vargas, Founder/Chairman/CEO
American Latino Veterans Association

"Identity Alchemy offers a roadmap to guide us on our way home. A path forward as we walk each other home. And home is actually that inner place of security, self-love, acceptance and a sanctuary."

— Kim LeClaire, Creating, Collaborating, Connecting
Impassioned Educator

"I wholly understand the importance of Pérez and Wheeler's first step—acknowledge that the ugliness of the past is a reality, and we all get to choose the future we want to pursue."

— William "Wild Bill" Vaughan, Retired Marine
Infantry Officer, Recovery Chaplain, and Director
of Recovery, Sanctuary Farm & Rest House

"If you've been searching for a way forward, this is it. Read this book. Do the work. Reclaim your life. You deserve healing. You deserve wholeness. You deserve to live fully."

— Nancy Rosado Santiago, HLX+ We are
many We are one | Founder, CEO

"Identity Alchemy should be required reading for leaders, educators, healthcare professionals, social workers, and anyone committed to guiding others through adversity—or breaking free from trauma themselves. Knowledge is power, and Identity Alchemy equips readers with the insights and tools needed to confront these realities, transform dysfunction, and foster resilience."

— Gil Juarez, Manager & Coach

"Reading Identity Alchemy is like hearing her voice speak directly to the truth inside you, with a strength that is both fierce and deeply healing. This is what the world needs right now: solutions!"

— Clem Harding, Aka Coach Clem, Coach of the Year 25/26
Yorkshire Prestige Awards, England

"What makes Identity Alchemy truly invaluable is its focus on integrative mind-body healing. It treats trauma itself as the missing link in conditions often dismissed as merely physical."

— Alessandro Tavares, M.D., Pediatric Urologist

Who This Book Is Not For

It is by going down into the abyss that we recover the treasures of life.

— Joseph Campbell

This book is not for everyone. We say that with love and also with honesty.

If you're looking for a quick fix, a magic pill, or a feel-good slogan to slap over your pain, then put this book down right now. Seriously—don't waste your time. This isn't a book you flip through while scrolling social media, hoping for a momentary high.

Because the truth? This work is real. It's raw. It's for the ones who are ready to get their hands dirty with their own life.

If you want someone else to save you, this book isn't for you.

This book isn't for those who are more committed to their past than to their dreams.

If you're waiting for the perfect moment, the perfect conditions, or the perfect person to show up and do the work for you, you won't find that here.

It's not for the ones who want to talk about change and aren't willing to feel the sting of growth, the discomfort of honesty, or the discipline it takes to rewrite your own story.

Because here's the thing: this book asks something of you.

It asks you to look at your life—really look. To face the parts you've been avoiding, to feel the emotions you've been numbing, and to take responsibility, even when it's easier to blame.

It asks you to show up again and again, even when it's messy, even when it's inconvenient, even when you don't feel like it, and even when no one is watching.

So, if you're not ready to invest your time, your energy, your heart into something bigger than a temporary distraction—this isn't for you.

If you're not ready to do the inner work, set this book aside for now. You will know when the time is right.

When that time comes, you'll be ready to get curious about:
- The emotional charge that keeps you stuck.
- The patterns you repeat without seeing the triggers.
- How your unhealed wounds unintentionally impact those around you.

You'll also be ready to face the fear of what happened in those missing memories. And when you do, the right people, opportunities, and breakthroughs will appear.

That is when you can commit to the process, trust the journey, and find the courage to be both shocked and enlightened by what you discover.

And… if you are ready now…

If you're tired of living half-alive.

If you're ready to step into the kind of life that pulls you awake every morning, the kind of life that feels like freedom, like purpose, like coming home to yourself…

Then this book is for you.

This is for the ones who are willing to do the work—not perfectly, not instantly, but consistently.

This is for the ones who want to thrive.

This is for the ones who are ready to live—really live—and are brave enough to believe that their best life is worth fighting for.

Foreword

By Dr. Rebecca Corbin, President & CEO, NACCE

We all face seasons in life when we feel profoundly disconnected from others, from our sense of purpose, and sometimes even from ourselves. These moments can creep in quietly or they can erupt suddenly, shattering relationships, trust, and the very foundation we thought was solid. Often, it is trauma, both the visible and the hidden, that pulls us into this place of feeling lost, isolated, and disempowered.

In my own life, I've experienced the heartbreak of fractured relationships and the longing to repair them. There were times when I wanted to bridge the gaps and heal the hurt. I found myself without the tools or language to do so. My desire to connect and move forward was deep and sincere. Like so many of us, I carried unhealed parts of myself that stood in the way.

Through these experiences, I learned that true transformation begins on the inside. Until we face and tend to our inner wounds, even our best intentions can falter. Healing isn't about simply "fixing" what is broken; it's about uncovering the parts of ourselves that have been hidden, neglected, or silenced and bringing them into the light with compassion and courage.

That is why *Identity Alchemy* speaks to me so deeply. This book is not about quick fixes or surface-level changes. It is a courageous invitation to embark on the inner journey required for lasting transformation. Rocío Pérez and Dr. David Wheeler take you on this inner journey, encouraging you to face your shadows, embrace your whole self, and reclaim the power and purpose that have always been yours.

Unhealed wounds derail people even though they may be gifted, ambitious, and resourceful. Their achievements may feel fragile, slipping away even though they seem secure. This leaves them bewildered, discouraged, and trapped in a loop they can't seem to escape. In my role as President and CEO of the National Association for

Community College Entrepreneurship (NACCE), I have the privilege of witnessing people transforming their unhealed experiences every day. Across our nation's community colleges, I see students, educators, entrepreneurs, and leaders striving to rise above their challenges and create brighter futures for themselves and for the communities they serve. The principles in this book mirror that same journey: moving from disconnection to connection, from surviving to thriving, from pain to purpose.

Carl Jung wrote about the importance of acknowledging the "shadow," those hidden aspects of ourselves we often deny or avoid. By courageously confronting our shadow, we begin to integrate all parts of who we are. At the same time, we must nurture the child within us, the part of us that longs to be loved, seen, and accepted. Together, this inner work becomes the foundation for living our most authentic and joyful lives.

As a co-author of two books on educational entrepreneurship, I understand how challenging it is to frame ideas into compelling invitations for action. Rocío and David have done so with clarity, grace, and profound wisdom. My hope is that as you read *Identity Alchemy*, you will feel supported in doing the deep work of self-discovery and healing. May these pages inspire you to connect with your shadow, uncover the life experiences that made you who you are, embrace your inner child, and rise into the fullness of who you were always meant to be.

When we do this work for ourselves, it creates ripples of transformation that extend far beyond us to the greater good. This is the kind of change our world needs now more than ever.

With love,

Rebecca Corbin, Ed.D.
President & CEO, NACCE

A Letter to David from Rocío

Dear David,

As I sit here, tracing our journey, words feel impossibly small to capture what you've meant to this work—to me. Others have turned away from the emotional violence of my experiences. You leaned in. You witnessed. You held space.

Our story began unexpectedly—across continents, through a computer screen during an online seminar that would change everything. What started as a simple accountability partnership transformed into something profound. *The MindShift Experience©* was born from lived experiences, not textbooks. It was forged in survival's fire, refined through more than 60,000 souls who dared to believe transformation was possible. You saw its heartbeat before I understood its pulse.

At the start of the year, I was elated. I believed my memoir was written exactly as I wanted. I invited you to edit, expecting a few technical refinements. Instead, we embarked on a one-year odyssey of excavation and revelation. What began as "Can you help me edit this?" became a sacred dive into the psychological impact of my wounding childhood experiences, unearthing truths that were ready to be heard and pain that was ready to heal. Your care allowed me to embark on a journey of self-discovery and profound healing.

You cried with me. Laughed with me. Held space for Little Rocío's pain. You invited me to see what I did not see, staying present when memories overwhelmed me, when my voice cracked, and when tears flowed uncontrollably.

Your expertise was alchemical. You transformed fragments of pain into a powerful narrative. You created a container so sacred that healing became inevitable. You heard my words—you felt their reverberations, understanding that healing is a spiral of remembering, releasing, and becoming.

From the book's title to its visual design, your creative vision and professional knowledge captured the essence of the book. It's a roadmap. A compass. A lighthouse for those navigating the complex terrain of healing.

I carried my story in silence for decades. Fragmented. And then you came along and showed me how to weave those fragments into a tapestry of resilience. Through your compassion and expertise, you showed me what was possible—my true authentic freedom. I am now me.

These pages pulse with a life force that is both mine and something greater. Your fingerprints are everywhere as a fellow traveler who understood transformation's terrain.

Thank you for being a guardian of this story's sacred transmission.

With love,

Rocío

A Letter to Rocío from David

Dear Rocío,

It is truly an honor to know you. The journey we've taken together has been amazingly extraordinary.

I met you at the beginning of the pandemic during a personal growth and development seminar. I knew you as a successful businesswoman and coach and you knew me as a professor of psychology at Robert Morris University. We started having weekly calls during the seminar. What began as simple discussions, soon blossomed into rich conversations about human behavior and cognition. Each week, we would share our experiences—always finding something fun and meaningful to explore together.

You came to me with your memoir, looking for some final edits. We dove in together, excavating the details of your life with curiosity and care.

Throughout the process, I kept asking myself, "Were the stories you had written vivid enough to create a movie in my mind?" If they were not, I'd ask you questions: What happened here? What do you mean by this? How did you get here? There's a block of time missing—what's the story there? Sometimes, a single written word, when examined, would expand to three new stories.

My role from the beginning has been to keep your words as authentic and true to your voice as possible. At first, that meant helping to rearrange what you had written to create a clearer emotional arc. As time went on, it became something deeper—a true collaboration, where my primary job was to create a safe space for you to share your truth.

I started noticing a pattern. You would begin telling me the story behind what you had written. I'd stop you and say, "Write it down." That became our mantra. Rather than letting powerful insights vanish into the ether, you would go off and write a multitude of pages, capturing the full story in your own words.

You have shown incredible bravery throughout this journey. There were days when the memories were overwhelming, and tears would come as you wrote. We were doing all of this over Zoom, and sometimes the emotional weight of what we were uncovering was too much for both of us—we'd each lie down on our respective sides of the screen and breathe. There are parts of your story that bring tears to my eyes every time I read them.

In addition to the amazing resilience you showed growing up in a horrific environment, I honor you for using that pain to build something powerful. You have turned your experiences into the gold of transformation, both for yourself and for the many people you have helped through your coaching and *The MindShift Experience©*.

When we began this journey back in January, we had no idea where it would lead. I remember during our first working session, you believed you had already gone through the healing process. I gently told you that you might have more to go.

Writing this memoir required you to look deeply and honestly at the details of what happened to you. Someone once asked me if examining the details erases the story. My answer? No. It doesn't erase the story— details dissolve the denial. And it's in that space, where denial is no longer standing in the way, that healing begins.

Thank you so much for inviting me to take this journey through the dissolution of denial with you. The transformation in you is absolutely astounding! I am excited to continue working with you and others on your memoirs.

With love,

David

Message to the Reader

Dear Reader,

Welcome to *Identity Alchemy*. This book is a testament to resilience, empowerment, and our profound ability to heal and live fulfilling lives. Whether you seek personal healing, support others in their healing journey, or want to understand the psychological impact of wounding childhood experiences, these pages are here to serve you.

For Rocío, writing *Identity Alchemy* has been one of the most transformative experiences of her life—decades in the making—filled with deep pain and profound healing. Along the way, she cried many tears and worked with various professionals to bring this book to life. The process invited her to confront difficult truths, revisit painful memories, and explore the darkest corners of her past. In the midst of this darkness, a quiet, persistent light remained within her. That light guided her, providing resilience in the face of despair and purpose despite pain. She came to understand that healing resides in turning pain into power, hardship into wisdom, and silence into a voice.

For Those Who Have Lived This Truth

For anyone who has felt trapped, caught in cycles they can't seem to break, struggling with self-doubt, emotional overwhelm, or relationship difficulties, this book is for you. Your pain was real. Your truth has always mattered. You were enough. Deserving of love, protection, and belief. Worthy of being seen, heard, and cherished. Healing is a deeply personal journey, requiring a unique, individualized approach. The journey is yours to take. You have the power to create your path toward healing and the process demands dedication, patience, and self-compassion. Your resilience runs deeper than your wounds, your potential is greater than your past. The very experiences that have challenged you are preparing you for your greatest victories. Your journey toward freedom begins the moment you recognize that cycles can be broken, patterns can be transformed, and struggles are shaping you into the powerful, authentic person you always were. Every step you take brings you closer to reconnecting to your authentic self. Support is available to you. You are worthy of living a fulfilling life.

For Those Who Support Others

Your belief matters. Your willingness to listen without judgment creates sacred space for healing. Your presence shows them that their journey toward wholeness is witnessed and honored. The extraordinary support you provide might take a toll on you. Take care of yourself, too. Your well-being provides the foundation for the healing to take place. Together, we can create a world where every person knows their inherent worth and is committed to healing.

For Those Seeking to Understand

Pay attention to what is being said. The people who lived these experiences have created profound resilience within themselves. They developed tools to endure the unendurable, to understand the unfathomable, and they emerged with wisdom that can light the path for others. Understanding this reality helps us recognize the courage it takes to heal, the strength required to transform pain into purpose, and the wealth of tools that can be used regardless of the environment they now find themselves in.

In addition to that, the healing process generates new neural pathways which expand their mental capacity to problem-solve and bring unique solutions to challenges of work and life. This synergy of resilience skills and expanded problem-solving skills is the undeniable gold of the healing process the world desperately needs.

Within these pages, you will find reflection exercises to help transcend the psychological impact of wounding childhood experiences, break free from cycles of pain, and reclaim a sense of self. You will discover strategies for reparenting, self-coaching, and cultivating resilience, along with practical steps to build a life filled with meaning and connection.

As you read, we invite you to reflect, explore your path, and grow. Thank you for allowing us to share the journey with you. Our deepest hope is that *Identity Alchemy* helps you discover the light within yourself and provides tools to thrive.

Thank you,

Rocío Pérez, IMBA & Dr. David Wheeler
The Identity Alchemists

Message to Mental Health Professionals

Dear Therapists,

We wrote *Identity Alchemy* with the heartfelt intention of making a meaningful difference in the lives of those navigating the complexities of complex childhood trauma.

Drawing from our own journey and decades of experience in education, personal growth, support work, and coaching people through life transformation and leadership development, we sought to create a resource that empowers individuals to overcome obstacles—both real and perceived—and build a fulfilling life on their own terms.

This book is a compilation of strategies, insights, and practical tools that have helped individuals move beyond trauma, providing an innovative approach to healing. We believe that by equipping readers with resources, they can embark on a journey of self-discovery, resilience, and empowerment.

Why This Matters to Therapists

As a therapist with expertise in complex childhood trauma, you are uniquely positioned to guide individuals through their healing journeys, offering professional support and insight. Complex childhood trauma presents profound challenges that require a deeper understanding of its long-term impact. This book serves as a valuable resource to complement therapeutic interventions, offering practical exercises, self-reflection prompts, and healing roadmaps that clients can integrate into their daily lives.

Therapists without expertise in complex childhood trauma can recommend *Identity Alchemy* as a resource to their clients. When used as a supplementary tool, this book empowers therapists to support their clients with greater empathy and insight.

Additionally, this work offers its healing power to helping professionals—those compassionate souls who hold space for others' pain while carrying their own unspoken wounds. For therapists, coaches, and healers who support others, *Identity Alchemy* provides an invitation to transform your own experiences into professional mastery. When you heal yourself, you become exponentially more effective in your work in guiding clients to breakthroughs.

How Therapists Can Use This Book

1. *Supplementing Therapy Sessions:* Incorporate exercises and reflective prompts to deepen client engagement.
2. *Client Empowerment:* Encourage self-paced healing by recommending this book as a tool between sessions.
3. *Support People Awareness:* Helps you understand the extraordinary resilience of people who lived through horrific experiences and provides tools to support healing while honoring the healing process.
4. *Helping Professionals:* Reflect on your own personal journey. Healing yourself expands your capacity to help others.

Your role as a therapist is very valuable in guiding individuals toward healing. *Identity Alchemy* is here to support both you and your clients on this journey. Through complex childhood trauma-informed care, compassion, and continued learning, you can empower individuals to transcend the past, reclaim their lives, and step into their potential.

Thank you for your dedication to healing,

Rocío Pérez, IMBA & Dr. David Wheeler
The Identity Alchemists

Purpose of The Book

*I*dentity Alchemy is a beacon for anyone who has ever questioned their worth because of what they've lived through. It gives individuals access to understanding their past, reconnecting with their power, and creating fulfilling futures. A new intentional identity, purpose, and community can arise through healing and self-discovery.

The goal is to provide new insights, tools, and discoveries, helping readers see life through the lens of someone who has been there, endured that, and deeply understands them. This book is an invitation for people who have experienced the impact of wounding childhood experiences to tap into their own strength and rewrite their identity and their future from a place of power.

Rocío Pérez is living proof that the human spirit, when met with the right tools and tenacity, can alchemize pain into purpose. Along with Dr. David Wheeler, she shares her and her clients' experiences to invite others to embark on their own healing journeys, believing we all came into this world as worthy human beings. The world desperately needs us to show up as our truest, fullest selves.

Core Message

This journey of profound transformation shows readers that, even facing adversity, they possess the inner strength to reclaim their lives, create their futures, and forge meaningful connections. This serves as powerful proof of the ability within each individual to be brutally honest with themselves in order to overcome challenges, thrive, and create a brighter, more fulfilling life.

Book Structure

Aligned with themes of empowerment and resilience, the chapters serve as stepping stones in the *MindShifting©* process—a model for self-empowerment and healing that emphasizes awareness, self-discovery, and action. Through this model, readers can:

- Be present to their current reality and be free from the triggers of the past
- Understand the missing elements in their upbringing that led to their struggles
- Reparent and coach themselves toward healthier perspectives and actions
- Have tools to create a roadmap for personal growth leading to a happy, healthy, and fulfilling life
- ***Know that no past is too dark to overcome***

Key Features
- *Personal Stories:* Real-life healing journeys to inspire hope and illustrate concepts
- *Practical Tools:* Affirmations, journaling prompts, and thought-provoking questions
- *Healing Roadmap:* A possible path to healing through awareness, self-compassion, and experience processing

Book Description

"Only those who will risk going too far can possibly find out how far one can go." — T.S. Eliot

From Seventh-Grade Dropout to International Bestselling Author: A Story of Unbreakable Spirit.

Rocío Pérez didn't just survive—she transformed and brought others with her. Born into a life where violence was served like meals and trust was shattered by the very people meant to protect her, Rocío endured savage beatings, sexual assault, and a family's public denial of her suffering. She slept in closets, anchored herself against concrete floors during her abusers' brutal beatings, and was abandoned on kitchen floors after being raped—somehow, she kept going. At five years old, actively contemplating suicide, a vision seared into her brain—her future self teaching children with joy. That vision became her North Star, the future she would live into reality.

From that darkness, she alchemized pain into purpose.

Rocío went from seventh-grade dropout and teen mom to earning a dual MBA, becoming an international bestselling author, speaker, and creator of *The MindShift Experience©*—the world's first comprehensive self-coaching system. For over three decades, she has helped more than 60,000 people rewire their thinking, rebuild their confidence, and reclaim their power.

In collaboration with Dr. David Wheeler, *Identity Alchemy* reveals how complex trauma hides in the invisible corners of our minds, bodies, relationships, and leadership. Through raw storytelling and practical strategies, Rocío and David expose the patterns of limiting experiences and share tools for reparenting, self-coaching, and emotional resilience.

This book is for:

- People with unhealed wounds seeking understanding and a path to healing
- Parents determined to break the cycle of inherited generational patterns
- Educators who want to reach beyond behavior and touch the heart
- Leaders ready to support others with compassion and emotional intelligence

Rocío's journey through rape, poverty, abuse, abandonment, and inherited patterns of abuse is not sanitized—it is real. And so is her triumph. Her story reminds us that resilience is about facing the truth and choosing to live authentically anyway.

Identity Alchemy is a beacon for anyone who has ever been confused about their world, their relationships, their worth because of what they've lived through. It invites readers to write their future from a place of power.

Rocío Pérez and Dr. David Wheeler are witnesses to raw experience meeting empathy and compassionate expertise, inside of a safe healing space, allowing the human spirit to alchemize pain into purpose.

ABOUT THE AUTHORS

Rocío Pérez, IMBA, Author, Speaker & Leadership Consultant, Creator of *The MindShift Experience©*

Rocío Pérez, IMBA, is an author, speaker, and creator of *The MindShift Experience©*. She has written and co-authored books on leadership, personal growth, and empowerment, including:

Unstoppable: 7 Steps to Becoming a More Intentional Leader
Imparable: 7 Pasos Para Convertirse En Un Lider Más Productivo
FORTALEZA: Stories of Strength Drawn from Mind, Body, and Soul
And the upcoming titles:
Fortaleza: Historias de Fuerza Surgidas de la Mente, el Cuerpo y el Alma
Ripple Effects: Daily Practices for an Extraordinary Life
Fortaleza de la Mujer Latina

As a leadership consultant, she draws from research, professional practice, and lived experience to help people gain awareness of their behaviors, recognize patterns, and create intentional change. Her work integrates cognitive, somatic, and experiential approaches that support individuals in moving beyond limiting experiences. She is a transformational speaker who uses her journey to encourage others in their growth.

Rocío is a leader whose voice emerges from lived experience, deep introspection, and a courageous journey back to the self she once carried in silence. Her work is rooted in emotional honesty and the belief that healing is not a straight line. It is a cycle of remembering, releasing, and becoming. Through her writing, Rocío invites readers into this process with her, offering a perspective shaped by vulnerability, strength, and the unwavering human capacity to rise. Rocío writes for those who have carried their stories quietly, believing they must face the darkness alone. She writes to remind them that transformation is possible, that courage can be cultivated, and that reclaiming one's voice is an act of profound freedom.

Dr. David Wheeler
Author, Coach & Psychology Professor

David Wheeler, Ph.D., is a psychology professor at a four-year university and a licensed massage therapist with more than four decades of experience exploring how people grow, adapt, and reshape their lives.  Trained in Physiological Psychology and Applied Experimental Psychology, he has examined the interplay between mind, body, and personal meaning. His university teaching has included psychological well-being, identity development, and the practical ways people navigate change across their lifespan. Alongside his academic work, David is a Life and Career Coach who helps individuals clarify their direction, recognize limiting patterns, and move toward a more authentic expression of who they are. His approach blends scientific insight, somatic awareness, and creative problem-solving to support deep personal transformation

Beyond the world of psychology, David finds creative inspiration in conceptual photography and the fluid, fast-paced challenge of underwater hockey—two pursuits that keep him grounded in curiosity, presence, and the art of seeing life from unexpected perspectives. *Identity Alchemy* reflects his long-standing commitment to helping people understand their inner world and create meaningful, self-directed change. His work is shaped by a deep respect for the courage it takes to explore personal history and an ability to hold space for the full spectrum of human emotion. He listens for what lives beneath the surface, helping people transform fragments of experience into a coherent and empowering story. In every collaboration, his aim is to create a compassionate container where remembering, releasing, and becoming can unfold with integrity and clarity.

MY HEALING JOURNEY

Acknowledgments

To *my abusers.* I express my deepest gratitude for making my life a living hell.

To those who inflicted pain, betrayal, and suffering, without realizing it, you became my greatest teachers.

Your cruelty nearly took my life. My soul forced me to seek healing—to rise above and transform my pain into strength, my wounds into wisdom, and my suffering into purpose.

I've experienced the lack of belonging, safety, security, connection, and attachment to my biological family. Every painful experience has been a teacher and an essential piece of my growth and transformation, shaping me into the person I am today and offering me a diversity of perspectives that I cherish deeply.

These experiences have allowed me to see the world through a unique lens. They've gifted me with resources that others may not possess and fostered within me a creativity that empowers me to solve problems many might walk away from. My challenges have become my greatest strengths, and my resilience has become the unshakable foundation upon which I've built my life.

If I were to change even a single thing about my past, it would alter everything I've become—and I wouldn't trade that for the world.

I've released the pain that once held me captive. I learned to break cycles instead of repeating them, to love unconditionally instead of fearfully, and to extend grace—to my abusers and to myself.

Through the chronic adversities I experienced, I reclaimed my power, and I discovered the treasures that were always within me. I discovered the depths of empathy, compassion, and unconditional love—where there was none.

And for that, I am eternally grateful.

To every soul who supported me, I extend my deepest gratitude. Your presence was part of the path, helping shape the contrast that made clarity possible. To transformational voices like Tony Robbins, who illuminated alternate modalities and cracked open new perspectives with boldness and intensity, and to Marianne Williamson, whose wisdom helped me Return to Love and reminded me of the gentleness within. I give thanks to the countless YouTube creators, podcasters, and thought leaders who shared their knowledge freely, and to pioneers like Dr. Joe Dispenza and Dr. Gabor Maté, whose work helped me make sense of the invisible patterns within. I honor Dr. Ardeshir Mehran, my trauma specialist, who saw me, heard me, and got me completely and profoundly. And to Dr. David Wheeler, thank you for being an extraordinary coach, a trusted friend, and a brilliant mentor who consistently held a mirror up to my greatness. To all the therapists and professional coaches who have walked beside me and continue to support me with wisdom, encouragement, and skill throughout the years, thank you for pouring into my growth and helping me reclaim pieces of myself, one step at a time. Every single one of you, in your way, contributed to my healing—and for that, I am deeply, irrevocably grateful.

To those who have chosen to confront their past, to break free from cycles of suffering, and to reclaim their power—I honor you. I want to acknowledge you for your journey. Reclaiming your life takes courage, resilience, and a firm commitment to yourself. Your strength is remarkable. Your willingness to heal is an act of self-love. And your journey, no matter how difficult, is leading you toward freedom, peace, and a life fully lived. By choosing to read these pages, you have already taken a powerful step toward *Identity Alchemy.* Whether you are at the beginning of your healing journey or deep in the process of transformation, know that you are seen, you are heard, and others support you.

To those of you who walk alongside the impacted souls—whether as partners, friends, family members, or caregivers—I see you. I hear you. I am here with you. I honor the patience, presence, tenacity, and profound love you offer, often without recognition, and sometimes moment by moment. Your willingness to stand in the discomfort, to listen without fixing, to see the invisible, to hold space when the pain feels too heavy—this is sacred. Complex trauma is not linear, nor is it easily understood. Your consistent, unconditional support is a lifeline—one that makes healing possible. You have made it possible for us to enjoy what it feels like to live a happy, healthy, and fulfilling life. You are part of the miracle. And for that, I acknowledge you, thank you, and hold deep reverence for the role you play in our becoming.

I am grateful to all of you for including this book in your life's journey.

With love and gratitude,
Rocío Pérez, IMBA
The Identity Alchemist

Introduction

*"The only way to make sense out of change is to
plunge into it, move with it, and join the dance."*

— Alan Watts

Freedom is often described as escaping darkness into light. My journey feels more like navigating a vast and turbulent ocean—a force of nature both daunting and transformative. The ocean is the chaotic experience of life, shaped by my past of abuse, neglect, and intergenerational patterns of abuse. The relentless waves violently toss me about, making me struggle to keep my head above water.

At first, I fight the ocean, resisting its pull. Each relentless wave is a reminder of the pain I long to escape—memories of words that cut to my core, blows that sting my fragile body, and the loneliness that defines my childhood. I struggle to find solid ground. Exhausted, I surrender,   and find the ocean is my guide. Opportunities begin to appear in the vast waters around me. Small, significant tools appear around me like driftwood. A sturdy plank becomes my lifeline, and fragments of wreckage form my makeshift raft. Each piece symbolizes a lesson learned or a moment of clarity. In time, I learn to move with the currents, letting them propel me towards healing with resilience, courage, and resourcefulness. The storms do not disappear. Each swell and ebb offers a new lesson, a fresh perspective, and a chance to transform the pain of the past into the strength of the present.

My path is shared with others. I see others tossed about in the same ocean. My purpose includes showing them how to use the driftwood to build their own raft—empowering them to ride the waves to their own healing.

The story of the ocean is a reminder that life's challenges can feel overwhelming, and within the waves lies the potential for growth and transformation. We do not always get to choose the waters we're thrown into. What is there is the opportunity to choose how we navigate them. And when we learn to ride the waves, we heal ourselves and create ripples of healing in our families, communities, and the world.

The captain of a ship facing heavy waves steers directly into them, confident in the strength of their vessel to push through to the other side. Alternatively, they may choose to ride with the waves, using them to their advantage and gaining a boost forward. Most people are sideways to the waves, leaving them vulnerable to being tossed about at the mercy of the waves.

Being the captain of your own ship requires awareness, adaptability, and self-trust. It means understanding that while you may be adrift in the ocean, you can control how you respond to it. To take command of your life, start by setting a clear destination—whether it's healing, success, or personal growth—and charting a course that aligns with your values and aspirations.

Resilience is your anchor, keeping you steady during the storms. Cultivating mindfulness and self-awareness allows you to recognize when to adjust your course or push forward with determination. Discipline and consistency serve as the wind in your sails, driving you toward your goals even when motivation wanes.

Most importantly, remember that you are supported. Seek guidance from those who have navigated similar waters, reflect on your experiences and learn from them, and offer your encouragement to those adrift. Work with a mental health professional who helps you build your muscle of awareness and reparent yourself so that you can build your resilience. Life's ocean can support you with the right mindset, tools, and resources on your journey toward the horizon of your dreams.

Chapter 1: Brother's Share

*"As long as you keep secrets and suppress information,
you are fundamentally at war with yourself."*

— Bessel A. van der Kolk

It is a winter afternoon, the kind where the cold seeps into your bones and makes every memory feel sharper, more defined. I left a community event, my mind buzzing with the conversations, the connections, the hope. I am driving to meet my brother, carrying with me the decision to publish my memoir—to tell my story, to break the silence that holds our family captive over the generations.

He is a sentinel of our family's most brutal secrets, standing watch over a landscape of pain so vast and deep it swallows entire worlds. His job is to lock away our stories, to keep the bruised and battered truth of our origins sealed behind an unspoken code of silence.

The picnic table sits in the cold, harsh light of the store's overhead fluorescents. The breeze carries the muted sounds of people eating, conversations blending into a soft hum that feels distant and irrelevant. My brother sits across from me, his hands rough and scarred, telling a story without words—each callus a testament to survival.

"Your brothers don't want you to speak of this," he says, his voice low and weighted with generations of shame. "Our family does not want you to speak of this." His fingers curl slightly, as if gripping invisible chains, his dark eyes lock onto mine with an intensity that can cut through steel.

My stomach tightens. A cold ripple moves through my chest and I stay focused on him. The wooden bench feels solid beneath me, grounding me to this moment. I taste the sharp, clean winter air and let his words settle like dust.

"Brother," I say, my voice emerging from somewhere deep in my ribcage, "I'm not doing this for me. I'm doing this for the people we can save."

When he begins to speak, I am watching his dam slowly crumble. "We were beaten like savage, caged animals," he says, his hands tightening into fists. The words are raw and unfiltered, dragged from a place of profound pain.

All of a sudden, the floodgates open up. He is no longer censored. He recounts the horrific conditions we lived in, the abuse endured at the hands of mother and father. I see his pain—it lives in the tremor of his voice, in the way his eyes glaze over, in the tight set of his jaw. The memories are etched into his skin, carved into the very fabric of his being.

"Most of us ran away," he continues, his voice breaking. "We ended up in the hands of adults who took advantage of us." The words hang in the air like smoke, thick and choking. I feel every syllable in my body—my heart racing, my skin electric with remembered terror.

My brother opens up to me about the horrific abuse we endured. The world around us dissolves, leaving only the old wooden table, the winter light, and the truth spilling into the open.

His voice is a torrent of whispers. Each word is a piece of a shattered mirror, reflecting fragments of a childhood stolen, of innocence brutalized. I listen. I witness. I hold space for the pain that lived in silence for so long.

In this moment—fully alive, fully present—I know with absolute certainty that I am doing the right thing. By breaking our silence, by giving voice to our story, I am creating a lifeline for others who are trapped, fighting, and searching for a way home.

When the truth is spoken, it opens up a pathway to healing.

Chapter 2: How Do I Fit In?

*"When we can no longer change the situation,
we can only change ourselves."*

— Viktor Frankl

I am the picture-perfect person. Where does it come from?

The night is flawless. Forty guests fill my home, laughter bounces off the polished walls of my showroom-like house. The party unfolds like a carefully composed symphony of sights, sounds, and sensations. Every detail is picture-perfect—the décor, the lighting, the ambiance, the food. I glide through the crowd, owning the space, commanding the room, being effortlessly charming, radiating grace and certainty.

"You're such a presence—like royalty," a friend remarks. "You must have been treated like a princess growing up."

I smile and think, "Princess—ha! I was a tortured slave."

This whole illusion of a perfect life is the facade I put up to fit in. The party is a work of art, crafted with exquisite attention to detail. My tailored suit matches the belt, shoes, and purse. My son appears to be perfect. My degrees hang proudly on the walls, proof of my existence. My accolades stretch far and wide—billboards, media interviews, magazine articles, newspaper spreads. I am seen. I am admired. My life is a masterpiece, curated with precision. My persona and presence reflect this perfectly painted image.

Despite this facade, I feel like I do not belong in the social circles I hang out with. I wear a leaden mask and costume that look like perfection but weigh me down like a suit of armor, keeping me separate. No one in my circles experienced the hell of my childhood. I wear the mask and costume to fit in. I become the costume. And no costume ever covers up the truth—my life has been different than theirs.

Beneath it all, a question gnaws at me: Where does all of this come from?

I am unstoppable—I keep going no matter what. I always land on my feet. I keep moving forward. I keep achieving. I keep performing the role of the woman who has it all, who needs no one, who is perfect. If I stop moving, if I stop performing, if I stop being the woman everyone admires, then maybe they'd see what's beneath the accolades, beneath the perfect exterior, behind the flashing cameras and polished veneer. I am trapped—locked in a prison of wounds, unspoken memories, and buried fears. If I came out from my armor of perfection, would the world see the horrific person my abusers believed me to be—the one who was raped, tortured, and ostracized? I want to be seen as perfect. The real question is whether I am ready to see myself without the mask.

Am I willing to strip away the illusion?

Am I willing to set Little Rocío free? To release the weight of expectation? The burden of survival? The belief that I have to be everything to everyone, while being nothing to myself.

For so long, I wanted to be perfect. I wanted to fit in. I wanted to belong. I wanted to feel normal. I am no longer wanting.

For so long, I waited. I waited to eat. I waited to rest. I waited to acknowledge my own existence. I am no longer waiting.

Now, I am aware that my childhood coping strategies shape my reality. With that awareness comes clarity and understanding. I go from being the archaeologist—digging through the ruins of my past—to the architect, designing the life I choose to live.

As I step forward, I have dropped the masks, the illusions, and the need to prove my worth. I accept I have always been enough and have always had the power inside of me to live the life I desire.

I no longer need your validation in exchange for my silence.

Chapter 3: Channeling My Inner Picasso

"You never know how strong you are until being strong is your only choice."

— Bob Marley

I am a child channeling my Inner Picasso, resourceful beyond measure. Art is my sanctuary—a silent refuge amidst a backdrop of neglect and abuse. In second grade, a structured classroom coloring activity provides a brief escape from the nightmares I face daily at home.

My teacher roams through the rows of desks and calls out each object. I feel a surge of excitement as I diligently color my pictures using every shade of gray from the stub of my pencil and every shade of purple from the stub of my crayon. The classroom is alive with the sounds of childhood—the screech of chairs and the scratch of crayons on paper. The scent of wax mingles with the earthy aroma of clay from previous class projects.

Mother resentfully buys me school supplies at the beginning of the year. Spitefully, she says she will beat me if I ask for more. As the year progresses, my original school supplies dwindle. Alternating between my only pencil and my only crayon, I pour my soul into the paper. Every stroke of those stubs carries me one step farther from the harsh violence of my home. I am a second grader channeling my Inner Picasso, resourceful beyond measure, making her masterpieces.

By the time I reach the image of the dog, the pencil is gone, and only the stub of my purple crayon remains. My teacher and her assistant freeze in front of my desk like oak trees. What did I do wrong? They look at me in disbelief and with sharp disappointment say, "Rocío, are you color blind? Why are your dogs purple?" Their words cut to the core of my being. I look from my teacher, to her assistant, then down at my tattered cardboard school supply box. I open it, glance inside, and say, "It is the only color I have."

The Kindness of My Teacher

The kindness my teacher shows me the next day is unlike anything I have ever experienced at home. The last kids scurry out. The classroom is empty. I am alone, packing my things, when my teacher walks up.

With an intense presence, she quietly hands me a brand-new box of sixty-four Crayolas. The box bursts with every shade I ever dreamed of—colors I have only watched other children use, names I whisper to myself like magical enchantments: Lavender, Orchid, Violet, Mulberry, Magenta—sixty-four perfect points at attention in neat rows—a world of possibilities. I stare at them for days, afraid to use them at first, in awe of their beauty, full of possibilities—all I can imagine, all I can create—waiting for me inside that box.

In addition to the crayons, she surprises me with a pair of brand-new shoes. Her eyes meet mine, soft and knowing. My teacher noticed my old shoes, the holed shoes, the ones I wore with pride, despite the soles flapping at every step. I take the new shoes. She smiles. No one else witnesses this kindness, and I feel it—her compassion, quiet and real—a glimpse of what compassion can feel like.

Her understanding and generosity give me hope more than the material things she gifted me. I see in her actions a willingness to notice my struggles and respond with empathy, something that is glaringly absent from my life. Her kindness speaks volumes, teaching me without words that there are people in the world who care, who help without judgment or strings attached. It is a moment of warmth and safety, a moment that whispers to me that I am seen and valued.

The Redemption of My Teacher and the Non-Redemption of Mother

My teacher's kindness redeemed the moment when she had questioned my color vision. Mother's hatred and violence remained an unhealed wound. My teacher saw what was missing and responded with care, choosing to uplift and empower me. The box of crayons and the shoes symbolized more than their utility; they symbolized hope and possibility. My teacher became a figure of redemption, someone who showed me the impact of thoughtful actions. Mother's rage was the embodiment of cruelty. It was a two-fold lesson: one lesson of the power of kindness to heal and the other lesson of the resilience required in the face of torture.

What I have experienced on my healing journey

On my healing journey, I've often traveled back in time through the power of my imagination, cradling my Little Rocío on my lap. My purpose is to create a new, beautiful memory that is bigger than any violation or lashing. I nurture her with the warmth and security of a heartfelt embrace. Gazing into her eyes, I reassure her that she is loved, wanted, and safe. Instead of memories of abuse, we hold hands and dance, reveling in the joy of movement. We shared countless tea parties and play rounds of Ring Around The Rosie, with laughter and joy echoing around us. We delight in dressing up in princess clothes together. We venture out on imaginary shopping trips, choosing the beautiful little girl clothes I daydreamed of wearing. Each moment I spend with Little Rocío allows me to reconnect with my inner wisdom and beauty.

Most importantly, I've affirmed the sense of worth and belonging in that reparented child, telling her repeatedly that she is cherished and special to me. I've framed her beautiful artworks and displayed them proudly for her to see. I've celebrated her, showering her with the praise I was always denied. Through this journey, I have blossomed, shining so brightly with love and joy. I am now an adult channeling my Inner Picasso, resourceful beyond measure.

The frightened part of my child has healed. She's traveled forward through time to meet me—the woman she has become—the one who triumphed, who fought back, who refused to let the darkness win. The frightened child and the fierce woman are one.

She now knows that the abuse was never a reflection of her worth, about something she did wrong, about being unlovable, or carrying the burden of the shame. She understands that staying safe was her job then. Now her job is to be free to create, free to enjoy life. In other words, free to be human.

Reflections
Channeling My Inner Picasso

We invite you to explore these questions with curiosity and self-compassion. Use them to reframe challenges into opportunities for growth, gratitude, and empowerment. Share your responses with trusted people so you feel heard and understood. Revisit the questions over time to celebrate your growth.

1. Describe an experience that has shaped your life.

2. What was something you did to escape that experience?

3. What did you think, feel, or believe at the time of this experience?

4. What decision did you make about yourself at that moment?

In this book, *Identity Alchemy*, we examine both the pain and the treasures; so, now let's reflect on the gold created from that experience.

1. Identify the lessons that emerged from this experience.

2. Acknowledge any false beliefs or misunderstandings you held at the time.

3. What inner strengths or beliefs about the world showed up from that experience?

4. Where specifically were you resourceful beyond measure in that experience?

Affirmations
Channeling My Inner Picasso

Your thoughts, feelings, beliefs, voice, and actions create your reality. Each day, choose three affirmations and speak them out loud. Hearing your own words turns affirmations into living declarations that reshape your mind. Speak with intention and feel the words settle deep within you.

1. I am worthy because I exist.
2. I am an artist of my own life.
3. My creativity is my sanctuary.
4. I design my future with intention.
5. I create new, beautiful memories.
6. I channel my Inner Picasso daily.
7. I am resourceful beyond measure.
8. I paint my world in any color I choose.
9. I am both the nurturer and the nurtured.
10. Kindness is a mirror reflecting my inherent worth.

Chapter 4: The Great Escape

"Change is the law of life. And those who look only to the past or present are certain to miss the future."

— John F. Kennedy

I was cruising down a California highway when I said, "Enough." I had been avoiding my healing journey like the plague, even though I was desperate to escape the pain of the repeated hells I was reliving. Despite the outwardly perfect life I showed to the world, I knew a more peaceful life existed. My intensive personal growth experiences had been too gradual in peeling back the layers. I wanted to stop my pain immediately. *I craved a radical metamorphosis.*

Who could guide me?

Right away, a person came to mind. She is a powerful coach whom I met a couple of months ago. She shows up in spirit. With her, I feel a presence gently holding space for me in a way that was right for me. She nurtures my inner child—that child within me who feels left alone in a storm—cold and unseen—longing for love that never comes. She creates a sacred atmosphere that provides the safety to begin the deep inner work I have long been afraid to face. With her, my soul feels a calming, grounding sense of safety and care that transcends words.

I stopped the car. I grabbed my phone and stared at it for an eternity. My hands trembled, and my heart hammered with fear, excitement, and anticipation of the unknown. Right now, on the side of the highway, this was the moment something deep inside me shifted. I said to myself, "I am ready to do my healing work now!" This was my hidden gem speaking—the hidden gem that had guided me throughout my life. My familiar voice of resistance had stopped me from making this call for the last six weeks. Was I now choosing to step into the tempest of my transformation? Was I now ready for this call to my coach?

When she answered, my words came out with raw urgency: "I am ready to heal. I am ready to do the work." The declaration hung in the air, powerful and irreversible. I made a bold invitation, "Guide me in a 24-hour healing session—a deep dive into my soul—to break through the walls my fear had built."

"Yes, I will guide you, Rocío," she replied.

Relief and terror washed over me.

"When do you want to do it, Rocío?"

I knew this was it—the most massive, bold action of my life, and there was no going back.

I said with urgency in my voice, "As soon as I can get there."

The Journey Begins

Confidently striding onto the airplane, ascending the narrow aisle to the window seat, summoning me, I could feel a strange lightness in my body. I made the phone call, scheduled the appointment, and booked my flight to freedom. The runway flowed past my window. The stillness before the liftoff mimicked the hesitation in my gut. As the plane ascended, so did the anxiety in my body. It sat in my throat like unshed tears, vibrated in my legs like unspent fear. My palms were damp, fingers gripping the worn armrest. I was on my way to see my Coach—to heal, to face the truths I had spent years burying.

The setting Southern California sun disappeared further behind us, with each mile, dragging me toward my fate. My reflection in the window was ghostlike against the dark blue sky. I was going to face the ghosts that had terrorized me in order to transcend the horrific childhood experiences that had shaped my life. This was the moment—the one I'd been both yearning for and avoiding for so long.

My mind kept racing—a relentless stream of questions playing on repeat.

What would the 24 hours look like?

Was I afraid of what I would find out?

Would I sit stunned as memories flooded back?

Would I cry the tears locked away for years?

Would I break apart completely?

Would I rebuild into something stronger?

Would I grieve the death of my old self—someone I'd known my entire life?

What if the person I've been was only the cocoon incubating the new person about to emerge?

What if the tough persona I had created was about to die? I had been locked in battle with the world. I had climbed metaphorical mountains without gear because there was no other way. I pushed forward through each brutal step because standing meant being taken down by the avalanche of chaos that surrounded me. I became a master of making things happen through sheer will and determination, never knowing what it felt like to create from a place of peace. Building from quiet strength was a foreign concept. I had always warriored through the storm—transforming every obstacle into another battle to be won.

Would I be able to give up the warrioring for true freedom?

What would happen when I open the locked doors in my mind, guarding my buried memories, unfelt pain, repressed anger, and shame?

What treasures would be revealed—courage, confidence, wisdom, fierce spirit, reclaimed power, and all the hidden gifts that had carried me through hell?

What would my new life look like? I knew this would change me. Those closest to me wanted me to stay the same because my healing threatened their comfort. I wondered if my new life of speaking truth and setting boundaries would mean stepping away from limiting relationships that feared my growth and authenticity.

As Colorado approached, I dreaded the welcoming, sacred, healing space generated by my coach. I wanted healing, the fluffy-wuffy kind that left all these questions unanswered.

And that's not how this works.

Healing may not arrive neatly packaged, painless, and polite. It can show up raw. Disruptive. Demanding. It may ask you to sit in the rubble. To feel what you've buried. To hear the echoes of the past.

Healing requires truth…

And truth peels back layer after layer. The truth is there to help reclaim your wholeness. Real healing honors you as you recognize your authentic self.

The tarmac slammed against the landing gear, violently snapping me into the brutal realization that this was really happening. I was doing this. I was choosing to heal, choosing to transcend the past. I was a fierce rebel, taking on the monsters of my life with a mixture of excitement and terror.

Arrival

Night descended across the Colorado mountains as I arrived at my coach's office. The snow caught fragments of moonlight and scattered them like a masterpiece across the frozen landscape. Oh, shit! Things are about to get real! Each step toward her door felt heavier and heavier with the premonition of what was about to be unleashed within me.

The warmth greeting me as I crossed the threshold was a stark contrast to the dread I had entered with. My coach's embrace wrapped around me like a lifeline. Her office had been created as a sanctuary, every detail intentionally arranged to welcome the transformation that was about to happen. I carefully set down my belongings—my purse, my coat, my fears, my anxieties—and filled my copper tumbler with water.

As we settled into our meditation chairs, I felt the familiar armor sliding into place. I could feel it—again. Like clockwork. Like ritual. Like reflex. The bulletproof armor was preparing to deliver me to the familiar performance stage, which gave me an illusion of safety. First, the chest plate of composure—impenetrable, polished to perfection. Then, the gauntlets of performance—flexible, and always ready to deflect, protect, perform.

And the **MASK**… Oh, the mask! It wasn't any mask. It was one I had sculpted over decades—chiseling it with precision, molding it with practiced smiles and well-timed nods. As it positioned itself on my face, I could hear it whispering, "Ready? Here we go again!" The familiar inner playlist kicked in—measured, logical, efficient, well-rehearsed monologues ready to be played to the world.

There was no hesitation. No internal debate. My body knew this dance. I was on autopilot. My breath adjusted—shallow and steady. My eyes scanned the environment, calculating the terrain. My ears tuned in for cues, tones, subtle shifts. I was in my armor, ready to fight once again in the illusory battlefield I had always fought in.

Yet, I was in her office. There was no battle here. She eased us into the conversation. Gently guiding us into the process. We were having a pleasant conversation about recent life experiences. It was two friends catching up over a tea party. I was talking about all the fluffy wuffies in my life. Everything was perfect. Everything was polished. Everything was safe. I was comfortable in the armor of perfection that enveloped me.

She was asking probing questions, which were ricocheting off my armor. I had my safe way of being—my guarded, untouchable way of being. I was going to answer her questions with the carefully rehearsed answers I wanted her to hear.

Like mother, I had mastered the illusion of a perfect life. Mother spoke eloquently, acted properly, and forced me to share the story of perfection with everyone. Mother had forbidden me from telling anyone about the hellish cage she and father kept me in. Her words were my jail cell—my solitary confinement. The fear she instilled in me locked away the truth of my childhood. Even though this illusion of perfection was forced on me, I longed to live in a world where everything was perfect. The script of perfection had become my armor, my defense, my way of keeping the real story buried behind a dam of well-manicured lies. My childish belief was that unacknowledged pain could be denied.

My armor of perfection was serving up a bunch of bullshit pies to my coach—happy with the superficial interactions I was having. My heart longed to be free, to feel, and to fly. My armor stood strong, battling to protect me from the very love my heart was aching for. My heart was craving a radical metamorphosis and was wondering if this experience was going to be worth my time. My coach sat there, silent, steady, holding the space, allowing moments of quiet. Moments of silence when I slowed down long enough to hear my thoughts, feel my feelings, and connect with my heart. Exhausted, I tapped into my humanity. Burning tears ran down my face.

All Hell Breaks Loose

Time stretched into an eternity… In that moment, a lifetime happened.

My armor shattered. The things I had deeply buried exploded into my awareness. There was no turning back. My mind had left the room. It was reliving the brutality, the torture, the betrayals, all the things I had numbed myself from experiencing to stay alive. I was caught in the torrent of memories of the violent rapes and beatings. ***No, I was not just remembering my life—I was reliving the traumas.***

My Super Power: I Can Float

The memories remain crystal clear, yet the body sensations were lost.

The cold living room floor against my back feels like ice. Mother's brutal blows to my ribs are all I can feel. The room looks so big from down here. The walls stretch up forever to the faraway ceiling. So tiny. So alone. So empty the house—a vast, cold void. Nobody hears. Nobody comes to help. How did I get here?

El Chubasco by Carlos y José is playing on the radio. I am enjoying the bright, bouncy rhythm and singing along with the music. Out of nowhere mother slaps me, "Stop singing". Her blow splatters me onto the floor. My four-year-old mind does not comprehend. What did I do? I was just singing a song. Did I do something bad? Did I forget something? Did I break something? I was trying to be good… I'm always trying to be good.

My ears are assaulted by her screams. They crash into me, sharp and hard. Her voice is everywhere—so loud it feels like it's inside my head. "I hate you to my core. You're not worthy of life. You're a bastard. I found you in a dumpster and had pity on you. You should've never been born."

Endemoniada. She's out of control. Her eyes don't look like mother's eyes anymore. They're the devil's eyes. She is the devil.

Her shadow moves toward me, big and dark. Her big, heavy hands are brutal, hitting with a heat that burns through my skin. Her kicks slam into my ribs. Kick after kick. Stomp after stomp. My scrawny little body skidding across the cold, rough living room floor.

I curl into a tight steel ball. I bite my lips to hide the pain. The air is filled with the dust swept up by my body. My mouth tastes salty from the tears gushing down. My tummy feels sick. My chest feels tight. My heartbeat thunders in my ears, pounding in my chest, trying to fly away.

I cried until my voice left my body because it hurt to the depths of my soul.

I gasp for air. I try to scream. I want to say I am sorry. Maybe then she will stop.

What did I do wrong?

I don't understand the beating.

I want her to smile at me.

Maybe she would hug me.

Why does mother hate me?

I want her to hold me.

I don't understand what I did wrong.

I'm trying to be good—so good. I try so hard to be good.

I just want her to love me.

It hurts. It hurts so much.

I don't cry anymore. Crying makes her angrier. I float up. Up to the ceiling. Disembodied, I watch the silent movie of a little girl's small body getting brutalized below.

It doesn't hurt when I'm floating.

I gripped my chair, my body frozen between past and present. Memories relentlessly crashed over me. Different memories, different moments, different versions of the same nightmare. Different familiar faces—who I was desperate to have loved me. The weight of it all pressed down on my chest, stealing my breath, my voice, my life. I wanted to run, to shove all the horrific memories back into the Pandora's box where I had hidden them for so long.

"Get me the hell out of here! Stop the movies! I don't want to experience this again!" I screamed at my coach and at the tempest in my head. "Stop the thoughts! I can't take it anymore. Get me the hell out of my thoughts. I don't want to see them." In that moment of desperation, I bolted from her office and vanished outside into the dark of winter, standing in the snow, barefoot, frozen, desperate. I could not escape the memories.

Constant Impact

The room is sparse and cold, a one-bedroom apartment that feels more like a prison cell than a home in a poverty-stricken side of a small town in Colorado. It is wintertime, and the chill seeps through the thin walls, making everything feel even more desolate and unwelcoming.

Two beds sit on opposite sides of the room like silent witnesses to the horror that is about to unfold. The space between them feels both too far and not far enough—a cruel stage for mother and father to perform their twisted ritual of violence.

Brothers are nowhere in sight. I am alone with the monsters in this barren space with only the two beds and the cold, empty air between them. The room is a coliseum. In father's hands, my scrawny 13-year-old body becomes the projectile traversing the arena. My body lands with a thud on the thin mattress on one bed and splatters onto the wall. The bed frame groans beneath the relentless pounding of his sledgehammers disguised as fists as they rain down blow after blow on my small body. The game continues even when he tires of it. He snatches me up and hurls me across the room to the other bed, where mother waits to take her turn.

The punches came left and right as my head lurched side to side, each blow snapping my neck like a rag doll while my limp body jolted with every vicious strike to my torso. I could feel my ribs absorbing the impact, my small frame convulsing with each hit as I became a human punching bag caught between two people who were supposed to love me.

Back and forth I go, from bed to bed, like a game of human ping-pong. The distance between those two beds becomes the measurement of my pain—a cold space that I fly across again and again.

That day, my childhood dies more each time I am thrown from one side to the other. A primal instinct kicks in. I know with absolute certainty that I am the one who makes it stop, or they will kill me.

When father comes at me again, I see my chance. I sink back onto my back leg, my hips coil, and fighting for my life, my right leg releases the built-up anger and fear onto him as my knee connects with the balls of my torturer. He doubles over, gasping, his face contorting in pain, crawling to the bathroom.

Mother's reaction is the most disturbing part of all. She runs into the hallway and drops to the floor, laughing with joy. "You finally got him!" she cackles, while chalking up another point in the sick game of familial abuse.

Disoriented and livid, I yell at her, "Are you crazy? How can you do this to your child?"

The world slams shut. Her response is gone—forever lost from memory. Another post-beating blackout.

The empty room is left alone—no warmth, no comfort, no safety. Two beds, four walls, and the echoing sounds of violence in the winter cold. The most disorienting part isn't the impact—it's realizing that when the throwing stops, I don't know how to move myself anymore.

No Such Thing as Permanence

A few days later, I feel the shift in the air before he even announces it—that electric tension that makes my skin crawl and my stomach clench into knots. Father's decision is made, and when that happens, the world bends to his will whether it wants to or not. No piece of paper with official letterhead, no lease agreement with its neat black signatures, no landlord's threats or legal consequences will ever stop him from doing exactly what he pleases. We are off to the next place to begin anew. I watch him pacing the living room, his heavy footsteps making the thin floorboards groan beneath his weight. The sound echoes through the walls like a countdown, each step marking time until the inevitable.

"Get in the car, we are moving," he declares, his voice cutting through the stale air with the finality of a judge's gavel. The words hang heavy in the room as I hear them, knowing what they meant—for us and for the inheritors of the mess we'd leave behind.

We abandon the apartment like abductees pulled into a silent sky by aliens from outer space. There is the lingering scent of last night's dinner. The dirty dishes are stacked in the sink, their crusty surfaces catching the harsh fluorescent light. The stains on the carpet remain as permanent markers of our existence here. The holes he'd punched in the walls during his rages gape like open wounds, unfilled and unrepaired.

The thoughts of scrubbing floors or wiping down counters, of returned security deposits, or the normal rituals of departure, never even cross his mind. I can see it in his eyes—that wild, unfocused look of someone operating purely on instinct.

My hypervigilance kicks in. Where are we going? I scan the room for everything we will abandon—furniture, belongings, a life. Nothing comes with us. The musty smell of the old apartment grows stronger, as if the walls themselves know they are being abandoned. We walk out with the clothes on our backs, leaving everything else to rot and be discovered by whoever comes next.

He is already mentally gone, I can tell by the way he looks through everything instead of at it; his mind calculates escape routes rather than responsibilities. This is our reality in its cruelest form, leaving destruction in its wake without a backward glance. No conscious effort toward what needs to happen, no consideration for consequences or other people's realities. It is pure, selfish momentum carrying us toward the next temporary stop, leaving behind another apartment full of damage and unpaid debts, another set of people who would curse our names when they discover what we leave behind.

I feel the familiar weight of powerlessness settle over me, knowing that wherever we land next, this scene will play out again. With him, there is the endless cycle of arrival, destruction, and inevitable flight with only the clothes on our backs. In this life, there is no such thing as permanence

The Laughter Dies, Safety Dies

New Year's Eve holds a profound meaning for Mexican families— it is more than marking the passage of time. It represents continuity, culture, and the unbreakable bonds that hold families together, no matter how much physical distance has been between them, no matter how different their experiences have been.

The next landing spot is Houston, Texas. We have a stopover for a few days at my grandmother Maria's house. This unexpected reunion leaves me excited. Never before have I enjoyed the tradition of a New Year's Eve celebration in my grandmother's home wrapped in a cocoon of family.

The focal point is the kitchen, filled with the cultural ritual of making tamales. The sweet aroma of canela cooking, the scent of my grandmother's masa flour, and spiced pork impregnates the air. The warmth from the stove radiates to every corner of the home. The most important ritual of the celebration is sharing stories and passing down traditions from generation to generation. The anticipation of the celebratory tamales sits sweetly on my tongue. Tamales are love wrapped in corn husks, tradition folded into every bite. What truly nourishes us is being together.

The familiar weight of hypervigilance lifted from my shoulders this morning when mi abuela's soft hands gently caressed me. The walls hold decades of family photographs instead of the echoes of violence. The house hums with the kind of safety I have been starving for—the sound of family without fear, laughter without looking over shoulders.

Brothers disappeared into my grandfather's bedroom hours earlier. The familiar sounds of Nintendo bleeps and bloops mixing with their muffled laughter create a soundtrack of childhood innocence.

I sit cross-legged on the living room floor, talking with my cousin Maria. We sit in conversation, basking in the warmth from the space heater. My grandmother's voice floats from the kitchen, melodic and soothing as she calls out instructions to my 16-year-old uncle, Angel.

My cousin Maria is a couple of years older than me. In my grandmother's house, those years might as well be decades. She carries herself with the quiet confidence of someone who belongs—because she does. Raised by my grandparents since birth, Maria has earned a place in the home unavailable to me. She is allowed to hang out with the men, to occupy forbidden spaces, not because she is better or smarter, but because she is theirs in a way I can never be. Maria moves freely between worlds. In Maria, I see what safety looks like: the ability to exist without fear, to speak without calculating the cost, to live without the hypervigilance of walking on eggshells. She is living proof that it is possible to simply be a child in a home.

The lively sound of Corrido music from my grandfather's large boombox fills the living room. Father, grandfather, and two uncles toast with small glasses of Presidente. Their animated voices share tales of sweet adventures of long ago. They laugh and one-up each other with every story. I hear the pure joy that threads through their words, their voices fluctuate with emotion, and each melodic change pulls me deeper into this beautiful, sacred moment.

Suddenly, father hears me giggling, his head whips up from his beer—eyes sharp as broken glass. They lock onto my eyes across the room.

I spring off the floor the moment I see him—father—coming fast, too fast. I gasp for air. My stomach knots. The hairs on my arms stand at attention. My skin prickles with fear. What did I do? All I know is that I'm in trouble as he darts toward me.

His raspy, angry voice drops to a menacing whisper, slicing through the room, barking out a command as he violently thrusts his hand toward the kitchen, "You don't belong here with the men! Get the hell out of the living room—go to the kitchen where you belong!"

The words crack like a whip. My ears ring. Sounds muffle. Time suspends itself in that moment before impact. I see the calluses on his palm as his hand draws back. I smell the soap my grandmother uses to wash the dishes, impregnating the air. I hear Angel's innocent giggle from the kitchen.

All of this exists in the same instant when his hand violently connects to my cheek with the sound of a thunderclap. I slam against the door frame—wood against bone. Stars burst behind my eyes. The taste of copper explodes in my mouth as my teeth cut into my tongue. I stumble—no, ricochet—into the kitchen, dizzy, seeing flashes of light. My heartbeat thunders in my ears. I feel lightheaded. My body feels like it's floating outside of itself.

I smell the pork tamale filling cooking on the stove. Swallowing tears, hoping for air, my face is throbbing. What is happening? Before I can even think, mother's hand brutally impacts my face. Busts my nose. Blood pours from my nose, and her words cut even deeper.

"You're not even worthy of life," she hisses. "You're a bastard. I found you in a dumpster and had pity on you. You were a curse to have been born."

Mother yells at me, "Get the hell out of my sight."

Like a soldier under fire, I tiger crawl across the kitchen floor, then stand, trying to steady myself, my vision blurring, and stagger out of sight. I do what I've been trained to do: Obey. Move. Disappear. Get out of sight.

And then… there's father. Again. His fist connects with my jaw before I can even protect my face. I am embedded into the door frame again. "Go to the kitchen where you belong."

Before the pain registers, mother is there again. Her open palm cracks across my cheek, snapping my head to the side.

I am their punching bag in a brutal match where I am the one who loses.

My pulse pounds in my ears, louder than my thoughts. My eyes dart around the room, scanning for a way out. My skin tingles with the electric charge of fear, every muscle tight and ready to run.

No time to think. No time to breathe. One explosion, one impact after another. The relentless, unpredictable, merciless attacks blur into a cycle that feels like one continuous heartbeat of chaos.

And in the midst of it all, the voice of mercy comes like a fresh breath in a storm. My grandmother's quiet words whisper from the corner of the kitchen table, "If you don't want her, you can give her to us." That whisper is the first thread of hope I can grasp—an acknowledgment that someone sees me, maybe even believes I deserve better.

Then—I hear him. My uncle Angel roars like a lion charging to my defense. At 16 years of age, when most teenagers worry about homework, football, and weekend plans, he leaps head-on into my nightmare with the fierce, selfless bravery that the adults in my life do not show. Angel takes the stand that the abuse is going to stop with him. With wisdom far beyond his years and a heart that refuses to look the other way, he chooses to protect me. In this moment, a 16-year-old teenager becomes the hero that grown men and women fail to be, proving that true courage is measured by the willingness to stand up when it matters most.

He has seen enough. He steps in with fire in his voice and anger on his tongue. "How the hell can you say that to your own child?" he shouts. "She's here because you opened your legs. This isn't her fault!"

Angel's words ring out like thunder, impacting my grandfather, who has been minding his own business. He boldly stands, voice booming, "What the hell is wrong with you? Why are you hitting her?"

The words slice through the room. The air hangs heavy, thick with sweat and tension. My heart is already slamming against my chest. Every breath is sharp with dread. Father's face twists, eyes blazing with that familiar ruthlessness. I recognize the pattern about to unfold.

His rough hand locks onto my arm, and the linoleum burns my skin as he drags me down the stairs, each thud of my body echoing louder than the shouts of protest from above. The banister blurs past in streaks of wood and shadow as foreboding erupts into reality.

The Corrido music plays on, oblivious. The laughter dies. The safety dies. I realize that even in my grandmother's house—even in the place I have believed is sacred—I am never truly safe. I know I have to escape.

And then… nothing.

Just blackness.

Angel tells me decades later that I am dragged down the stairs to the bare concrete floor of the laundry room and beaten unconscious.

You Know They're Going To Kill Me

January 3rd—I escape the death march of my existence.

My window of time is small—frighteningly small. Tonight, the road of no return leads to Houston. Outside, I hear the scrape of metal as father works on the Datsun sedan. Inside, mother paces in sharp, clipped steps, her voice tight with urgency as she decides which possessions will make the cut. The very thought of cramming two adults and five children into that tiny sedan squeezes the air from my lungs. It already feels like a coffin on wheels—suffocating, stuffed with silence and fear.

8:00 AM

I watch mother lift her blue makeup case. Every woman in the 1980s seems to have one, its matte finish cool beneath her fingers, its small mirror catching the dull morning light. Today, there is no makeup inside. Instead, she tucks in our immunization records, faded family photographs, and brittle papers that smell faintly of dust and ink. The clasp snaps shut with finality. This caboodle is no longer cosmetic—it is her treasure chest of survival, a fragile box holding the proof of our existence.

10:00 AM

Mother and father in the basement send me upstairs to watch brothers. Yes. Yes. Anything to escape the sounds of mother and father's voices as they rise in pitched battle, determining the fate of the unclaimed space in the car.

Ascending the basement stairs, the thought circles endlessly in my mind. "How am I going to escape the torture and enslavement at the hands of mother and father?" My pulse hammers, my body quivers with urgency. I know I must ask my grandmother for help,

At the top of the stairs, I slip through the narrow shortcut by the pantry. The hallway stretches long and dim, the walls pressing in, the air stale and heavy. I muster every ounce of trembling courage, internally rehearsing the words I will force past my lips as I stand before my grandmother. I deviate from my assigned mission of caring for brothers in the living room.

I darted into my grandmother Maria's room, stand firmly in front of her, and lock eyes. I am compelling her to see the humanity beneath my pain. Terror and courage collide in my chest like thunder. My throat closes, my breath shakes, my mouth as dry as the desert. In a voice carefully composed to convey that this is my only chance, the words gush forth, "You know they're going to kill me."

Her eyes pool with tears, and silence swells until it nearly crushes me. Then she breathes, barely audible, "I know."

The words shatter me. My chest cracks wide open. "I need you to help me," I plead, voice trembling, body shaking so violently I can hear my teeth click.

In front of me, she freezes, paralyzed between fear and love, torn between truth and loyalty.

Off to the side, my uncle Angel steps forward and says, "I'll help you." His eyes lock on mine. He has seen my bruises. He has heard my bloodcurdling screams. He knows. He is the only one in the house with enough balls to help me.

A flickering spark of hope enters my darkness. My grandmother nods in agreement, moved by his courage. Together, they choose me. Together, they choose to help me escape.

4:00 PM

I find my window of opportunity and ascend from the basement. I see my grandmother and Angel. They shove me into the closet. The smell of starched clothes fills my nose, sharp and clean. I fold into the corner, back against the wall, the cold metal frame of the rollaway bed a barricade before the door. Shirts and trousers cascade over me, the fabric scratchy against my cheek, their weight my shield.

The waiting is torture. Every second stretches long, every sound razor-sharp.

Mother and father notice my absence and initiate a sector search through the house, with their rage echoing off the walls. Not in the basement. The thunder of footsteps on the stairs. Not in the kitchen. Not in the living room. Not in my grandfather's room.

Father's voice rips through the air, closer, closer. "Where the hell is that bitch? I know you're hiding her!" Father shouts. Mother's voice cuts sharply, "We'll call the cops. You'll pay for this."

His shadow looms over the closet.

I freeze to stone. The air is filled with dust and fear. Is my breath too loud? Is my heartbeat too heavy? The slightest movement would betray me.

His hand reaches for the rollaway bed.

"Leave it!" Angel says, firm, unflinching.

The moment hangs heavy. Father is contemplating Angel's 6'4" football player's frame. Father withdraws, suspicious and unwilling to press further. They give up the search, determined to get on the road to Houston.

6:00 PM

Mother and father slam the doors as they leave to gas up the Datsun. Like always, they take the boys with them.

Seizing the opportunity, Angel reaches into the closet and says in a hushed voice, "Give me your hand." I reach up, arms trembling, and grasp my lifeline. He pulls me out of the closet. Collapsing, I stammer, "My legs are numb." His frame wraps around me like armor until I can stand on my own.

The Datsun's taillights fade into the darkness, swallowed whole.

This is it. My moment. Adrenaline floods me. A momentary glance at the clock. I sprint out the door and run in the opposite direction of my executioners. The cold night air slashes against my face, biting through my thin windbreaker, settling into my bones. My shoes slap the pavement, every shadow alive with danger, every sound sharp with pursuit. I do not look back.

And then—I see it. Angel's red getaway sports car screeches around the corner at the agreed-upon place. I fling open the door. He shouts, "Duck!" I throw myself onto the passenger floorboard, willing myself into an invisible ball. Angel speeds away. The smell of oil and dust fills my nose, I am trembling with relief while the fear of being caught vibrates through me like the roar of the engine. I am trembling with the sound of my own heart pounding in my ears and the sound of the tires tearing up the road into the cold darkness.

Let's Go Back Inside

My coach caught up to me and said, "Let's go back inside, Rocío."

There is a war inside my head. Why would I want to go back inside? One part of my mind wanted to skim the surface, to heal enough to get by. The other part—the one I had buried for so long—the one that had brought me here—screamed to get out.

My body turned to my Coach, pleading, "Get me out of here. Get me out of my thoughts. Make it stop! I will pay you the full amount if you stop this and let me go." My coach looked at me and asked with steady resolve, "What's happening?"

She wants to know what's happening. I do not know what happened or what did not happen. What am I thinking? What should I be thinking? Why now? Why do I have to experience this? I cannot do this. I am too ashamed to share my experiences even with my coach. Why does healing hurt so much? I had a perfect, pollyanna life, and now the relived experiences are shattering the illusion of the perfect life I had created. I do not want to relive those experiences I had run away from when they happened.

Please, stop the flashbacks!

I had endured every type of abuse. Now, my subconscious was forcing me to confront it whether I wanted to or not. The memories kept coming. My thoughts spun out of control. It felt like an intense tennis match, my thoughts volleying back and forth with no end in sight.

Silence Spreads Like a Blanket

We drive to a nearby 7-Eleven. My heart pounds as I step into the fluorescent light, the hum of the coolers buzzing in my ears. I find a payphone, lift the heavy receiver, and call mother. My hand shakes as I press the buttons. When she answers, I lie: I tell her I'm at the airport; I tell her I'm pregnant; I tell her I'm not coming back.

For a couple of days, I lay low at my aunt's house in a neighboring town. Mother and father search for me, their "little slave," like jaguars desperate for their prey. For two days, they search, and. Finally, they give up and leave for Houston without me.

Three days later, I leave the hideout at my aunt's place and move back to my grandparents' home. Mother, father, and the boys are gone. I breathe without fear catching in my throat. I tell myself, "Here, I can start again."

Peace is short-lived.

I traded the hell of life with mother and father for the hell of life at my grandparents. The memories of mother and father's abuse claw at me, raw and unhealed. Outside me, my cousin Maria and my uncles drag me into their chaos. Jealous, reckless, and drunk, they force me into a world no child should ever know. They make me smoke cigarettes, make me drink alcohol, and pull me out of school to party. To them, it's a hilarious initiation. To me, it's survival. Breath by breath. Moment by moment. I want to numb the pain of the abuse I am now living.

One night, I'm still thirteen years old, and my uncles are drinking in the front seat of my grandfather's blue van. Their laughter spills out into the night. We are parked by the park across the street from the house. Maria and I are in the back seat. Suddenly, red and blue lights explode behind us. The police car pulls up. My stomach drops. My breath catches in my throat. The officer's flashlights blind me.

"Out of the van!" they sharply order.

"Face the van!" "Arms behind your back!"

Cold metal bites my wrists as the handcuffs snap shut.

"Spread your legs!" Then the pat down. The reading of my rights.

They shove me into the back of the squad car. My reflection stares back at me from the glass, wide-eyed, stunned. I sit in silence, my world collapsing.

Unbeknownst to me, mother and father were so intent on vengeance that they file a runaway report, which is still active. On paper, I am missing. In the eyes of the law, I am not a 13-year-old girl. I am a runaway. A criminal. Booked at the station. Fingers pressed against the black ink pad. Fingerprints rolled onto the report. Mugshot taken. Then the cell door slams shut. The concrete walls close in. I am a child locked away.

Under interrogation, I tell them I am living with my grandparents. Hours later, my grandfather picks me up. I am released to him because mother had signed away her parental rights to my grandparents. In deafening silence, we go home.

I walk into my grandparents' home. The living room is engulfed in shadow. The kitchen light spills across the floor. My uncles gather around the table. My grandfather's voice cuts through the air, furious, commanding. He yells at them, "You're supposed to protect her, not get her into your chaos."

Chaos is all this family knows.

My uncles spend their days drinking, their nights partying. One evening, when I am fourteen, they and their adult friends cheer Maria and me on as they force drinks into our hands, egging us on with cries of "Faster! Faster!" They laugh as they show us how to shotgun beers, timing us, watching us stumble. I'm dizzy, unsteady, spinning. I stagger into a bedroom nearby and pass out.

Later that night, the nightmare reemerges. I am jolted from unconsciousness by the horror of one of my uncles raping me. I scream, "Leave me alone!" His harsh whispers demand I "hush" as if my terror is the problem. I fight, I cry. The house is full of people. My screams for help echo through the house. I know that everyone hears, and no one saves me. The silence spreads like a blanket, thick and suffocating.

In this family's math, the answer is simple: one predatory uncle versus one disposable granddaughter. The solution? Remove the "problem". Ship the evidence back to Texas. Back to parents who already know how to keep secrets—who have mastered the criminal art of willful blindness.

Betrayal has a rhythm. It passes from one generation to the next like a curse. Parents to children. Aunts and uncles to cousins. Grandparents to grandchildren. Each taking their turn. Each choosing silence. Each choosing to protect the abuser rather than the child.

Days later, I am packed like damaged goods to be sent back to mother and father. Back to the hands that have already taught me how betrayal feels. The circle is complete, the pattern perfect – from one house of horrors to another.

Let It Out. Let It All Out

I was overwhelmed with the intensity of the experience of release. All I could do was hold on while my system purged itself of a lifetime's worth of concealment. My body convulsed with deep, wracking coughs that tore through my chest, leaving my throat raw and my lungs burning.

I stumbled to the bathroom, hunched over the sink, gagging—my body physically ejected decades of buried experiences. My body was purging what my mind had unlocked. Everything was releasing at once. Vomit. Tears. Unearthly sounds.

I gripped the sink's edge, my knuckles white, my reflection in the mirror a blurry mess of fear and pain on the edge of something. The emotions that had been trapped for so long were clawing their way out, and my body was paying the price for their freedom.

And then my Coach said it.

"Are you afraid that people will know what you've been through? Do you want others to think you are perfect?"

Her words punched me in the gut so hard I could barely breathe. The dam was gone, and there was no turning back. My voice tore out of me, raw and jagged, as I yelled, "Yeah, you're right, they all want me perfect, flawless, untouchable—and I'm so damn tired, I'm exhausted, I can't do this anymore."

Tell it like it is, Rocío! Let it out! Let it out!

I'm so damn tired, I'm exhausted, I can't do this anymore.

Desperate for rest, my body drained, my mind at war, I crawled into bed. And as I began to sink into the mattress, another relentless wave hit. No, not again. I was back on my feet, stumbling toward the bathroom. More needed to come out.

I barely made it in time—vomiting, peeing, purging. Sitting on the toilet, I heaved into a bucket, my body emptying itself in every possible way, all at once.

The same brutal rhythm repeated: collapsed in bed, mattress swallowed me, another wave tore through, staggered to the toilet, barely in time. My mind desperately fought to keep the memories locked up while my body expelled decades of buried truth.

Amid the chaos, my Coach's voice cut through.

"Let it out. Let it all out."

Let it out? How could I let it out? My whole life, I had been told that it was my fault for what happened to me and that it was shameful.

As I sat there, helpless, vulnerable, exposed, she asked, "What happened, Rocío?"

"What Did Your Father Do To You?"

This was it. I wanted to run. I was still holding on to the shame and pain of what father did to me.

The relative safety of daylight retreats. Darkness awakens. The monster in my home comes alive, ready to unleash his terror. I sleep in a closet to stay safe. I see the street light streaming through the window. Father comes in. I dart under the bed. His long arms searching for the scared, silenced girl, pressing my entire body against the wall under the bed, avoiding his reach. Still, he grabs me. Violently dragging me out. Raping me and abandoning me on the kitchen floor.

The family finds me there the following mornings and turn my terror into their entertainment. In the evenings, they gather to laugh at the "sleepwalker" who wanders the house at night.

What they refuse to see is that I had been violently awoken, raped, and abandoned—repeatedly until I am 9 years old.

Over time, things get horrendously worse. In these moments, my mind shuts down. I dissociate from my body because the pain is too unbearable. It is as if it is happening to someone else—some other little girl.

Age 3: It Begins

I am sleeping on the living room floor. Father arrives home after the bars close. He picks me up from my sleep, takes me into the kitchen, and sits me on the kitchen sink. I stare into the darkness of the night through the kitchen window, seeing the ghostly reflection of the kitchen on the glass. He pushes my head against his crotch. I don't understand what is happening. I don't know what to do. In a desperate attempt to divert his attention, I ask for one of the staples of our diet, "I'm hungry. I want an egg." No diversion. I am only three years old. I am so confused and afraid.

Age 5: The Triangle of Betrayal

I sleep in the room before the bathroom. Why do I know it is July 25th? That is my next older brother's 7th birthday. Father picks the early morning hours of that day to rape me.

My oldest brother gets out of bed to go to the bathroom, passes my room, and lets out a scream. I am dissociated, not in the room, not aware of what is happening. The scream brings me back into the room. The scream wakes mother and birthday brother.

The entire house erupts into chaos.

Father scrambles for words, his voice cracking as he tries to defend the indefensible.

Mother's voice explodes like an injured animal, raw and primal, echoing through the house. "How can you do this to me?" she screams at the top of her lungs, her rage directed at his betrayal of her, rather than my pain. Her fury is a living thing, wild and untamed. It is for herself. She is raging, not because he violated her daughter, but because he dared to betray her.

He apologizes to mother, his words tumbling out in a desperate attempt to save himself. His apology is to her, as if I am not even in the room, as if my body, my pain, my violation are secondary to his need for her forgiveness.

Without missing a beat, he points the finger of blame directly at me. "It is her. It is her fault. She's the one who did it."

Then birthday brother—the one whose special day this was supposed to be—turns to look at me. His eyes are hard and accusing. He joins in the blaming of me. "It's your fault. You ruined my birthday!" he hisses, as if my rape is a calculated disruption to his celebration. He chooses his resentment over my pain, his disappointment over my devastation.

I stand there, invisible in my own nightmare. They are making me the bad person. They should be upset with what father did to me. I feel so empty and alone. I feel the blame.

My violation is not the tragedy. I am the problem. I am the one who ruined everything. Inside me, the violated little girl cries.

Mother exclaims, "Largate! Leave!"

Brothers stand frozen, their faces pale, eyes wide with shock. They hear every word, every accusation, every denial. The air is thick with tension, suffocating, unbearable.

Father drapes his blue suitcase over the bed and fills it with his clothes. He nonchalantly takes his humiliation out the front door.

I listen to the crunching of the gravel on the street beneath his brown cowboy boots as his silhouette disappears into the distance.

The momentary feeling of safety shatters as mother shouts to brothers, "Bring him back!" Brothers are happy to see him home as he often worked in different cities; so, they joyfully run to fetch him.

When father returns, mother and father face each other like players in some twisted game of London Bridge, their bodies form an arch of deception above my small head. I stand there in the triangle they created, trapped in the geometry of my own destruction, watching them stare into each other's eyes, oblivious to my existence.

The air between them cracks with something that feels like electricity and tastes like poison. Mother turns to father and says, "I forgive you."

Those words haunt me for decades like a dagger to the heart, "I forgive you."

What I wanted to hear was, "How can you hurt our child?" "What you did was unforgivable." Instead, there is the devastation of watching her choosing a man over her daughter.

I stand there in that triangle of betrayal, my small body frozen in shock, as I watch mother and father trade my life for their comfort. The ground beneath my feet feels like it is dissolving. The walls seem to tilt inward. The very air I am breathing turns to ash in my lungs.

In that moment, I learn the cruelest lesson a child can learn: the people who are supposed to protect me, sacrifice me for their own shared delusion. That my pain is less important than their peace. That I can be standing right there, visible and vulnerable, and be erased by their need to pretend everything is fine.

The triangle closes around me like a trap. Above me, they find their resolution. Below me, the foundation of my childhood cracks wide open, and I fall through into a darkness that takes decades to climb out of.

No one checks in to see how I am doing. I am five years old, expendable, my truth is negotiable, and I am being raised by monsters who only care for themselves. My inner strength tells me I have to take care of myself. The geometry of that moment—mother, father, and blamed child—became the blueprint for my adult relationships. I had been taught, in the most visceral way possible, that my role in this family was to absorb the shame that belonged to everyone else.

And I stood there, small and shocked and utterly alone, learning to carry a burden of shame that was never mine to bear.

Age 5: The Reprieve

Immediately, mother directs brothers to go to the next-door neighbor's house to phone her aunt and summon her. When my great aunt arrives, she goes straight to the kitchen to speak with mother. I hide behind the wall, sneaking around to hear what they are talking about. I overhear mother telling her that I am a bad person and need to be exiled. I feel as if my entire existence is a mistake.

I am taken away in my great aunt's white Cadillac to her home, a place free from the brutal hands, cruel voices, and midnight violations. My great aunt and uncle take care of me. They feed me, clothe me, and keep me safe. I hold onto that feeling of safety as tightly as I can.

My great aunt takes me on sporadic visits to mother and father. I think it is every other week, but the exact timing escapes me. Stories are a patchwork here—a puzzle of my childhood I reconstruct from scraps of memory and the accounts of the people willing to talk about it.

The visits lack humanity or connection. I am like a ghost moving through the house, simply existing, surviving. It feels like I go there to get punished. Mother's hatred for me and her lack of connection are earth-shattering, destroying whatever spirit I build while staying with my great aunt and uncle.

I am standing on one bed and mother is sitting on another. She tells me to go tell father that I hate him. How do I navigate her crazy request? Instead of visiting family, I am stepping into a world of strangers, people with nonsensical expectations from whom I am disconnected.

The ground beneath me feels unstable. Instead of being my safe harbor sheltering me from the storm, mother is the storm. Over and over again, mother's words inject their poison, "You are unworthy of life! You whore. You husband stealer. You slut. You bitch. You prostitute. You stripper. You're trash. I found you in a dumpster and had pity on you. You were jealous of me, and you stole my husband by having sex with him."

The confusion is constant, a swirl of fear, shame, and disorientation that leaves me unsure where I even belong.

Back at my great aunt's house, things are stable. They buy me new clothes. I go to first grade like a normal child. I had my own bedroom and sleep in my own bed. I am honored. They dress me up when they take me to celebrate my 6th birthday at Chucky Cheese with my great aunt, great uncle, and their adult children. This is the first and only time in my life that my birthday is acknowledged.

I remember next Easter vividly. My aunt takes me to the store. When we get to the end cap, there were yellow, green, and blue stuffed Easter bunnies with a small basket on their bellies. My aunt tells me to choose the one I want. I chose the blue one, holding it like a sacred gift.

Age 6: Returned To Hell

In June, first grade ends.

Unexpectedly, father demands my return home.

Safety disappears. I immediately know I am being returned to hell. I am terrified to go back. I am shaking and trembling. I can feel it in my bones, in the pit of my stomach, in the way my breath catches and refuses to release.

I can feel my great aunt's terror, too. It radiates off her like heat, thick and suffocating. She is helpless to resist father's threats of death. Although father's threats are always in private—whispers in corners where no one else can hear—he carries through on them. She knows what waits for me with mother and father.

She reluctantly takes me back to the family secret. Her jaw clenches, her eyes avoid mine as she loads me and my blue Easter bunny into the car. The drive is silent, each of us trapped in the silence of impending doom.

Unable to confront mother and father, she drops me off and rapidly departs.

I stand there, a stranger in a place that is supposed to be home. The air itself feels hostile, charged with invisible threats. I am emotionally numb, feeling disconnected from these people who are supposed to be family. The lay of the land has shifted. There are new rules. They have an agreement that father is to stay away from me. Now I am public enemy number one.

The mines are everywhere, buried beneath every word, every glance, every gesture, waiting to detonate at any point in time into a beating. Secrets are required of me. Father's threats echo in my mind. Mother's demand to stay away from father keeps me scanning for danger. I move carefully, quietly, as if the floor beneath me might crack open and swallow me. I navigate danger every single minute of every single day.

There was a time when he picks me up and puts me on top of the fridge. He thinks it is a cute little game. I freeze—panicked. I'm going to get in so much trouble. Mother does not want me near him. I sit there, high above the kitchen floor, my legs dangling, my heart pounding, fearing the height and mother. This time mother ignores it, and continues cooking, and brothers continue their game of tag below. I see everything from up there—the way they avoid eye contact with me.

I remember times when it is so unsafe to walk around the house, especially when mother and father are together. I am not supposed to see them. I am not supposed to exist in their presence. When I do appear, when I dare to be visible, father turns to mother and says, "See? She's jealous of us." His words twist reality, painting me as the problem, the intruder. He chalks up another point in the game of family dysfunction.

Nights blur into days and days into nights. Time loses meaning. I am always seeking safety around these monsters, vigilant for the inevitable attack. There is no sense of safety—not by day, not by night. I am always on guard, always listening, always watching, always waiting for the next strike.

I am a child living in a war zone, and the enemy is everywhere.

One afternoon, while venturing outside the house, my bare feet on the bare dirt, the scent of motor oil hangs in the air, sharp and heavy, as I approach the driveway. There, half-hidden beneath the car, father is working. I can hear the faint scrape of his tools against metal, a sound that feels ordinary. Suddenly, he rolls out and locks eyes with me. His hands are smeared with grease. With an emotionless face, he says, "I'm going to visit you tonight."

In that moment, fear floods my body like poison. At six years old, I am warned—trapped before the danger even begins. He leans closer, his voice low and threatening, each word is like a knife: "If you tell anyone, I'll kill your mother. I'll kill your great-grandmother." Father demands silence. He enforces it with threats of death. "Not a word to anyone." My voice is silenced even before the upcoming "visit". I am hushed while being raped.

The family secret. The horrors are kept silent. No one names the abuse, and everyone knows. There is an unspoken contract. They know what happened, and no one is allowed to say anything. Keeping silent keeps them from owning the shame. The silence of the shame of all the horrors belongs to the family. It moves through our house like smoke—thick, suffocating, and invisible to anyone on the outside. And the shame lingers for decades. I can see it in the way their eyes avoid mine, in the quick change of subject when the past echoes in the silence, in the aching loneliness of existing without acknowledgment. The truth is buried under generations of denial, and the cost is our collective soul. What happened to me is buried beneath a silence that screams louder than any words ever can.

Age 6-7: The Dungeon

During the summer of my sixth year, my body begins to rebel. My skin is a screaming canvas of my external chaos—raw, angry eruptions that flare without warning like volcanoes releasing lava. The doctors murmur in puzzled tones. I watch their faces as they examine my skin, their brows furrowed, their mouths tight, and their pens scraping across charts as they document their confusion. Unexplainable. They run tests, prescribe medicines, try treatments—nothing works. I see the uncertainty in their eyes, the way they glance at each other as if searching for answers neither of them has. No medicine can cure what is happening to me. No treatment can stop it. I am left hopelessly watching my own body betray me in ways no one can explain. The doctors are deaf to the story my skin is shouting—the story of a child whose body is rejecting the environment that is supposed to keep her safe.

The bumps on my skin grow, spreading like wildfire across my arms, my legs, my torso. At times, they scab over, oozing and crusting with a rotten scent that makes people recoil. I see the disgust, fear, and revulsion on my family's faces when I go near them. I can smell it myself—sour, decaying, burning. It makes me want to run out of my body.

One day, a group of my aunts sit outside on the porch, their voices loud in disgust. They retract their bodies to avoid me. "She has rabies," one of them says, her tone certain, as if she has diagnosed me herself. "It's because she hugged our next-door neighbor Don Prudencio's dog, who they said had rabies." They nod in agreement, their faces twisted with worry for themselves. They believe I am contagious, I am dangerous, I am something to be avoided.

Father's solution is to build a quarantine room. In his blueprint, it keeps the family safe. He calls it protection. I know it's a cage, a dungeon. He hammers and saws, measuring everything except his heart. The walls go up, separating me from the family. When it's finished, I am incarcerated. The heavy door closes behind me, separating me from the world.

The room is the size of the twin bed it contains, with the walls confining me on all sides. No room to move, no space to walk. I sit on the bed because there is nowhere else to go. One single window is my contact with the world. I attach my face to the glass, my breath fogging the pane, my fingers tracing the edges of the frame. I watch brothers run around outside, their laughter floating through the window like a cruel reminder. I am so close to them, yet impossibly far away.

It is hell being in that room. The silence is suffocating. The loneliness is unbearable. The walls press in, stealing the air, stealing my hope. I am a child, alone, watching the world through a window, wondering if anyone will ever let me back in. Mother warns me, "¡Quedate, maldita! No te salgas."

One day, it is too much for me. I escape through the window, my feet hitting the ground with a soft thud. Freedom. Air. Space. I run toward my visiting cousins, their voices calling to me, their arms open. All I want is to play, to be a child, to feel normal.

Mother sees me. She storms toward me, her face twisted with rage. "Maldita! porque te saliste." She grabs me, her hands brutal and unforgiving, and drags me back toward the room. I fight, I scream, I beg—to no avail. The pointy heel of mother's stiletto shoe held in her hand strikes my head—excruciating pain—imprinting punishment on my skull for daring to leave. The door slams shut. The lock clicks. I am trapped again. I sit on the bed, my body aching, my skin burning, my heart shattered. All I want is to play with my cousins. All I want is to be seen, to be touched, to be loved. Instead, I am locked away, with no attempt at a solution. Only isolation.

The house is tomb-silent that summer day. I feel the oppressive heat pressing against the windows. The air hangs thick and motionless, as if the world itself is holding its breath. Mother and brothers have vanished. All I know is the terrifying certainty that I am alone with him.

He enters the room. The temperature seems to drop despite the blazing summer heat. His shadow falls across my small frame like a death shroud, and I know what was coming even before his hands touch me. He begins to rape me, my six-year-old mind disassociates from the experience.

I remember staring through the gap at the top of the curtain, my eyes fixed on the world outside the window. The summer sun is blazing, painting everything in cruel brightness while darkness consumes me from within. I hear the sound of the free souls playing outside. Life continues in a world I am no longer part of.

I learn how to disappear while still breathing. How to numb the pain by leaving myself behind. To endure the unendurable by becoming no one at all.

My body becomes a stranger to me. I experience the rape as something happening to someone else—a girl who looks like me—a shell I abandon to float at the ceiling. The disconnection is complete and merciful. My spirit hovers above the scene like smoke, watching the crime happen to the shell of a body that was once me. I cannot feel my own skin. I cannot feel the bed beneath me. The only feeling is a desperate, primal instinct to be anywhere but here.

The summer light keeps streaming through the gap above the curtain, indifferent to the darkness being carved into my soul. And somewhere floating above it all, the part of me that is pure and untouchable watches and waits for it to be over, counting the moments until I can find my way back into my own body.

In the dungeon, part of me keeps reaching for warmth, longing for someone who can sit and be with me and for something that actually protects instead of imprisoning me. Instead, I learn to catalog pain.

The physical pain of mother's beatings, unbearable, yet somehow more bearable than what father did to me. Her beatings leave bruises I can see, wounds that have names. His penetration brings excruciating pain and instant dissociation; my mind flees my body the moment he touches me. I live through her rage by staying in my body. I live through his violation by leaving my body and floating to the ceiling.

The daggers of emotional pain mother's words plunge into my heart—"You are not good enough, everything is wrong with you." It's a yo-yo game: pulling me close to be friendly, then shoving me away, showing me again and again that my life was sacrificed for her entertainment. Father's emotional cruelty is different—the cold indifference, the way he looks through me as if I am a disposable object for his use.

I learn that protection and imprisonment can wear the same face.

Age 7-8: The Promise of Protection

In the summer of my seventh year, we relocate to another city. One more pointless move to a destination unknown to me. As father loads our personal belongings into the back of the pickup truck, all of the children except me are loaded onto the long bench seat. Mother, so twisted in her jealousy, sees me as competition. She places me on the floorboard at her feet to isolate me from father. The heat of the engine burns through the metal beneath me. The tremor of the road vibrates against my skin. The smell of oil and dust fills my nose. All I see is the swing of my siblings' legs dangling above me as the thick darkness of the night stretches beyond the windows. Shadows rush past too fast to name. My young brain is asking, "Is there something wrong with me?" My body is caught up in the pounding truth that two hours is a very long time when you are staring at your family's feet.

The night of the move, we have a gallon of milk and a loaf of bread for five children and two adults to share. I dunk my slice of white bread into the milk and suck every drop from it, wanting it to be something hardy, something that will fill the hollow ache in my stomach. It is never enough.

We arrive at the new house, which stands alone at the edge of everything, secluded at the end of a long driveway like a fortress of secrets. This is the same house that mother and father first lived in after they married. The scent of the sewer clings to the air, seeping into my clothes, my hair, my skin. We are next to the city sewer treatment plant. On the property is a backyard slaughterhouse. I can smell the blood of the game, pigs, cows, and other animals that father slaughters in the slaughterhouse—thick, disgusting, not safe to breathe.

After the move, I feel alone. Not allowed to have friends. No contact with the extended family. A constant fixture of life is the group of bikers who come by almost daily. I am scared as they ride by on their motorcycles with .22-caliber rifles strapped to their backs, their engines roaring like thunder, their eyes cold and unreadable.

I spend my days taking care of what mother demands. I wash dishes, do laundry, hang the clothes to dry, change diapers, look after the children, sweep the floors, and clean the house. When mother is napping or watching her telenovelas, I escape outside. I generate make-believe worlds, baking mud pies, playing with horny toads, and daydreaming of the life I will have in the future—inside my imagination, where I am safe.

One day, I tell mother I am hungry. She is brutal. She makes me eat an entire pan of chorizo and eggs—enough for five children and one adult—and viciously yells at me that I am taking food from her children and to never ask her for food again. She stands there in anger, her eyes blazing, and makes me eat every bite even though I want to vomit. My stomach churns, my throat tightens, and I force it down because I have no choice. I learn that hunger is safer than asking. My tummy hurts so bad.

The Promise That Breaks Me

I am alone with mother in the kitchen, waiting to be bossed around to do whatever she needs. Father is at work. The boys are playing outside. She makes what sounds like a promise, like protection. "You tell me if 'HE' touches you again."

A few nights later, I am sleeping under her side of the bed to stay safe. The monster rolls her to his side of the bed and reaches for me, and strokes my genitals. Something fierce erupts inside me—I fight back, my small body fueled by rage. He now knows I am going to resist; so, he stops.

The next morning, I tell mother what happened, as she had instructed. Instead of the protection, I expect, she looks at me with cold eyes and denies that he would ever touch me. She says, "You are lying! He did not touch you!" I am not believed. Her disbelief hits harder than any physical blow ever can. Trust breaks inside me. I feel alone in the world. There is no protection here.

I know with devastating clarity that I am alone in the world and have no one to turn to. The person who promised to protect me has chosen him over me. Mother keeps me away from father. Her jealousy sees me as competition, as a threat to her position. Her actions are malicious, cloaked in the language of protection.

Brutally Beaten and Left Behind

Mother and father are taking the boys with them for the day. They tell me I am not going. The bikers scare me. I want to go for safety. I am scared to stay home alone in this house at the edge of everything, where no one can hear me scream. In spite of all they do to me, I want to go with them for safety. The imaginary threat from the bikers scares me more than the real torture from mother and father.

I beg them. I plead. "Please, let me go. Please don't leave me here." I even get in the car, climbing into the back seat, my small hands gripping the edge of the door, my heart pounding with hope that maybe they will let me go with them.

Father is having none of it. His face twists with rage. He yanks me out of the car, his grip brutal and unforgiving, and drags me into the house. He throws me into the bathtub, and my body slams against the cold porcelain. The icy water crawls up around me, soaking my clothes, chilling my skin. I am shaking from the cold and fear, gasping for air, terrified at what is happening.

Then comes the garden hose. He unleashes thwack after thwack on my skin—my arms, my legs, my back—each strike deep and burning.

"¡No me vuelvas a decir que quieres ir!" "Don't ever flipping ask me to go again."

I protect my head. I scream. I cry. I beg him to stop.

He doesn't. A few minutes of beating lasts an eternity.

The door slams shut. The sound of the car engine fades into the distance.

The icy water swallows me whole. It's not just cold—it invades every angry welt left by the hose. My body is numb, my heart is hollow, and I am alone in the middle of winter, in an unheated house.

The lesson is clear: wanting safety is punishable. Needing them is dangerous.

I am eight years old, and I have learned that I am on my own.

Age 9: A Rare Moment of Freedom

I am nine years old. In a rare moment of freedom to be a child, I am outside engaging in a game brothers call World War III. The rules are to chase down and attack the enemy with rocks. I am the enemy. They are the attackers. In a brutal volley of rocks, I sprint toward the house, my heart pounding, desperate to escape. As I run for cover, my right foot slips. The fall. The impact. The sharp edge of the concrete stair meets my skull with a sickening crack. A searing jolt of pain shoots through me. It feels like my head splits open.

For a moment, I lie there, stunned, ears ringing. I feel the blood streaming down my face. It is not warm like I expect—it is a cold trickle over my cheek and down my chin. My fingers tremble as I reach up and touch it. My hand comes away slick and red. I am terrified.

Mother comes out to bring in the boys. Dizzy and shaking, I force myself up and stagger toward mother. With tears in my eyes, I hold out my blood-covered hand and plead, "I need help!" She glances at me. Shock is absent. Concern is absent. A blank stare as she says, "Go close the back door. It's 6 PM." There it is—cold indifference—the demand to lock up the house for the night. I stand there, blood dripping onto the floor, waiting for something—anything. Arms remain at her sides. My pain is ignored by mother. There is the expectation to shut the door, because it is time. That is what matters. Not the blood. Not the wound. Not me.

I feel invisible. Ignored. Uncared for. Unimportant. My injury means nothing. My pain means nothing. I mean nothing.

I do as I am told. I walk to the back door, lock it, and make sure it is secure—like every night. The all-important, unchanging routine must go on, even with blood dripping from my head, even as dizziness threatens to pull me under. I press my hand against the wound, feeling the coolness of my life spilling out. Brothers sit there, staring at me, emotionless. I sit on the edge of the bed with an expanding puddle of blood on the cold concrete floor beneath me. The world moves on as if nothing is happening.

My wounds go untreated. Hours after the injury, father arrives home in the wee hours of the morning, being greeted as a hero come to save the day. In a flurry of activity, brothers excitedly tell him about my injury as I walk out of the bedroom. Mother awakens and joins us. He escorts us from the living room into another shared area with a twin bed. He instructs me to lie on the bed, and he examines my head wound. The family circles the dimly lit operating theatre, their faces a mixture of awe and curiosity. He shaves my head and cleans the wound.

Father instructs mother and brothers that he has things under control, and they can go back to bed. Once again, leaving me alone with him. In that vulnerable moment, as I lie bleeding, father violently whispers for me to be quiet, and he slips his hands under my t-shirt and fondles my undeveloped breasts.

That is the last time he touches me.

Too late... The damage is carved so deep into my soul that it takes decades to excavate. I learn that when I fight back, when I tell the truth, when I follow the rules—I am alone, unprotected, and blamed for the very violence that is destroying me.

My Coach Asked Again

"What happened, Rocío? What did your father do to you?"

My mind is at war. The shame fights to keep me silent, trapped, safe. The future fights to reveal, release, heal. I look at her—then away, staring at the wall, desperate to escape, searching for a way out. The shame overwhelms me. It lives in my soul like a tattoo I did not choose. My family threatened me into secrecy, forbidding me to speak the truth. I realize the shame belongs to them. It is not mine to own.

All I want is to disappear into the safety of silence. My throat tightens, my body tenses, and my mind scrambles for a distraction. And the truth keeps knocking. The truth catches me. Each question she asks is a mirror, and in every reflection, I see the fractured parts of me that I have locked away.

I force myself to confront what had happened to me—again and again. Each time my coach asks a question, I ask myself a deeper one: "Rocío, what did you come here for?" "I came here to heal" is my response.

I came here to help people heal. Leading others into liberation while bound in chains is unworkable. Healing is about freedom for me and becoming a safe place for other people's stories. I understand in that moment that my breakthrough is personal and sacred. Every layer I peel back becomes a path for another soul to follow.

"It's time to tell the truth. It's time to face reality."

Slowly, I turned back to her. I faced the pain head-on. For decades, silence was my prison. I had resisted the pain of the memories. I looked her in the eyes, and overcoming the extreme shame I was feeling, I told her everything I had remembered.

I spoke the truth.

I am coughing it up—decades of silence erupting from my body. The dam breaks. I lose control. I pee more. Over and over, the cycle continues. The more I release, the more I access. By speaking the horrific life experiences aloud, shame loses its power. With every truth I speak, another wave crashes through me. For over an hour, I empty it all.

I have had an invisible chain tightening around my voice, my spirit, my freedom. Every unspoken memory added weight to the chain. With every horrific experience I give voice to, another link of that chain loosens. I feel it falling from my neck, my shoulders, my chest. Every word becomes an act of rebellion against the silence, an act of self-love that says, "This no longer owns me." Releasing the pain means acknowledging what happened while choosing my own identity. Freedom lives in the expression. Freedom lives in the truth. I declare, with bold compassion and unshakable clarity: what happened to me is real. Who I am is separate from what happened. I am the woman who rose—I am me.

And then it stops. I surrender everything. I collapse into bed, exhausted beyond measure. Something inside me shifts. I sink into the silence, my mind still, the heaviness released from my body. Fighting ceases. Running stops. Pure, unfamiliar relief washes through me as the pain leaves my body.

Elevated, Powerful, and Free

Today, I stand in a place of profound transformation. Through this journey of healing, I've allowed the healing process to occur. Rather than blocking out or denying the memories of childhood experience, my memories are clearer than ever. Fractured memories have transformed into vivid, completely embodied experiences—each moment now painted with pristine clarity and truth—experienced with all of my senses—seeing, hearing, feeling, knowing. The searing emotional charge that once enveloped my reality has been liberated by the intense flames of healing. I've given myself complete permission to acknowledge and re-experience that which I once denied. Those feelings that previously overwhelmed me have evolved into quiet echoes. They exist alongside me. The power they held over me exists in the past. The traumatic memories now rest in peace.

The unresolved childhood experiences used to be my puppet masters. I no longer feel the intense feelings I once felt—the ones that consumed me with unworthiness, anger, pain, and sorrow. Now, I choose how the gifts of my experiences serve me. I stand as the sovereign—the queen of my own experiences—having full power over myself. I look at these memories from my position of strength and authority, seeing them with perfect clarity. Like standing on a high balcony, I observe the garden of my memories below. Every detail remains vivid, while I remain elevated, powerful, and free.

I now speak my first language, Spanish. I now understand it. Those childhood experiences occurred in my first language. When I locked away the experiences, I locked away the language, too. Now that the experiences have been released, my first language has also been released.

Taking Your Power Back

We stand at the window and watch our breath fog the glass. We feel the past pulling at us. We reach for will, for grit, for the part of us that says "Do it anyway." We realize will is a blunt instrument against a nervous system that remembers. People say, "You need more willpower." Here's the truth: willpower moves the body while triggers control the mind.

When a trigger hits, your brain's alarm system hijacks everything. Logic shuts down. The nervous system floods. Survival takes over. You cannot "will" yourself out of a triggered state. That is neuroscience. The body remembers what the mind tries to forget. Until we reconcile the past and rewire our nervous system, willpower remains a useful short-term tool that is ultimately unsustainable.

Triggers act like an emotional vortex. High-achieving people set a vision, declare goals, and create a plan. Then something small, real or perceived — a rejection, a delay, a doubt, a feeling, or a memory — pulls us right back into old patterns. The past hijacks the present. Our nervous system hijacks us when we need to take action. We push harder. We force more. We exhaust ourselves. We react to threats that exist in memory, demanding responses in the present.

Transcendence means reconciling the past to create what we desire in the present. Willpower fights emotion. Transcendence goes beyond that to rewire your nervous system. This is the foundation. This is the work that makes any other technique, practice, or strategy work. Rewiring the nervous system means teaching your body that the threat has passed. It means creating new neural pathways where safety lives.

Memories from past experiences convince us that threats are happening now. Our nervous system erases the boundary between then and now. We blow up. We blame. We belittle. We do what we do. We are under the false belief that our current reactions are based on current experiences. We react to the ghosts of the past instead of reality.

When you understand that your reactions belong to the past, you get to step into the present moment with clarity. You can transmute the experiences that once broke you into the wisdom that now empowers you.

When you see the distinction of the present being separate from the past, you liberate yourself from the prison you created. This means dismantling the carefully constructed identity with all of its Illusions, fears, meanings, thoughts, emotions, beliefs, automatic actions, and stories you lived to release the authentic person you have always been.

Reconciling the past means facing your experiences. It means feeling what you buried. It means meeting the younger version of yourself who learned that the world was unsafe, that love was conditional, that clarity required disassociation. It means repetition, patience, and compassion for yourself.

This takes intention and showing up again and again, especially when your old self begs you to stay the same. When you reconcile the past and rewire your nervous system, you can access transcendence— the practice of meeting the trigger as it arises, feeling it in the body, naming it, and responding out of choice rather than reflex.

Willpower is force; transcendence is flow. When we hold transcendence, success stops being something we chase and becomes something we channel. Our bodies soften. Solutions appear. We hear a different voice inside—calm, curious, precise. Our actions feel aligned. We embody success.

We breathe. We feel the old weight lift. We see a wider horizon. We hear our own clear voice say, "We will lead with presence." We press our palm to our heart and we know: willpower alone is only one tool. We must reconcile the past and rewire our nervous system so it stops hijacking us when we need to take action. Transcendence is the practice that turns that tool into a life.

The transformation of pain into gold follows its own timeline. It takes what it takes. It is about un-becoming—shedding the old identity— and it is about becoming—embracing your authentic identity. This is fundamentally a transformation of how you engage with the world and how you define what's possible for your life.

This alchemy happens through intention and consistent action, especially at times when your old self begs you to stay the same. It is a moment-by-moment practice, staying committed to the processes, and showing up again and again. Healing demands being responsible for your present, for your future, and for the ways you contribute to your own suffering.

The most empowering part: you must choose it. Only you can do it for yourself.

Freedom lives in the realization that every moment is a new moment. Past experiences exist in the past. Your freedom exists in the now. Creating habits is surface work. Transcendence is the deep work of rewiring your brain.

Breaking Free: Understanding and Healing from Complex Trauma

Complex trauma is a silent epidemic. It affects people of all ages, cultures, and backgrounds—shaping their emotions, relationships, and sense of self in ways they may not even recognize. Whether stemming from real or perceived childhood neglect, abuse, domestic violence, bullying, or systemic adversity, its effects may last a lifetime if left unaddressed.

I'm telling you the story of my experiences so you can reflect on your own story. You are the expert about your life. You know the inner work you can do that will lead to healing. For me, it was talking to little Rocío, "Hey, little girl, I love you. You are special, you are safe, you belong, I am proud of you, I am here for you, I believe you, I understand you."

Growth requires awareness, courage, and intentional consistent action. It demands your participation.

Impactful life experiences come in different forms. People dismiss the significance of their life experiences by comparing them to others' experiences. Here is a list of experiences often dismissed or overlooked. Reflect on them and notice which ones bring up memories.

Impactful Experiences List

Relationship / Interpersonal

- Bullying, exclusion, ostracization, teasing, rejection, abandonment, being strung along
- Divorce or separation from a loved one.
- Infidelity (discovering a partner's betrayal)
- Gaslighting or emotional manipulation over time
- Estrangement from family (cut off, disowned, ostracized)
- Losing a close friendship (sudden rupture, ghosting, or betrayal)
- Being betrayed by a trusted person (friend, mentor, spiritual leader)
- Childhood neglect (emotional or physical)
- Separation from a caregiver (foster care, deportation, parental incarceration)

Violence / Crime / Oppression (experienced, witnessed, or indirectly impacted by)

- Combat or war experience
- Violence
- School shooting or workplace violence
- Domestic violence
- Discrimination or hate crimes (racism, homophobia, ableism, etc.)
- Sexual assault or harassment (rape, being prostituted)
- Being held captive or kidnapped
- Having your life threatened
- Near death at the hands of another
- Mugging or assault by a stranger
- Stalking or cyberstalking
- Arrest or incarceration (personal or of a loved one)
- Witnessing police brutality
- Human trafficking or forced labor experience
- Familial trafficking
- Slavery or indentured servitude
- Terrorist attack or being a first responder
- Genocide

Health / Medical / Bodily
- Accidents (sports, car, medical, paralysis)
- Healthcare experiences (cancer, illness, life-changing diagnosis, missed diagnosis, invasive surgery, near-death hospital stay)
- Malpractice
- Rehabilitation or nursing home stay
- Pregnancy and delivery
- Experiencing a miscarriage or stillbirth
- Sudden disability or loss of ability (blindness, hearing loss, amputation)
- Extreme body image pressure (eating disorders, shaming, medical weight issues)
- Chronic illness or caregiving for a severely ill family member
- Child with special or severe needs
- Psychological hospitalization
- Illness or loss of a pet

Environmental / Travel / Place
- Natural disaster (earthquake, hurricane, flood, wildfire)
- Aftermath of a natural disaster (displacement, losing a home, famine)
- Losing the farm or livelihood due to environmental factors
- Pandemic or epidemic
- Plane crash or near-miss
- Car accident or close call
- Roller coaster ride or thrill-based somatic experiences
- Being stranded in a remote place (lost while traveling, hiking accident)
- Exposure to hazardous conditions (toxic spill, radiation, chemical accident)
- War zone exposure as a civilian or aid worker
- Cultural displacement (moving to a foreign country and facing isolation or hostility)
- Displacement because of armed conflicts

Social / Economic / Structural

- Severe poverty or homelessness
- Housing displacement (eviction, fire, etc.)
- Sudden job loss, redundancy, being fired or laid off
- Getting kicked off a team
- Being extremely successful then losing everything
- Financial hardship (loss of a scholarship, bonus, subsidy, savings collapse)
- Lawsuit or legal entanglement
- Addiction in the family (living with or losing someone to substance abuse)
- Public humiliation (shaming, harassment, social ruin)
- Being falsely accused of a crime or wrongdoing
- Single parenthood
- Hostile living environment (marriage, roommates)
- Hostile physical environment (gang wars)
- Constant vigilance because of dangerous animals
- Food insecurity or famine

Death / Loss

- Death of a loved one (parent, partner, child, friend)
- Sudden or unexpected death of a loved one (suicide, accident, overdose)
- Accidental harm to someone else (causing injury or death, even unintentionally)
- Loss of a financial asset or inheritance
- Loss of community or cultural home (through gentrification, forced migration)

Identity / Psychological / Existential

- Religious or cult experiences (spiritual abuse, indoctrination, excommunication)
- Identity crisis (loss of cultural, sexual, or personal identity)
- Chronic loneliness or social isolation
- Failing to meet expectations in testing, job interviews, auditions, or academically
- Gaslighting leading to loss of sense of reality
- Psychological breakdown or burnout

Reflections
The Great Escape

Are you ready to break free? Do you say "Enough!"?

If the answer is NO, then put this aside and come back to it when the time is right for you.

We invite you to explore these questions with curiosity and self-compassion. Use them to reframe challenges into opportunities for growth, gratitude, and empowerment. Share your responses with trusted people so you feel heard and understood. Revisit the questions over time to celebrate your growth.

Below are reflection questions designed to help you explore the patterns, beliefs, and hidden wounds that may be shaping your life. These questions are meant to be sat with, felt, explored deeply, and shared with others. Details destroy denial. Courageously remembering the reality of your experience(s) frees you.

A. Join us by writing down your memories. For the first exercise, choose any life-changing experience you remember and write the story of what happened. Refer to the list of Impactful Experiences to see if any of them bring back memories.

B. The next step is getting curious about your initial written, recalled experience. Expand on your story in **Exercise A.** Ask yourself the questions that follow. This version is likely to be more detailed than your initial, written recollection. As you heal, more of the memories surface. The italicized sentences are examples from Rocío's stories.

   1. What details are missing? Where do you dance around the truth? *When my coach asks me what happened, I speak in abstractions. I protect the abusers by hiding the details of their abuse.*

   2. What are the bodily experiences? *The body sensations that I feel are: suffocation when mother smothers me with a pillow, pain in my lower back, tightness in my chest, and horrible headaches.*

3. What do you hear, see, feel, know, sense, or believe at that moment? *I hear mother yelling demeaning obscenities at me. I know she is angry. I feel rejected. I believe she cares only for herself. I am irrelevant to her.*

4. Rephrase words that are too gentle to more accurately describe the impact of the experience on you. *I shift my language from using the word "incest" to the word "rape". I call things what they are. Instead of saying, "I had a difficult time," I say, "I went through hell".*

5. What do you believe about yourself and the thing that hurt you as a result of this experience? *I believe distance equals safety. Closeness equals danger. The people who should protect me are the ones who hurt me.*

6. What parts of the experience impact you the most? *What impacts me the most is mother laughing as she tortures me.*

7. How does this experience shape you? *This experience teaches me that trust is a trap. Kindness is a mask. Good intentions are illusions people wear to get close enough to destroy me.*

8. How do you cope with the experience? *I cope with the experience by numbing myself through schoolwork. I become a Spelling Bee expert, writer, and math wizard.*

9. What happens right before this event? *Recollecting that I am listening to the music right before mother slaps me to the floor.*

10. What happens right after this event? Memory fractures. *The beatings are so severe that my mind shuts down. I black out. What happens next exists in a void I cannot access.*

Affirmations
The Great Escape

Your thoughts, feelings, beliefs, voice, and actions create your reality. Each day, choose three affirmations and speak them out loud. Hearing your own words turns affirmations into living declarations that reshape your mind. Speak with intention and feel the words settle deep within you.

Reparenting and Self-Healing
- I am my source of love and validation.
- I nurture and care for myself.

Truth-Telling and Detail Recovery
- I am my truth.
- I am powerfully witnessed and acknowledged.

Body Awareness and Healing
- My body is safe.
- My body is healed.

Sensory Integration
- I experience things as they are.
- I experience all of my senses in the present moment.

Reframing Beliefs About Self
- I am loved and protected.
- I know my self-worth.
- I am responsible for my own actions.

Trust and Safety
- My boundaries keep me safe.
- People honor my worth and well-being.

Integration and Transformation
- My life experiences are my freedom and joy.
- I fully experience my humanity.

Memory and Healing
- My healing journey is unique.
- Complete memories are the key to freedom.

10 Essential Questions to Help You Seek Professional Mental Health Support

Recalling these memories might have brought to light issues that may be best handled by a professional mental health provider. Finding the right mental health support is a crucial step toward healing and well-being. Here are ten thoughtful questions to guide you in choosing the right professional and ensuring you get the support you desire:

1. What specific challenges or concerns am I facing that make me consider seeking professional help? Identifying your struggles helps you find the right type of support.

2. What type of mental health experience best fits my needs (e.g., therapist, counselor, psychiatrist, coach, religious leader, nonprofit organization, participant-led support group, community leader)? Understanding the differences between these roles ensures you seek appropriate care.

3. What qualities do I value in a mental health professional (e.g., empathy, experience, communication style, credentials)? Knowing what you value in a provider helps you find someone who aligns with your preferences.

4. Does the professional have experience or specialization in dealing with my specific concerns? Checking their expertise ensures they have the right skills to support your journey effectively.

5. What methods do they use, and do these align with my preferences? Understanding their methods (see Chapter 32: Available Therapies) helps you feel comfortable with the process.

6. What are the financial considerations? Does the provider accept my insurance or offer sliding-scale fees? Clarifying costs upfront ensures that therapy remains sustainable for you.

7. What are my goals for seeking professional support, and how will I measure progress? Setting clear goals helps you stay focused and track your personal growth throughout the process.

8. How comfortable do I feel opening up to this professional, and do I sense a connection during the first session? Trust and rapport are key elements of effective therapy.

9. What logistical factors do I consider, such as session frequency, availability, and whether they offer in-person or online sessions? Ensuring that their availability and format work for your lifestyle helps maintain consistency in your care.

10. Am I ready and committed to investing time and effort into the healing process? Recognizing your readiness helps you engage fully in the journey and make the most of the support offered.

These questions can help you make informed decisions, ensuring that you find the right mental health professional to support your healing and growth.

Chapter 5: My Journey to Thriving

*"As long as you keep secrets and suppress information,
you are fundamentally at war with yourself… The
critical issue is allowing yourself to know what you know.
That takes an enormous amount of courage."*

— Bessel van der Kolk

I immersed myself in personal development and devoured every resource I could find. I listened to Anthony Robbins, Wayne Dyer, Deepak Chopra, Marianne Williamson, T. Harv Eker, and countless others who inspired me to believe transformation was possible. I attended over 100 conferences and spent 35-40 hours a week pouring time, energy, and money into desperately searching for answers in the external world. What I discovered was that healing was an individual experience. I had to look inside of me to find the pathways to my healing. No one outside of myself knew the truth of my childhood. What was missing for me was the realization that I had been denying this truth. The weight of this denial became heavier than the pain itself.

I began writing this memoir because I wanted my pain to have meant something. I wrote with the intention of helping others. In the process of writing, I discovered that I was in denial of the truth about the horrific abuse I had experienced. I wanted to remain in my pollyanna-ish, fantasy world, which hid the true horror of my childhood. Deep down, the cracks in my illusion grew wider, and the shouts of truth became too loud to ignore. No matter how tightly I clung to the false sense of safety, reality bled through the gaps, demanding to be faced. Denial had shielded me, and it had trapped me in an invisible jail cell.

I was ready to confront my past so that I could transcend it. Was I remembering correctly? Was I overexaggerating? I reached out to brothers, aunts, uncles, and those who witnessed the abuse, saw the impact on me, and supported me running away when I was 13. I wanted reassurance that maybe my memories were distorted, that maybe I had imagined some of the pain.

What they revealed shocked me beyond my worst fears. My aunt began gently and firmly, "It was worse than what you're describing." My uncles, Angel and Sergio, painfully said that they had tried to save me. They had seen the horrific abuse and had fought against it. They were powerless to stop it. The weight of his helplessness lingered in his voice.

They told me that even my four-year-old body was in terror of father. I feared his presence, his voice, and his evil energy that engulfed us all. It was a darkness too deep to outrun. When he was gone, I desired that he would never come back. Something deep in my soul knew. Like a dog senses danger before it arrives, I experienced a creeping darkness that seeped through the walls, the air thickened, pressing in on me, an invisible force gripping my small frame with terror. I felt father's presence long before the rumble of his tires echoed down the street, before his car turned the corner, before the roar of the engine reached my ears, I would instinctively dart under the table, clutching the legs so tightly they had to pry me away. The fear was constant, keeping me bracing for the unpredictable. Fear had shaped my every move, long before I had words to explain it.

I had contacted them, longing for comfort—for someone to tell me, "No, it wasn't that bad. You're remembering it wrong." Instead, I was met with the truth that I had endured something that was even more brutal than I had allowed myself to remember. And worse than confirmation was the way they spoke with a certainty that shattered any remaining doubt. There was no room for misinterpretation, no space for hoping I had been mistaken. It was worse than I remembered.

And that realization was heartbreaking. I sat with the weight of it, the grief, the anger, the sorrow, and the shame. As painful as it was, something else happened. I discovered that acknowledging the truth was the beginning of my new life. When I confronted my memories, the release was undeniable. With every tear shed and every truth acknowledged, the grip the past had on my physical body loosened. It was like an exhale after a lifetime of holding my breath. The weight of the denial had settled deep into my being, manifesting as a constant tension throughout my body. I had been encased in stone—trapped in an unyielding shell. And facing the horrific experiences of childhood cracked the surface, breaking me free from the casting that had held me captive for so long.

The Pain That Liberates Us

The truth doesn't always come wrapped in comfort. Sometimes, it arrives like a hurricane blowing through the stories we've built to protect ourselves, exposing us to things we avoided seeing.

We minimize the impact of our experiences, especially when we compare them to other people's. Your experience of life being different from someone else does not mean that your experiences are not severe enough to justify your pain. Repression can come in many forms: shame, guilt, self-blame, minimization, avoidance, dissociation, repression, reframing, denial, normalization, etc. This repression may compound to have more impact than if we had dealt with the experiences when they happened. By repressing the past experiences, we become untethered from our life experiences—both in the present and from the past.

For so long, I questioned whether I was making the memories bigger than they really were. Was my trauma even real enough to justify my pain? After talking with my aunt and uncle, there was no doubt. I am free to own my pain. The shame belongs to the abusers. In telling my story, I want the millions of others who have felt the same doubt, the same fear, the same burden of wondering if their pain is real—**it is**. Despite the pain, the truth is what sets us free.

My healing became an inner journey, one that required me to face myself and take ownership of my growth. I committed to daily self-healing practices: affirmations, visualizations, and bold, consistent action. These daily practices helped me reframe my experiences and shift my thoughts, feelings, beliefs, actions, and language patterns. Through these practices and with all this searching, I came to the profound realization that the answers I sought were within me.

At first, mine was a personal pursuit, fueled by an insatiable curiosity about my human potential. I wanted to understand the mechanics of change—what allowed me to break free from my perceived and real limitations and step into my fullest, most powerful self. I had devoured the wisdom from the greatest minds in coaching, neuroscience, and leadership. If there were a way to unlock my highest potential, I was determined to find it.

I started deciphering what I learned from these top professionals—extracting the core principles, techniques, and insights that aligned with my belief about what creates a fulfilling life. The deeper I explored, the more I realized something crucial: transformation went beyond information; it included experience. Learning it for myself ignited something deeper. I was committed to applying it, testing it, and shaping it into something transformative that others could experience in a profound, life-changing way.

I desired to give people a direct path to self-discovery—a path that could avoid the years of searching, frustration, and disappointment I had experienced with generalized approaches. The truth I uncovered was this: what we seek already exists inside us. We are the ones who can embark on the journey of self-healing.

For centuries, people have examined what makes people highly successful with the goal of recreating what they have by imitating what they do. This has led to the belief that success is simply a matter of willpower and forced action. This approach falls short, especially for those who have experienced complex trauma. What I discovered is that transcending these life experiences is necessary before modeling the habits of high achievers has an impact.

Nervous system regulation is an essential part of healing and growth. True transformation requires a deeper reprogramming of the self—an intentional process of integrating what was missing from our formative experiences.

Many of us move through life with an invisible void left by formative experiences absent during our critical developmental years. For some, that missing piece is safety and security; for others, it is connection, attachment, empathy, or even self-awareness. These fundamental aspects of human development shape the lens through which we perceive and interact with the world. Our responses, perceptions, and even our capacity for connection are unconsciously shaped by these gaps. Transformation is about reprogramming our inner world to include what was absent. This means actively learning what was missing in our development. The coping strategies that once kept us safe—whether emotional detachment, hyper-independence, passive-aggressive behavior, people-pleasing, or defensive reactivity—must be examined and, when necessary, released.

To recognize our wholeness, we must teach ourselves what was missing in our past. We must cultivate the feeling of safety for ourselves. We must practice empathy. We must recognize the comfort of secure attachment. This process is necessary for true transformation. Healing is about building those parts of ourselves missing from our upbringing. Through this intentional process of learning, unlearning, and integrating, we can step into a fuller, more complete way of being—one that allows us to respond to life from a place of wholeness.

This process of transformation also requires the development of self-efficacy, emotional intelligence, resourcefulness, and intentional goal-setting. As we reprogram ourselves with what was missing, we must cultivate the belief in our ability to influence our own lives, deepen our capacity to understand and regulate our emotions, and set meaningful goals that align with our newfound wholeness.

The Roller Coaster of Success: Why Some Achieve and Lose It All

In my work with clients, I have seen a recurring pattern—a roller coaster ride where they achieve extraordinary success, then lose it all, often without understanding why. No matter how talented, driven, or capable they are, their success repeatedly slips through their fingers. This cycle leaves them confused, frustrated, and feeling powerless to break free.

Many of these individuals have the external resources to be successful—knowledge, skills, abilities, education, money, networks, or opportunities. However, time and time again, I see that these external resources are not enough. The missing piece is an internal, fundamental program that must be built from within.

When you lack a deep sense of worthiness, security, connection, or self-trust, no amount of external achievement can compensate for it.

The absence of this internal foundation distorts your ability to see what is possible, limits your capacity to sustain success, and often leads to self-sabotage or unconscious patterns of collapse.

Until you do the internal work to reprogram yourself, the cycle continues. When you recognize and internalize what was missing—whether it be safety, self-worth, emotional security, or a sense of belonging—then you can get off the roller coaster and create success that lasts. True transformation starts by unleashing the internal resources to sustain external success.

When you learn to intentionally use the coping mechanisms required by your environment—resilience, adaptability, resourcefulness, or hyperawareness—alongside your newly developed internal foundation, you become unstoppable. No longer held back by old patterns, you can channel your coping strategies into strengths, using them with intention rather than as unconscious reactions. This is the point where you expand, evolve, and create a life of lasting fulfillment and impact.

Success as a Reflection of Your Internal Programming

Success is what you choose it to be—deeply personal and shaped by your values, desires, and vision for your life, rather than meeting external expectations or comparing yourself to others.

True success is about having the ability to create and recreate success in any form you desire. Whether that means personal growth, meaningful relationships, inner peace, career achievements, or simply feeling aligned with who you truly are, you get to decide what success looks like for you.

When you process and integrate your past experiences, you develop greater self-regulation, resilience, and emotional agility—the real precursors to sustainable high performance.

The reprogramming and rewiring of your nervous system lay the foundation for true success. Then the long-term strategies for success—like discipline, focus, and perseverance—become truly effective and actionable. The roller coaster of success, which was dependent on external circumstances become transmuted into something you can generate, sustain, and reshape as desired.

Who you become in the process of healing is what leads to sustainable success.

The Right People Can Help

Transformation begins the moment we see what has been hidden, when we name it for what it is, and when we feel the impact it has had on the choices we make and the lives we live.

Awareness Opens the Door to Freedom.

Softening my armor was a process of constantly taking intentional action. It happened in those spaces where I felt safe enough to speak my truth, to voice what I had endured, and to share what I had felt. It was in the places where I discovered that anger was allowed. Where disgust could surface without being met with judgment.

Each of these openings led me from one step to the next. They gave me the chance to do what I now understand as the real inner work. And the truth is, every single layer is the real inner work. Complex trauma is a series of experiences stacked on other unresolved experiences. It takes courage to unpack what needs to be unpacked at and to transcend what needs to be transcended.

Healing often reveals itself backwards—the freshest wounds rise to the surface first, demanding to be seen and spoken. Layer after layer gets peeled away until the buried seed of pain is revealed. What matters most is the sacred act of unpacking itself, allowing each fragment to surface in its own time. Healing takes what it takes.

Some people believe they can do it on their own. We are meant to do this with others. The right people can help us. People who listen deeply with empathy can hold the mirror; they can extend their hand. Even though the right people can help, it is like someone who has gone overboard. The person on the life raft can offer the rope. The one in the water has to reach for the lifeline. You are the one willing to do the work and reach for the lifeline to move forward.

In doing that work, something extraordinary happens. You build resilience. And that resilience becomes a foundation for everything else: courage, confidence, belief, and the ability to rise again and again no matter what life throws at you.

There's a saying: you grow through what you go through. And it's true. I told my therapist, "If I erased anything in my past, I would erase the person I've become." With the horrific childhood experience, I developed empathy for myself, a deeper connection with others, and a compassion for all of humanity with all of its struggles. This is what makes me the person who I am and I love all of me.

I've found purpose. I've discovered my mission. I know what I want, and I know how to support people. And over and over again, I hear the same acknowledgment, "Rocío, what's remarkable about you is that you grew through hell and now you are walking beside others on their journey out of hell, too."

Boat Exercise

Who do you want to accompany you on your journey? Here's an exercise called the *boat exercise*. Imagine you're in a boat on the water. You're the captain. And you get to decide: who are the five people you want on that boat with you? Who do you trust to ride the waves with you—no matter how calm or how stormy the journey gets?

Maybe there's someone in your life right now who clearly belongs there. Or maybe you realize there are gaps—roles no one currently fills. If so, you get to imagine: *Who would represent that for me? Who's the person who would have my back, no matter what?*

This is why I'm so fiercely loyal to the people who have shown me, over and over again, that they're truly in my boat. The ones who hold me, see me, and stay when the waters get rough.

Now, think about archetypes. Each person on the boat represents something essential and someone who:

- Creates **safety**: a place where you can take off your armor.
- Offers **security and protection**: who you know will defend your best interests.
- Brings **connection**: who listens deeply, who hears you.
- Nurtures your **sense of belonging**: who makes you feel you matter, no matter what.
- Sees you as **whole**: even in your healing.

The truth is, no one person can give us 100% of all of these. Some people may give us two or three of these qualities. Others may embody one, and they do it so beautifully that it fills us up. A therapist, for example, might be the one who sees us wholly. A best friend might be the one who creates belonging. A mentor might be the one who gives us courage and safety.

Ask yourself, *"Who would most support me right now?"* Who's in my boat? And even more importantly—why? Do the people in my boat help me grow, keep me stagnant, or drag me down?

A Journey of Healing and Transformation

Life will test you. Challenges are invitations to rise. The first step is rejecting the belief that struggle is permanent. A better life is something you create with intention and bold action.

Hope is an action to go beyond limitations. Your thoughts shape your reality, so speak to yourself with belief. Growth demands courage, persistence, vision, and determination. Even in adversity, resilience combined with mindset, visualizations, affirmations, and bold action can create results beyond expectations.

True healing is about giving up forcing outcomes, embracing stillness, and allowing peace to be a place of growth. The power to achieve the impossible is already within you. Transformation is for anyone willing to do the work. You have the power to reveal your true self.

Reflections
The Journey to Thriving

We invite you to explore these questions with curiosity and self-compassion. Use them to reframe challenges into opportunities for growth, gratitude, and empowerment. Share your responses with trusted people so you feel heard and understood. Revisit the questions over time to celebrate your growth.

Our invitation to you is to embrace self-love, rewrite your story, and step fully into who you are meant to be. Your future starts now.

1. **Who Will Join You:** Who are the five people who will join you on your journey? *List the five people who will be on your boat and how they will support you.*

2. **Redefining Self-Worth:** How have your accomplishments shaped your perception of self-worth? *In what ways can you begin to separate your value from external achievements?*

3. **Filling the Void:** Reflect on the ways you've sought love and validation from others. *How can you start providing those things to yourself?*

4. **Letting Go of Unmet Expectations:** What expectations did you have for love and support from your family? *How can you release those expectations and redefine love on your terms?*

5. **Creating Safety Within:** Describe what emotional safety feels like for you. *What practices or boundaries can you put in place to nurture this sense of safety?*

6. **Celebrating Personal Growth:** What are three things you love about the person you are becoming? *How have these qualities evolved through your healing journey?*

7. **Rewriting the Narrative:** What limiting beliefs from your childhood impact your self-perception today? *How can you reframe those beliefs into empowering affirmations?*

8. **Cultivating Self-Compassion:** Reflect on a time when you were hard on yourself. *How would you offer yourself kindness and understanding in that moment now?*

9. **Identifying Unmet Needs:** What emotional needs went unmet in your childhood? *How can you meet those needs for yourself today?*

10. **Thriving:** How can you transition from your past coping strategies to thriving? *What does a peaceful, fulfilling life look like for you now?*

Affirmations
The Journey to Thriving

Your thoughts, feelings, beliefs, voice, and actions create your reality. Each day, choose three affirmations and speak them out loud. Hearing your own words turns affirmations into living declarations that reshape your mind. Speak with intention and feel the words settle deep within you.

- I am worthy.
- I am thriving.
- I embrace my true self.
- I am patient with myself.
- I write my empowering story.
- I enjoy the peace I have created.
- I nurture myself with love and care.
- I am excited about where I am going.
- I am compassionate towards myself.
- I am the source of my own validation.

Chapter 6: Back to My Inherent Worth

"You are not who the world says you are, you are who you decide to become."

— Matshona Dhliwayo

The light they tried to extinguish. I always knew I was worthy because I felt it deep in my bones—like a silent, steady rhythm humming through my being. Even as a child, I could feel the light inside me. I loved to speak up. I dreamed big. I danced with life. I daydreamed of love, happiness, and connection.

The people around me tried to make me feel unworthy. Mother, brothers, teachers, family members, boyfriends saw me and my light made them uncomfortable. Little-by-little they responded with criticism, silence, punishment, shame, disapproval—subtle, sharp, and relentless. My light was dimmed by these attacks but never fully extinguished. Through it all, I knew that worthiness was something every person has because they exist.

When the World Tried to Erase Me: The Voices That Tried to Define My Worth

There were moments—so many moments—when I knew I was worthy. And the people around me worked overtime to convince me otherwise. Their actions, their omissions, their tones—all carried the same poisonous message: You are not enough.

The Chorus of Criticism

I can hear brothers' voices echoing like a chorus of mockery. "You have a long neck." "You can't play with us unless you can prove you're strong enough." "You're just a girl—you get periods." As if my biology made me less. As if my strength had to be earned through humiliation.

I remember the pretty girls in beautiful outfits with polished shoes and new toys. They walked together in circles of belonging. I was left alone, wearing hand-me-downs and carrying pebbles in my pockets.

In first grade, I found my way to school by myself—a six-year-old wandering the streets because even friendship felt out of reach.

Invisibility

Then came the boyfriends: "I hate that you don't serve me food." "You should bring me coffee." "You should dress sexier." "You work too much." "You're not allowed to be more educated than me." "You need to live for me." "Why are they calling you? I am the national figure; they should be calling me!" "I am the millionaire; they should be asking me to speak on entrepreneurship!"

They wanted me to shrink, to exist for their comfort, to disappear into domestic shadows, to become invisible. My voice, my dreams, my degrees, my accomplishments—it all made them feel small. So instead of rising with me, they withdrew love like a punishment. Why would I praise you to make you feel better about yourself while I am unacknowledged?

Aunts and uncles looked through me as if my child and I were invisible. Without a word, they stole my son's diapers, our coats, our clothes. I found a large box full of my belongings and showed it to my grandmother. Her response? "Leave them there, they will get mad if you take them."

Invisible. Disposable. Unworthy.

Lessons in Shame

Father told me coldly, "You will not redeem those Dairy Queen certificates because we don't take charity." They were not charity. I earned them at school through hard work and excellence. He made my achievement feel like a stain on our name.

Mother warned, "I'll beat you if you ever take anything from anyone." And she meant it. I remember the beatings. For cuddling up to my grandmother. For resting my head on my uncle's shoulder. For simply reaching for love.

Worth of a Woman

"You're despicable," mother spat at me. "You are unworthy of life." "You work for me and must give me your money." "You are nothing because you are a woman." "You must submit yourself to a man."

She said it with such venom, as if she truly believed I had no right to dream, to lead, to live freely. She tried to sentence me to a lifetime of servitude, silence, and submission.

Constant Disapproval

My cousins on welfare put me down. They had nice clothes and I had their hand-me-downs. "You're not pretty like us." "You don't wear nice things like we do." "You're poor—we're rich."

Every comment they said, every beating they gave me intended to put me down and erase me.

Academic Doubt

And in the classroom—a place that was supposed to be safe for minds like mine—I was made to feel defective. "You just don't get it, Rocío." "You're unplugged… disconnected." "You're never going to make it."

This might have been expected in elementary school; however, this was my master's-level Spanish literature class. I could read the words, hear them, and pronounce them, and have a complete lack of comprehension of what I was reading. I worked so hard. I would stay up to the wee hours of the morning and could not get it. They labeled me as less. They did not see how my comprehension of Spanish was locked inside the experiences with the family growing up.

No Support For You

I was eight years old, mother was helping oldest brother with his homework. I walked in and asked mother, "Can you help me?" She whipped around and growled at me, "I will never help you. Don't ever ask me for help again."

It was the anger in her face, the venom in her tone, and the finality in her voice I remember. I felt the sting in my chest, the heat in my throat, and my hands went cold. That moment I learned that it was dangerous to need support. That I had to prove my value through silence, strength, and self-reliance. That receiving love, support, or care was conditional. So, I became self-sufficient and hyper-independent because I knew my worth, and I was protecting it.

Armor I Wore

I stopped asking for help. I stopped stating my needs. I swallowed my voice to keep the peace. And I wore armor like strength—shiny on the outside, suffocating on the inside.

I learned love was conditional. I'd attract partners who mirrored the emotional neglect I experienced as a child. How I'd give more than I received—and then feel resentful, and unaware of it.

The real unraveling began the day friends asked me: "How can we support you?" and "How can I contribute to your success?" And I froze. My body tensed, and the automatic response spilled out before I could stop it: "I'm good." "I don't need anything." "I've got it."

Something inside me ached because I wanted to know how to receive their help. I had learned that needing others led to abandonment or pain. The fear was that if I let people in, they'd use my vulnerability against me.

Pattern Recognition

Despite all these attempts to extinguish my belief in my self-worth, a voice inside me kept whispering: I know the truth, my worth is inherent in who I am.

As I grew in my work—coaching powerful leaders, guiding transformational change—I began seeing the same patterns reflected in others. Engineers, doctors, entrepreneurs, and speakers, confident, strategic, and visionary in their external armor. While inside, they carried the childhood scripts that told them there was something wrong with them.

They sabotaged success, repelled money, rejected help, avoided love—and I understood them intimately. Because I'd done the same.

One of my biggest breakthroughs came while reviewing my finances. There were unpaid customer invoices, late payments, excuses, and broken promises. At first, I blamed others. Mary never paid. John was always late. Jasmine lied about the wire transfer.

Why were all these people so unreliable? I had a sobering realization: I was the common denominator. I was the one who created it. I was the one not enforcing my boundaries. I was tolerating disrespect because part of me believed that asking for what was mine would lead to rejection, someone being upset at me, or being ostracized.

Reclaiming My Power

That was my turning point. I began reclaiming my power. I started asking: Where did I begin to equate boundaries with being "too much"? When did I start confusing worthiness with performance? Why was I protecting myself like that eight-year-old girl still trying not to get burned?

The answers were liberating. In the past, people tried to tear me down—through criticism, silence, punishment, shame, disapproval, and doubt. I was conditioned to believe in being unworthy. The great thing is that conditioning can be reprogrammed. When their voices got loud, when I walked to school alone, or when my last dollar was stolen from me, my soul always remembered my worth. I dug myself out from under the rubble of their projections. To find my way back, I started telling myself the truth again: I am worthy, lovable, capable. and enough. I love all of me.

Reclaiming Your Worth

If you recognize yourself in this story, if you've carried the voices of those who tried to diminish you, know that your worth was buried beneath their projections and your protective responses.

Recognize the conditioning. Notice where you dim your light to avoid rejection. Where you accept mistreatment because you were taught it was normal. Where you play small because the world conspired to make you believe you were unworthy.

Question the voices. Whose voice do you hear when you criticize yourself? Whose standards are you feeling compelled to meet? Whose approval are you seeking? These voices may be the echoes from people who buried your light.

Reclaim your boundaries. Start asking for what you deserve. Stop tolerating disrespect. Enforce your standard because you know your worth.

Practice receiving. Allow others to support you, help you, and celebrate you. Your independence was a reaction to your circumstances. Your true nature is being in community, receiving support, and giving it freely.

Remember your inherent worth. You are worthy because you exist. You are valuable the way you are. You have a place in the world because of your humanity.

Your Light Shines Brightly

I tell this story from a place of power. If you've been told you're not enough, you need to hear this: *They lied.*

You are who you've always known yourself to be. Now is the time to remember what you've always known deep down: You are worthy, empowered, and enough. And you are free from carrying their projections.

The light they tried to extinguish? It's still burning. It always has been. It's time to let it shine.

Reflections
Back to My Inherent Worth

We invite you to explore these questions with curiosity and self-compassion. Use them to reframe challenges into opportunities for growth, gratitude, and empowerment. Share your responses with trusted people so you feel heard and understood. Revisit the questions over time to celebrate your growth.

1. What messages about your worth did you receive as a child? How do those voices show up in your inner dialogue today?

2. When do you remember first feeling "not enough"? What was happening around you, and who was present?

3. In what ways do you dim your light or make yourself smaller to avoid rejection or criticism?

4. What coping strategies did you develop to protect your sense of worth? How are they serving or limiting you now?

5. Where in your life do you seek approval from people who are fundamentally unable to give you what you need?

6. How has your relationship with receiving help, support, or love been shaped by your early experiences of worthiness?

7. What would change in your life if you truly believed you were worthy simply because you exist?

8. In what areas do you tolerate treatment that reflects the unworthiness you were taught rather than the worth you possess?

9. How do you recognize the difference between your authentic voice and the voices of those who tried to define your value?

10. If you could speak to your younger self about their inherent worth, what would you want them to know?

Affirmations
Back to My Inherent Worth

Your thoughts, feelings, beliefs, voice, and actions create your reality. Each day, choose three affirmations and speak them out loud. Hearing your own words turns affirmations into living declarations that reshape your mind. Speak with intention and feel the words settle deep within you.

- I belong.
- I am free.
- I am strong.
- I am worthy.
- I am enough.
- I am powerful.
- I choose myself.
- My light is bright.
- My worth is inherent.
- Love finds me easily.

Chapter 7: Self-Compassion

"The moment you start treating yourself with the same love you'd offer a wounded child, true healing begins."

— Unknown

The choice between pain and abandonment. "We cannot control your pain anymore." The doctor's words hit me at my core as he delivered his verdict. His voice carried the weight of defeat, the admission that medicine had reached its limits with my shooting pain. "We need to burn the nerves that lead to your leg and your back so that you can stop feeling the pain. And we need to put some rods in your back." The words hung in the air like smoke, choking me with their implications. Surgery. Metal rods. Burned nerves. Three months of recovery where I would be as helpless as a newborn, dependent on others for the most basic needs.

All of this was a result of a head-on collision that nearly left me in a wheelchair. My body became a prison of agony that no key could unlock. For two years, I had been shuffling from doctor to doctor, my spine screaming with shooting pain down my right leg with every step I took. The simple act of standing became a negotiation with torture, each movement a reminder of my lack of control.

I needed traction on my back daily to function; my body stretched and pulled like a medieval torture device, giving me moments of relief from the fire that lived in my spine. Pain had become my constant companion, whispering reminders of my limitations with every breath, every movement, every attempt to live a normal life.

I contemplated the surgery and knew my son would need care while I was recovering. With my twelve-year-old son's face in mind—his eyes holding the innocence of childhood, believing that his mother could fix anything—I picked up the phone to call the one person who was meant to be my safety net. Mother. The woman who had carried me in her womb, who was supposed to understand that when your child calls in desperation, you answer without question.

"Mother," I said, my voice already heavy with the vulnerability I hated to show, "I need back surgery. The doctor says I'll be laid up for three months. I need help with my son." The words felt like admitting defeat, like confessing that my strength had run out, that I stood at the edge of what I could handle alone. Yet surely, she would understand. This was the moment when maternal instinct would override everything else.

Her response hit me like ice water in my veins: "Your uncle's going to be in town. I can't help you. I am going sightseeing with him."

The silence that followed was deafening. I could hear my own heartbeat in my ears, could feel the ground shifting beneath my feet as the reality of her words sank in. Her brother's vacation—her sightseeing, her entertainment—was more important than her daughter's surgery. More important than her grandson's need for care while his mother recovered from having her spine reconstructed.

I had to make a choice that no mother should ever face: live in excruciating pain that was slowly destroying my ability to function, or get the surgery I desperately needed and risk my son's well-being. If I got surgery, I would lose the ability to feed my son, to help him with homework, or to take him to school. We would have no one—no one to care for me, no one to care for him.

So I chose pain. I chose to live with shooting pain in my spine, with fire in my legs, with the daily torture of a body that betrayed the life I was trying to build. I chose to be in pain so my son would have stability, because the woman who gave birth to me had chosen sightseeing over maternal care.

Mother lacked the compassion that other mothers would give— the instinctive, fierce protection that was meant to make her drop everything and rush to my side. Instead, she offered me the brutal lesson that I was alone in this world, that even in my darkest hour, I can only count on myself.

Unfulfilled Yearning For Comfort

Two years later, my body betrayed me again. I had been diagnosed with precancerous cells that needed to be frozen away. The procedure, which sounded simple, left me feeling like I had been turned inside out, my body wracked with pain and nausea that seemed to seep into my very bones.

The surgery had me so sick that even breathing felt like work. Each inhale was a struggle against the waves of nausea that crashed over me like a relentless tide. I had learned the lesson too well to repeat the same mistake of asking mother for help again. The memory of her choosing sightseeing over caring for us was too fresh, too sharp, cutting out any illusion I might have had about her capacity for maternal care.

I lay on the couch after my son went to school, my body curled into itself like a wounded animal seeking comfort. The house felt hollow around me, filled with the kind of silence that amplifies every ache, every moment of vulnerability. In that vulnerable state, something primitive and desperate arose from the depths of my chest—a yearning so profound it felt like hunger.

I found myself craving something that lived in my imagination: the feeling of mother lying in bed with me, comforting me, her voice soft and soothing, telling me everything was going to be okay. I could see it clearly—her hand stroking my hair the way mothers do in movies, her body so close that I could feel her warmth, her presence filling the space around me with safety. The yearning was like reaching for water when you're dying of thirst.

Even as the longing consumed me, I knew with bone-deep certainty that it would remain a fantasy. Mother had no desire to be motherly to me. She lacked the tenderness that was meant to be as natural as breathing, as automatic as a heartbeat. The woman who had given birth to me was missing some essential piece of maternal DNA, some fundamental understanding of what it meant to nurture the child you brought into the world.

As I lay there drowning in my own desire for comfort, a friend stopped by to drop off a burger I requested—a small act of kindness that felt both precious and heartbreaking in its simplicity. That greasy paper bag contained more compassion than I had ever received from the woman who was supposed to love me unconditionally. It was the extent of the care I could expect, the full measure of support available to me in my hour of need.

The burger sat on the coffee table like a monument to my reality: I was motherless in the truest sense—she lived yet refused to be what I needed her to be. The mother I yearned for—the one who would rush to my side, who would hold me while I was sick, who would choose my well-being over hatred—existed in my imagination, a ghost of what was meant to have been yet lived only in dreams.

Compassion Missing

For years, I've wrestled with a truth that cuts through me like broken glass: compassion was something I desperately wanted, something I inherently desired, yet something that eluded me completely. It was like being born colorblind to kindness, unable to receive the very thing my soul was starving for.

I have spent my entire life pouring compassion out as if it were water from an inexhaustible well—offering it freely to others, feeling their pain as if it were my own, holding space for their wounds with the tenderness of a mother caring for her child. Being the recipient of that sacred gift was missing for me. That gaping absence of compassion in my life became twisted and tangled with the shame of being abused, creating a toxic knot in my chest that I carried everywhere I went.

Where normally there would be nurturing, love, and care flowing toward me like sunlight, there was neglect, cruelty, and harm—an endless winter that froze my ability to believe I was worthy of warmth.

Compassion Found

In a world where blood relations had taught me that love was conditional and care was earned through perfect behavior, I discovered what compassion looked like through people who chose me because they wanted to. When I was in my mid-forties, I lived with Carmen. Her family became the people closest to family I had—through the radical act of unconditional acceptance alone.

They were the ones who always welcomed me in, their door opening before I could even knock, their faces lighting up with genuine joy at my presence. There was no performance required, no mask I had to wear, no version of myself I needed to present to be worthy of their space. With them, I could simply exist and be celebrated for existing.

Carmen, her daughter Maya, and her granddaughter Lily had concern for me that felt foreign and precious—the kind of worry that comes from love rather than obligation, the kind of care that asks "How are you really?" and waits for the real answer. They ensured that I was included in their life as an essential piece of their family puzzle—deliberate, intentional, chosen. They made me feel special in ways foreign to my experience, as if my presence added something irreplaceable to their world.

Being taken care of was part of being family to them—a natural expression of love that flowed as easily as breathing. They taught me what it felt like to belong somewhere, to be chosen rather than tolerated, to be held by people who wanted to hold you.

I learned that family transcends who raised you—sometimes it's about who sees you, really sees you, and decides that you're worth keeping. They became my chosen family, my safe harbor, my proof that love without conditions actually exists in this world.

It was through Carmen, Maya, and Lily that I began to understand what it might have felt like to receive the love and nurturing I had been denied my entire life. One day, Lily burst into the kitchen, her little face streaked with tears, heartbroken and crying to her mom about something that felt earth-shattering to her seven-year-old world. Her friend had said mean things to her, and the pain was written across her features like words on a page.

I watched Maya's motherly instinct kick in instantaneously. She hunched over, scooped Lily up in her arms like she was the most precious thing in the world, and carried her to the bedroom to comfort and nurture her. The tenderness in that gesture took my breath away— it was so natural, so automatic, so full of unconditional love.

Lily emerged a little later, seeking comfort, and went straight to her grandmother. Carmen opened her arms wide, gave her a big, enveloping hug, looked Lily directly in the eyes, and listened with complete attention to everything her granddaughter had to say. There was no rushing, no dismissing, no telling her to "get over it"—just pure, focused presence.

That moment struck me like lightning, illuminating a darkness I had lived in without knowing. It was the first time I truly understood that compassion was one-directional for my entire life. I could give it to others, feel it for others, empathize with their pain until it became my own. Receiving compassion stayed beyond my reach. I had no frame of reference for what it felt like to be held in that sacred space of unconditional care.

Your Pain Matters

On another occasion, after one of Lily's swim meets, she came home with injured shoulders, her little muscles tight and sore from the competition. I watched, mesmerized, as both Carmen and Maya took turns massaging her back, their hands gentle and healing, helping her feel better with the kind of attention that said, "Your pain matters. You matter."

I stood there wondering with an ache that went bone-deep: What would that be like? What would it feel like for someone to care about my pain and actually try to help me heal from it? I thought back to my own childhood, searching desperately through my memories for even one moment of similar care. Emptiness answered. If I had ever gone to mother in pain, if I had ever asked for help or comfort, she ignored me completely or beat me for daring to need something from her.

The Tumor

On the eve of my 34th birthday, I wake with anticipation. I take the day off—my gift to myself—a slow morning, a couple of doctors' appointments, space to breathe. My first appointment is at 10 AM. I leave my nutritionist's office with a smile, already picturing a leisurely afternoon. At 11 AM, I'm in the grocery store across the street from my primary doctor, killing time before my noon appointment. A wave crashes over me. My body turns heavy, my head swims. I grip the cart, desperately attempting to steady myself. I am too sick to go to my doctor's appointment; so, I cancel it. Warrior mode kicks in as I drive the hour home, every mile a test of will.

I collapse into bed, the world spinning. At 5:30 PM, JJ arrives to take me out for my birthday dinner. JJ is my best friend—my adventure and travel buddy, the one who stands beside me through every season. He is the person I can lean on, no matter what life brings. "I don't feel well—I need to rest," I say. JJ insists, "Let me drive you. You can rest in the car." I refuse. I climb to my upstairs office, glance at a few documents on my computer, then surrender to exhaustion.

At 1:30 AM, pain splits my skull—a sharp, stabbing force. I stumble from bed, words tumbling out incoherently. I realize JJ stayed the night when he wakes up and urgently asks, "What's wrong?" I can't stand. His face blurs in panic. He urges, "Let's go to the hospital." I call the hospital; the attending doctor tells me they are going to call an ambulance unless I get to the ER immediately. Within minutes, JJ is racing me to the hospital. The pain is relentless. I curl up in a ball, crying from the intense pain in my head. I am thinking someone is stabbing me in the head. Doctor after doctor tries to control the pain, cycling through treatments and medications.

In the ER, under harsh fluorescent lights, a doctor looks me in the eye and says, "You need an MRI." I protest—"I have a birthday party." She holds my gaze and says firmly, "You need to cancel it." I refuse to cancel. I celebrate anyway, surrounded by friends. One leans in, voice low, "What will you do if they find something?" I answer without hesitation, "I'll celebrate. Before, during, after. That's who I am."

He enters the room without greeting me, moves directly to his chair, and says, "A picture says a million words." He reviews my file, lays out my options. In an instant, I step into warrior mode. "What do I need to know? What are my options?" He tells me the risks—stroke, death, the necessity of surgery. I listen, absorb, and choose action.

He enters the room without greeting me, moves directly to his chair, and says, "A picture says a million words." He pulls up the MRI on his computer screen and points to the image, showing me how the tumor mushrooms into my brain. His face is serious as he explains—in time, this will kill me. No one knows how long it's been there. I look at him and say, with absolute certainty, "This tumor has been there for years." I've complained to doctors about my balance, the ringing in my ears, again and again. Every time, they tell me it's just an infection. I've taken medication, courses of steroids, round after round. What I realize now is that the steroids have kept the tumor at bay—until now. This round I am currently taking isn't working anymore. The symptoms break through, and the truth finally comes to light.

He reviews my file and then looks at me with a gravity that lands hard. "The biggest risk is that you could have a stroke and die any moment." I stare at him, shocked—thirty-four years old, and he's talking about dying in an instant? Something shifts inside me. I go into warrior mode. For me, this becomes a business transaction: live or die. Every problem has a solution—my grandmother taught me that—and this one has a solution too.

He reviews my file and looks at me with a gravity that lands hard. He lays out the risks, every word heavy in the air. Something shifts inside me. I go into warrior mode, spine straightening, eyes locked on his. "Okay, doctor, what are my options?" I ask, voice steady.

He lays them out: invasive surgery, stereotactic radiation surgery, or let it take its course, which means death.

"The biggest risk is that you could have a stroke and die at any moment."

I stare at him, stunned—thirty-four years old, and he's talking about dying in an instant.

For me, this becomes a business transaction: live or die. Every problem has a solution—my grandmother taught me that—and this one has a solution too. I choose action, even when none of the options feel easy.

I decide to take matters into my own hands. I go home and obsessively research, diving deep into anything that might help. I change my diet even more—something I've been working on for years—and immerse myself in alternative therapies. I learn what foods cause inflammation and which reduce it, how to alkalize my body, how to do salt therapy, and how to support my healing from every angle. I refuse to sit with my arms crossed, waiting for the doctor to tell me what to do. He's already given me the diagnosis and the options, and now I see my path: I can do something about it, or let it take its course. I choose action.

JJ and Jack stay by my side. JJ stands by my side for years. Jack makes it his mission to keep me happy. I watch those around me fall apart as my stereotactic radiation surgery nears, and I realize—I am the one holding everyone together. The day arrives. My brothers, sister-in-law, my son and his girlfriend, my godmother, and JJ gather. None of us know how to deal with the situation, so we turn to reminiscing over the humorous life experiences people have had. They remind me of the time I tried to flush my son's frog down the toilet not knowing the frog was sleeping. I walk into the surgery room, my head anchored to the table with a Freddy Krueger mask—precision is everything. Blue light floods my vision as the procedure begins. I float in a surreal space, suspended between fear and surrender.

Afterward, I return home, weak and restless. JJ cares for me—up and down the stairs, rubbing my back as I cry, exhausted and unable to sleep because of the steroids.

The tumor was fused to the nerve. Medicine had done all it could. I decide to take things into my own hands.

My first act of bravery: leaving the house for a massage and facial. During the massage, tears slip down my cheeks, silent and steady, as I lie on the table. At that moment, I claim my health, my future. I decide to live as if everything is resolved, to move forward with courage.

Even in this moment, I hold myself together—moment by moment, breath by breath—choosing strength, choosing life, and comforting my family and friends through this ordeal.

Your Pain Doesn't Matter

Even now, as an adult, I continue to reach out to mother, and I am rejected. The pattern repeats endlessly—no matter what I'm going through, she finds a way to make it about herself.

 It took me years to tell mother that I was living with a brain tumor. The details of that conversation are seared into my memory with painful clarity.

We were sitting at her favorite Mexican restaurant, the familiar smells of cumin and cilantro filling the air, and I decided—this was the moment. I needed to share my truth with her, to let her know what I was facing.

On that beautiful winter day, with sunlight streaming through the restaurant windows, I told her everything. I opened up about my diagnosis, the procedure I had undergone, and the reality I was facing with this tumor that had grown in the very part of my body that had been forced to hear so much cruelty. I spoke about my uncertain future, about my fears, about the weight I was carrying alone.

Her response was like a slap across the face. Instead of compassion, instead of concern for her daughter who was sitting across from her, sharing something terrifying and vulnerable, she immediately turned the conversation toward herself. She told me about a time when doctors had suspected she might have a brain tumor. She went on to say how she had dramatically written letters to ensure her boys would be cared for if something happened to her.

Her experience had been a scare—a false alarm that ended with relief and normalcy. The contrast was stark: she walked away unscathed while I faced an actual tumor. As usual, she hijacked my moment of vulnerability and made it entirely about herself.

I sat there in that booth, the noise of the restaurant fading into background static, realizing with devastating clarity that mother had no space for my pain. She had no ability to feel what I was feeling, no capacity to hold my fear or offer me comfort. It was as if, no matter what catastrophe I faced, she had to be the one acknowledged, the one centered, the one whose experience mattered most.

I was left completely alone in my own pain while she relived her past drama, performing her own pain like a one-woman show that had no room for anyone else on the stage.

The Birth of Self-Compassion

This diagnosis is my wake-up call. I realize I have not lived. I have been chasing money, following a path that society expected of me. I remember my college counselor telling me, "You need to go into business and earn a double PhD." That was never my dream. I see now that I have been living someone else's expectation of what they thought I should be. No amount of money, no business, no project holds more value than my life and my family. At this moment, I choose to start living for myself.

That moment taught me something profound and life-changing: compassion comes from within. I had spent my entire life giving to others, believing that I had to be deserving before receiving it myself. I had been waiting for compassion from mother before being kind to myself.

If mother withheld compassion, I would offer it to myself.

If mother denied my pain, I would hold sacred space for it.

If mother turned away from my suffering, I would witness it with the tenderness I had always given to others.

And in doing so, I found something unexpected—comfort that grew into strength. Healing that transformed into power.

Birthright of Self-Compassion

For so long, I had been taught that compassion came after proving I was worthy through suffering, through perfection, through making myself small enough to deserve crumbs of kindness.

I now know that self-compassion is a birthright. Everything I had been seeking from the outside—validation, support, acknowledgment, the simple recognition that my pain mattered—was always within me, waiting for me to claim it.

I now know that I am allowed to feel, to grieve, and to acknowledge my pain without anyone's permission. I am allowed to give myself the love and kindness I have always poured out for others. And most importantly, I hold the power to treat myself with the compassion I have always deserved.

Because self-compassion was already mine. It was immediate. It was unconditional. It was mine to give myself. It was something I had always desired, something that belonged to me by birthright, something that lived in a place where no one—mother included— could reach it or take it away.

I am the one who decides, and I am the one who gives it to myself. And in that decision, I found healing.

Reflections
Self-Compassion

We invite you to explore these questions with curiosity and self-compassion. Use them to reframe challenges into opportunities for growth, gratitude, and empowerment. Share your responses with trusted people so you feel heard and understood. Revisit the questions over time to celebrate your growth.

Recognizing the Absence
1. When you think about your childhood, can you recall a time when someone showed you genuine compassion during a moment of pain or struggle?

2. What does it feel like in your body when you recognize that something essential in your early years was absent?

3. Have you ever found yourself able to give something freely to others that you've never received yourself?

Witnessing True Compassion
4. Can you remember a moment when you witnessed someone else receiving the kind of care you had always needed?

5. What emotions arise when you see others being nurtured in ways that were foreign to you?

6. How does your body respond when you observe genuine tenderness between others?

The Pain of Seeking Understanding
7. Have you ever shared something important about yourself with someone else and have had them make it about themselves?

8. What does it feel like when your pain is dismissed, minimized, or overshadowed by someone else's drama?

9. Can you identify moments when you realized that certain people in your life have no space for your suffering?

Physical Manifestations

10. Are there places in your body where you feel like pain or discomfort has taken up residence?

11. What physical sensations or patterns have you noticed that may be linked to emotional wounds you've carried over time?

12. When did you notice your body protecting you from impactful experiences by becoming ill?

The Turning Point

13. Can you identify a moment when you realized you had to stop waiting for others to give you what you needed?

14. What would it feel like to be kind to yourself without anyone else's approval?

15. How might your life change if you treated yourself with the same compassion you show others?

Claiming Your Birthright

16. What would it mean to believe that you deserve compassion simply because you exist?

17. How does this self-compassion feel in your body?

18. What would you say to yourself right now if you spoke with the same tenderness you'd show a beloved friend in pain?

Moving Forward

19. What does self-compassion look like in your daily life?

20. How can you honor your pain while also nurturing your healing?

21. What would change if you became the source of the compassion you've always sought from others?

Affirmations
Self-Compassion

Your thoughts, feelings, beliefs, voice, and actions create your reality. Each day, choose three affirmations and speak them out loud. Hearing your own words turns affirmations into living declarations that reshape your mind. Speak with intention and feel the words settle deep within you.

- I am worthy.
- I love myself.
- I am my friend.
- I treat myself well.
- I honor my feelings.
- I am kind to myself.
- I am gentle with myself.
- I embrace my humanity.
- I am patient with myself.
- I am compassionate with myself.

Chapter 8: Right Ear Revelation

"In order to change, people need to become aware of their sensations… Physical self-awareness is the first step in releasing the tyranny of the past."

— Bessel van der Kolk

As I sit writing this book, my fingers pause over the keyboard when one correlation emerges that sends chills down my spine—something so profound and new that it makes me question everything I know about my own body's wisdom. All of these horrific experiences that I recall with vivid clarity are anchored in my right ear.

The realization hits me like a physical blow as I recollect the metallic scrape of the cast-iron tortilla griddle. The sound is more than a memory floating somewhere in my consciousness—it is positioned specifically on the right side of my head, as clear and present as if mother is standing here cooking right now. I can feel the exact location where that sound lives, nestled deep in my right ear like an unhealed scar.

Then comes the flood of recognition. Father's voice—his verbal assaults and the whispered threats during his midnight rapes—all of it echoes from that same right side. His words enter my ears and burrow into that specific space and make it their permanent home. I can hear the exact timbre of his voice, the way it drops to that menacing whisper, the cruel satisfaction that drips from every syllable, all of it playing like a broken record in my right ear.

Every story I am writing, every horrific memory I am excavating from the depths of my buried past, comes with its own soundtrack—and that soundtrack is exclusively right-sided. The voices of people who hurt me, dismissed me, and abandoned me, all speak from that same location in my head. It is as if my right ear is a repository for pain, a storage unit for every sound that has ever wounded me.

Sixteen years ago, when the doctors diagnosed the brain tumor pressing against my right ear, they delivered the news with clinical detachment: "You've lost some decibels in your right ear." The words felt like another medical fact to file away, another challenge to overcome.

As I sit surrounded by the ghosts of these memories, all speaking from that same damaged ear, I understand that I lost more than decibels—I lost the connection to the memories stored in my right ear. My body has been protecting me, dampening the auditory sense that had been a conduit for so much of my pain. My right ear is the keeper of the wounds, which I am now ready to listen to.

Now, as I write these stories with full embodied awareness, I can hear everything with startling clarity. My childhood is no longer muffled or distant—it is immediate, present, demanding to be acknowledged. My right ear has awakened from its protective slumber, ready to release what it has been holding for so long.

I press my hand against my right ear, feeling the warmth of my palm against the side of my head that has carried so much pain. This ear that was damaged by a tumor, which lost its ability to hear certain frequencies, is now the very instrument through which I am reclaiming my story.

When we recognize what wired us and truly understand what impacts us, we start to notice the patterns—sometimes with startling clarity. Is it something I see that sets my nerves on edge? Am I more sensitive to a certain sound, a voice, a tone, or the way light falls across a room? Is it a feeling in my body—a tightening, a chill, a pang of emptiness?

In moments of dysregulation, all of our senses become heightened, and we are far more likely to be triggered by echoes of our past. It might be something we saw, something we heard, or something we felt long ago—suddenly brought back to life by a glance, a word, a sensation. Our bodies pick up signals instantly and automatically respond to what's happening now, conflated with every unhealed wound we are carrying.

Understanding how we interpret information—whether we see it, hear it, or feel it—gives us the awareness to pause, to ask: "What is this really about? Is this now, or is this then?" Because in those moments of dysregulation, we are reliving the sensory imprint of what hurt us most.

The body knows exactly when it is safe to remember.

Reflections
Right Ear Revelation

We invite you to explore these questions with curiosity and self-compassion. Use them to reframe challenges into opportunities for growth, gratitude, and empowerment. Share your responses with trusted people so you feel heard and understood. Revisit the questions over time to celebrate your growth.

Physical Awareness:
1. What part of your body holds your most vivid memories? Is it your stomach, your chest, your head, or a specific location?

2. When you recall impactful experiences, where do you feel them physically in your body right now?

Sensory Connections:
3. What sensations (hearing, sight, touch, smell, taste, or gut feeling) from your past can you experience with startling clarity? Where in your body do you experience them?

4. Are there specific voices, noises, or sounds that make your body react immediately? What does that reaction feel like?

Body Wisdom Recognition:
5. What might your body have been protecting you from by dampening certain senses or creating physical symptoms?

6. How has your body been your ally in survival, even when it seemed like it was working against you?

Healing Integration:
7. As you do your healing work, what sensory experiences are becoming clearer or more vivid?

8. How can you honor the wisdom your body has shown in protecting you while also allowing it to heal?

Present Moment Awareness:

9. Right now, as you reflect on these questions, where do you feel tension, warmth, tingling, or other sensations?

10. What is your body telling you about what it's ready to heal?

Affirmations
Right Ear Revelation

Your thoughts, feelings, beliefs, voice, and actions create your reality. Each day, choose three affirmations and speak them out loud. Hearing your own words turns affirmations into living declarations that reshape your mind. Speak with intention and feel the words settle deep within you.

- I sense peace flowing through me.
- I sense my connection to myself.
- I hear my inner voice speaking the truth.
- I feel sensations that guide me toward joy.
- I feel grounded in my body.
- I feel my body's incredible wisdom.
- I know my body creates perfect health.
- I see my body as my greatest ally.
- I sense perfect harmony in me.
- I see my body as beautifully whole.
- I hear my body's messages of love.

Chapter 9: What Is Family?

*"Sometimes family is not the people you are born to, but
the people who choose to stand by you, heal with you,
and help you become who you were always meant to be."*

— Najwa Zebian

What is family? Let me tell you what mine was. From the very beginning, my life was marked by a devastating lack of safety, security, stability, and belonging. Father's financial struggles and machista attitude meant that our family was constantly uprooted, moving from one house to another, one city to the next. Each time, we left behind what little we had accumulated and started over with only the clothes on our backs.

Mother did her best to carry the bare necessities of survival—birth certificates, immunization records, the cast-iron tortilla griddle, a tabletop stove, and a few cooking utensils. The transient nature of our lives made it impossible to create a home as a place of warmth, safety, permanence, or community.

It was a forced isolation for me. Father forbade us from having friends or inviting anyone into our home—he wanted to maintain control over our family and keep the abuse hidden from prying eyes. I constantly struggled to fit in, always the outsider moving into communities where others had known each other their entire lives. This ongoing disconnection left me without any sense of stability, without a place to call home, without a feeling of belonging anywhere. Each night, I went to bed unsure if I'd be in the same place when I woke up the next morning.

The Loneliness of Achievement

This sense of disconnection followed me relentlessly into adulthood. When I received my GED—one of my first accomplishments—I called mother and told her I would pick her up for the graduation ceremony. She refused to go, adding with casual cruelty that asking father would be a waste of time since he wouldn't be going either. I felt a deep, familiar sorrow wash over me that day. Even in one of my proudest moments, even when I had achieved something significant against all odds, I was utterly alone. The realization hit me like a physical blow: this was the family I had to work with. This was the love that would be absent no matter how hard I tried or how much I achieved.

After so much heartbreak, I chose to skip my bachelor's graduation—the pain of celebrating alone felt too overwhelming to bear. When I shared this heartache with my counselor, Benita, she gave me one of the greatest pieces of advice I've ever received: "Someday, you will have to create your own family."

When it came time to celebrate achieving my master's degrees, I chose to include those who had stood by me through the journey. Those were my true family. I dedicated my graduation party to my son, honoring his support and the sacrifices he had made alongside me. Mother refused my invitation to the celebration. Not satisfied, my younger brother showed up at her doorstep to pick her up. She refused—again. In that moment of rejection, I understood what Benita meant about creating my own family. It became clear that this new family did not include mother and father, who had rejected me as their daughter.

As time went on, my son created a family of his own, and brothers built their own families. Those families, at times, actively rejected me. Now it was time for me to create a new family of my own, built on love, acceptance, and genuine connection. I accepted the reality that my biological family was not the family I had always longed for.

What is belonging? In my adult life, I found glimmers of connection through relationships that filled in some of the gaps left by my childhood. Shirley and Dave became family to me—I called them Moms and Pops, and for thirty years, they were the closest thing I had to parents who saw and accepted me.

When my son graduated, Moms showed up. When my girlfriend asked to meet mother and father during my son's high school graduation celebration, my heart dropped because mother and father were absent. It was Moms who jumped in without hesitation and said, "I am her

Moms. What would you like to know?" Her words wrapped around me like a warm blanket, claiming me as her own—stepping into the role a mother was expected to play.

On holidays, they invited me into their home, offering me a glimpse of the love, freedom, and acceptance I had always longed for. Their family welcomed me with open arms, allowing me to simply be myself—no performance required, no conditions to meet, no fear of rejection lurking in every conversation.

Observing them, I began to understand what a family could actually be. I witnessed how it felt to belong unconditionally—to walk into a room and know you were wanted, to share your thoughts without fear of judgment, to make mistakes and be loved. Through their example, I learned that belonging is about being seen, accepted, and cherished exactly as you are.

This was the blueprint I would use to create my own chosen family— one built on choice, love, and the radical act of showing up for each other, again, and again.

My biological family sometimes uninvited me to Thanksgiving. Instead, I spent it with friends, creating my own version of family around tables that welcomed me. One Thanksgiving, my friend Jack invited me to his family's home in Northern Colorado to celebrate Thanksgiving with his family. Sitting in the driveway as we arrived, I asked him a question that had been haunting me for years. *"What is it like to come home?"* Jack looked at me, confused, and asked what I meant. I tried again, searching for the right words: *"What does it feel like to come home?"*

His answer left me completely shocked. *"This is the place where I'm accepted. No matter what I do, these people love me and accept me."* I sat there staring at him, wrapping my mind around what he had described. Unconditional acceptance—a concept foreign to me because it was beyond anything I had ever experienced.

The confusion on Jack's face shifted to a deeper understanding—even sadness—as he recognized that "coming home" was completely foreign to me. He had believed it was a basic human experience, and he was witnessing, in real time, the profound absence that had shaped my life.

For Jack, home was safety, acceptance, and love without conditions. For me, home had always been a place where love did not come at all. I never fit in. I had to be on my best behavior, and even then, it would result in rejection or being ostracized.

In that moment, sitting in his car outside his family's home, I realized I was searching for what Jack had always known—a place where I could simply exist and be loved for who I was, not for what I could do for them.

Alongside these revelations, I felt immense gratitude for my friends Carmen and her daughter Maya. They, too, modeled what Jack had described—what it truly meant to have a home, a sense of security, and a sense of belonging that I was learning to recognize. They embraced me as part of their family, inviting me to their family celebrations without hesitation or conditions. At Carmen's dinner table, I watched her beam with pride as Maya shared her accomplishments, the love between mother and daughter so natural and unconditional. At their holiday gatherings, I witnessed the easy laughter and comfortable silences that come when people feel completely safe with each other.

Through them, I began to understand that home was more than a physical place. It was the people who welcomed and accepted you, who made you feel like you belonged simply because you existed. It was the feeling of walking into a room and knowing you were wanted there because your presence alone brought joy to the people who loved you. These friends were teaching me, piece by piece, what unconditional acceptance looked like. They were showing me that the home I had been searching for my entire life was a feeling I could create with the people who chose to love me as I was.

Shirley, Dave, Jack, Carmen, and Maya showed me what a chosen family could look like—and the contrast with my biological family was stark and painful. Spending time with my chosen family was transformative. They were nurturing and encouraging of all family members, ensuring that everyone was nurtured, felt heard, and valued. Conversations flowed with genuine interest and support. Mistakes were met with understanding rather than judgment. Love was expressed freely and without conditions.

On the other hand, my biological family was functionally dysfunctional. They judged each other constantly, and the adults always had to have the upper hand, always had to be right. The nieces and nephews were perpetually corrected, challenged, and made to feel stupid. I watched helplessly from the sidelines, knowing that these toxic patterns could scar the younger generation for life, as they had scarred me.

The closest I had come to creating that feeling of family within my biological relatives was with brothers. Those rare moments of connection became precious to me—the closest I had to family, to a genuine sense of belonging. For a time, I organized holiday gatherings and brought us together, hoping I could create the warmth and acceptance I had experienced with my chosen family. When those efforts fell apart, I felt the loss deeply. With those fragile connections, I was left outside—caught between a rejected biological family and a chosen family where I was still finding my footing.

The Illusion of Belonging

For years, I've joked that wherever I sleep at night is where home is. When I travel, wherever I lay my head becomes home for that moment. I would tell myself with practiced confidence, "I am home everywhere I am." I believed this adaptability was a reflection of inner security, a sign that I had developed a deep sense of belonging and connection to myself and the world around me.

That joke, repeated so often it became my mantra. I saw it as a declaration of freedom. In reality, it was the opposite—a carefully constructed mask hiding the profound lack of belonging I carried within me like a stone in my chest. The truth I kept locked away was devastating: I felt unanchored—to place, to community, to self. My ability to "feel at home everywhere" was the coping mechanism of someone who had lived without true belonging, who had a false sense of peace with rootlessness because roots had always been ripped away. If everywhere could be home, then I could pretend that being ungrounded removed the pain. I called this adaptability—the ability to belong anywhere—so it felt like a choice rather than a wound. Beneath that cheerful facade, I was a woman searching, hoping, carrying the ache of a child desperate to feel like they truly came home.

I was 38 and felt completely disconnected from my biological family. Reflecting on my life, I wanted to make sense of decades of pain that seemed to have no purpose, no meaning, and no sense of belonging. I asked my friend, "Why was this life happening to me?" Then my friend shared something that would fundamentally change my perspective forever: "You belong to life." Those four simple words struck me to my core like lightning, illuminating the hidden gem inside—I belonged to existence itself.

Life itself has brought me here and kept me here, through every sexual violation, every beating, every rejection, and all the dark moments that almost destroyed me. Life had refused to let me go, even when I wanted to disappear, even when the pain felt unbearable, even when I felt completely alone in the world. I began to see that while having a traditional family or a singular place of belonging was missing, I belonged to something infinitely greater—to life itself, to the mysterious force that had carried me through every storm and delivered me to this moment of recognition.

This is Family

My lifelong quest for belonging has profoundly shaped me, driving me to build spaces where others can feel at home, even as I'm discovering what home truly means to me. Belonging to life became the inspiration for creating community for others. In every step of my journey, I have sought to create a sense of belonging, stability, and unconditional acceptance—for my son, for the people I've chosen, and for the communities I've been privileged to be part of. I've learned that sometimes the greatest gift we can give the world is the very thing we desired the most.

Today, I have come to accept my biological family for who they are. I no longer wait for them to embrace me as their family. Instead, I embrace the beautiful opportunity to create my chosen family, built on love, acceptance, and the radical act of showing up for each other.

The home I spent my entire life searching for was something I had the power to create all along. And in creating it, I discovered that belonging is about finding your place in the world and making space for others to belong too.

Throughout my life, I intentionally built connections with fierce determination. I made new friendships and invited new people to celebrate life with me—birthdays, holidays, accomplishments, and any other occasions worth marking. These celebrations were acts of rebellion against the isolation that had defined my past. They generated a sense of belonging, piece by piece, creating the family I always desired.

My own journey has taught me the profound truth that even without a traditional biological family. It is possible to move forward. It is possible to create connection, to find meaning, and to discover that belonging to life is the deepest belonging of all. I understand now the resilience it takes to start over, the courage it takes to rebuild, and the radical act of faith it requires to believe that you deserve love and belonging, even when the world has told you otherwise.

Reflections
What Is Family?

We invite you to explore these questions with curiosity and self-compassion. Use them to reframe challenges into opportunities for growth, gratitude, and empowerment. Share your responses with trusted people so you feel heard and understood. Revisit the questions over time to celebrate your growth.

Healing is a journey of unlearning pain, redefining love, and reclaiming belonging. Through reflection on both the wounds of the past and the treasures of the present, we can consciously create the family and sense of home we truly deserve.

1. What was the family you had growing up?

2. In what ways have experiences of safety, stability, or belonging (or the lack of them) influenced your understanding of family?

3. How have your experiences within your biological family—whether functional or challenging—made you reflect on your own role in the inheritance of generational patterns?

4. What was the most surprising realization you had about your biological family, and how did it impact your perspective on belonging?

How would you like your family to be?

1. What chosen family would you create if you could do that?

2. What lessons from your previous experiences made you desire that chosen family?

3. How would your chosen family help you redefine what belonging means to you?

4. In what ways would embracing the idea that "you belong to life" empower you to heal and move forward?

Affirmations
What Is Family?

Your thoughts, feelings, beliefs, voice, and actions create your reality. Each day, choose three affirmations and speak them out loud. Hearing your own words turns affirmations into living declarations that reshape your mind. Speak with intention and feel the words settle deep within you.

Creating Your Chosen Family
- Genuine connections flourish in my life.
- My chosen family forms naturally around me.
- Love and respect flow through my relationships.

Understanding What Home Means
- I am valued.
- I am wanted.
- I come home to myself.

Healing from Past Experiences
- I choose love.
- I honor my past.
- I approve of myself.

Building New Traditions
- I am worthy.
- I create my own traditions.
- I build beautiful memories.

Self-Acceptance and Worth
- I give myself compassion.
- I am enough exactly as I am.
- My worth exists because I exist.

Chapter 10: The Invisible Ancestral Script

"Family dysfunction rolls down from generation to generation like a fire in the woods, taking down everything in its path until one person in one generation has the courage to turn and face the flames. That person brings peace to their ancestors and spares the children that follow."

— Terry Real

The Survivor: generational patterns.

My grandmother declared without hesitation: "No man in my house will ever lift a finger." They walk past dirty dishes. They avoid the stove. They leave shirts wrinkled. They ignore dirty counters. Their hands are reserved for holding forks, for toasting beers, and for commanding others. Everything else—every act of service, every detail of care—falls to the women. My grandmother's words roll off her tongue like gospel truth, delivered with the certainty of someone who has swallowed the ancestral script whole, letting it run through her bloodstream unchallenged. She sees it as order, as the way things have always been and always should be.

What she was really reciting was the blueprint of the script that got inherited by everyone like a family heirloom, known or unknown. These words functioned as the operating system that governed how every person in our lineage automatically moved through the world, how we measured our worth, and how we taught our children to shrink themselves into culturally acceptable boxes.

The ancestral script was so seamlessly embedded in the fabric of daily life that it felt like truth. It whispered through generations. Women served. Men commanded. Children abided. Women's value was in their service. Their voice was secondary. Their needs came last. Men had to be strong and unfeeling. They demanded respect and could do whatever they wanted. Children didn't talk back to their elders. They did as they were told.

These messages disguised themselves as tradition or cultural pride. The ancestral script created Survivors who moved through life blind to their own survival. Women mistook servitude for love, silence for peace, and self-erasure for virtue. We carried these patterns in our posture, in the way we apologized for existing, in how we automatically stepped aside when men entered rooms, in the way we had learned to make ourselves smaller so men could feel bigger. Men constantly had to show their machismo and lead their family while lost themselves. Children lived in fear of the world, unable to understand, bracing for punishment that could come from anywhere at any moment.

The most insidious part of generational trauma is how it convinces us that our cages are choices and that our limitations are preferences. Women affirm that men are superior. Mothers pass this belief to their daughters—and even to their sons. We are the ones who keep carrying this limitation, planting it into generation after generation, and then blaming others for a belief system we ourselves create, sustain, and defend. This truth has baffled me my entire life. The ancestral script has been running in the background since before we were born, shaping our neural pathways and defining the constraints of our lives.

Like so many things in life, we believed our choices were our own. The truth ran deeper: they had often been scripted into us long before we were aware. This made it so challenging for the one who longed to break through but felt unable to. The battle involved more than willpower or desire—the invisible thread, the ancestral umbilical cord that bound us to the past, held the real control. These unseen influences lived in the background: the patterns of our mother, the behaviors of our father, the words of a grandparent, family member, cousin, friends, or the silent modeling of whoever shaped us most. Over time, these imprints became ingrained in our being, becoming part of the very DNA that guided us.

Roles

I grew up in a world where the air itself felt split between two rules— one for men, and one for women. The women moved like shadows, careful, quiet, and always yielding. Their words were soft, their steps measured, their worth tethered to how well they served. I watched them bow their heads, their eyes lowered as if they had been born already apologizing for taking up space.

The men, on the other hand, carried themselves like gods carved out of flesh. They walked into rooms and expected the air to bend to their presence. Their voices thundered, their decisions were unquestioned, and their worth was assumed. They believed the world belonged to them simply because they were men, and everyone else was there to serve their desires.

Mother's World: Where Women Were Less Than Men

In mother's house, this belief was ingrained into the fabric of daily life. Women were less than men. That was what I was taught, the rule I was expected to live by. I had to be subservient. I saw it in the way mother bent her will, in the way she shaped her words to avoid confrontation, in the way she instructed me that this was what it meant to be a woman. From the time I was little, I heard it repeatedly: men were the leaders, the rulers, the ones with inherent value. Boys were told they were special, destined, important. Girls were told we were helpers, servants, caretakers of their greatness.

Mother's voice sharpened this truth for me. She told me again and again, "You will never get married as a strong woman. Men want obedience. Men want submission. You will have no career, no independence, because your life must be about him—what he wants, what he needs. Your happiness is not the point." Her words were like chains she tried to fasten around me, reminding me of the fate she believed was inevitable.

How The Survivor Showed Up

In moments of stress, The Survivor showed up in subtle ways. My body would pull back, there would be a slight hunch on my shoulders, my hands would sweat when I would assert myself, the fawning smile on my face when delivering serious messages, and my voice would soften to that familiar whisper. It was so subtle, so careful, so determined to avoid disturbing the peace that most of the time I remained unheard with the intensity that my message deserved.

The patterns had embedded themselves so completely in my cellular memory that I carried them in my posture, in the way I entered rooms, in how I loved my own family. Even in business, I could feel myself shrinking into that familiar posture of fawning kindness, my words wrapped in such delicate layers of politeness that they barely registered as whispers in rooms that demanded roars. My voice floated across conference tables and family gatherings like air—present but insubstantial, easily dismissed, quickly forgotten. I could taste the frustration on my tongue as my words disappeared into the ether, swallowed by the same learned helplessness that had shaped my family's existence.

These were the patterns of The Survivor in me—familiar and comfortable even as they suffocated my spirit, knowing exactly which buttons to push, which fears to activate, and which childhood memories to resurrect. I could trace these patterns back through generations—mother's way of shrinking when confronted, my grandmother's habit of apologizing for existing, the family members around them who had learned that making themselves smaller, quieter, less threatening to the world around them was expected.

I had absorbed some of mother's ancestral patterns like a sponge. The way she would lower her eyes when speaking to father, the way her voice would trail off when she needed to be heard most, the way she would apologize for taking up space in her own home. She had learned the art of making herself small enough to avoid conflict, quiet enough to avoid confrontation, invisible enough to avoid harm. Unknowingly, I had learned these ancestral patterns because I had been raised by a woman who had been taught the same devastating lessons. I had become a master of the inherited silence, even though my body was screaming to be heard.

The Warrior within me could see the chains that had bound my grandmother, mother, and all the people around and before them. The Warrior understood that silence breeds danger, that shrinking equals death, that the inherited ways of being small pose the greatest threat to my authentic power. This Warrior broke the limiting beliefs that my family had taught me to accept as permanent pathways in the landscape of life, and that is why I did not belong.

The Battle

I lived between these voices—The Survivor pulling me toward submission, The Warrior lifting me into liberation. I felt the weight of the ancestral beliefs pulling me down, and at the same time, I tasted the sweet air of a future where I chose my own worth.

My body had become a war zone where ancient patterns clashed with emerging truth. This battlefield raged internally, invisible to outside observers. There were no visible wounds, no obvious casualties. On the inside, the war was devastating—my cells caught in the crossfire between ancestral pattern and authenticity, my body holding the patterns of the way things have always been while simultaneously reaching for healing. Every heartbeat drummed the rhythm of this internal combat, every breath drawn was contested territory between who I had been taught to be and who I was allowing myself to become. The battlefield stretched from the pit of my stomach, where fear lived like a coiled snake, to the base of my throat, where my authentic voice struggled to break free from decades of enforced silence.

In business meetings, I would feel The Warrior surge forward with brilliant ideas and bold strategies, then watch The Survivor pull me back into that familiar fawning posture, my body shifting between these two versions of myself, shoulders straightening with Warrior confidence, then hunching with learned helplessness, sometimes within the same conversation. The conflict was exhausting, a constant tension in my muscles of being pulled in opposite directions by forces that both claimed to have my best interests at heart—The Warrior knowing that my survival depended on breaking free from generational limitations, while The Survivor insisted that my survival depended on maintaining them. Some days, The Warrior would win, and I would speak my truth with a clarity that surprised even me, while other days The Survivor would triumph, and I would find myself apologizing for taking up space, dimming my light to make others comfortable, choosing silence when the moment demanded my voice.

Awakening

As awareness floods through me, I can feel something shifting. The invisible messages from my ancestors that have shaped me are becoming visible, and in their visibility, they lose their power to control me unconsciously. I am no longer a passive carrier of inherited limitations—I am an active observer, awake to the invisible forces that have been directing my life from the shadows.

The women around me see something different in me. They call me brave, tell me I have broken a pattern no woman in our family has ever dared to break. They praise me for standing tall, for providing for myself, and for being free from abuse. In their voices, I hear the echo of a new possibility—one where I am whole, strong, and unafraid to be both a woman and independent.

I am The Warrior—fierce, unbroken, and unapologetically alive. I am also The General, capable of creating ultimate victory in my life.

I know exactly what I want, and I refuse to be distracted by the voices of doubt that try to cling to me. I see the ancestral patterns—the chains of submission, silence, and limitation—and I refuse to wear them. I break those patterns with every choice, every step, every breath.

I do the work that my ancestors were too afraid to do. I do whatever it takes. When the path is steep, I climb. When the storm rages, I keep walking. When the odds stack themselves high against me, I find another way through. I put myself through university with a sixth-grade education when everyone else whispers it is impossible. I work multiple jobs to thrive—to provide, to build a life for myself and my son that is carved from resilience and love.

I am the one brothers turn to, the one family leans on when guidance and support is needed. Though I was told all my life I had no worth and to be subservient, I rise as a voice of clarity, of wisdom, and of leadership. I give from a place of strength—contributing to my family, my community, and the world around me.

And I lead by example. I step into spaces no woman in my lineage has dared to enter. I show the people in my life that they can dream bigger, go further, and become more. By going to college, by becoming a professional, and by being independent, I become living proof that freedom is a choice, and I choose it.

I believe anything is possible—and more than possible, it is probable. I refuse to limit my vision to what others say can be done. I see beyond the boundaries, beyond the walls, beyond even what the people in my life dare to believe is achievable. I move past lines of generational beliefs, chains, and curses to claim a space beyond their imaginations.

I am strong, resilient, resourceful, and proud of who I am—proud without apology. Determination fuels me, and no obstacle, no person, no expectation can stand in my way.

The real battle is fought within. And within myself, I win, over and over again.

Breaking the Invisible Inheritance

We often think that it's the big things that have the greatest impact—the life-altering events that demand attention, empathy, and the dramatic moments that leave visible scars.

In reality, it's the subtle things that make the greatest impact, the invisible threads that weave themselves so seamlessly into our being that we mistake them for our own authentic nature. I can feel the weight of this realization settling into my bones as I recognize how unaware I am of all of my ancestral patterns handed down like an unwanted family heirloom. These instinctive behaviors, gestures, and conversations flow automatically from my lips.

Writing these stories with full awareness of how trauma has shaped what I remember and how I communicate those memories, I can hear the difference. My voice on these pages is clear, direct, uncompromising. The woman writing these words stands apart from the woman who spent decades whispering when she should have been shouting.

The invisible messages from my ancestors that have shaped me are becoming visible, and in their visibility, they lose their power to control me unconsciously. I am no longer a passive carrier of inherited limitations—I am an active observer, awake to the invisible forces that have been directing my life from the shadows.

The very fact that I can see the battle between The Survivor and The Warrior means that The Survivor is receding and The Warrior is gaining ground. Visibility breaks the patterns' power. Recognition shatters their control. The Warrior in me is learning that the greatest battles rage within—against the inherited limitations that live in our own hearts and bodies. Visibility breaks the patterns' power. Recognition shatters their control.

I am a Warrior. Fierce, unbroken, and unapologetically alive. I break the ancestral chains with every choice, every step, every breath that is my own. I do the work that the people around me are too afraid to do, becoming living proof that freedom is a choice, and I choose it.

Reflections
The Invisible Ancestral Script

We invite you to explore these questions with curiosity and self-compassion. Use them to reframe challenges into opportunities for growth, gratitude, and empowerment. Share your responses with trusted people so you feel heard and understood. Revisit the questions over time to celebrate your growth.

"The first step to freedom is seeing the cage."

Recognizing Inherited Beliefs
1. What spoken and unspoken rules about gender, power, or worth were embedded in your family system?

2. How did the men and women in your family carry themselves differently? What messages did their body language convey?

3. What phrases or beliefs were repeated so often in your household that they became "truth" without question?

4. Which family member's voice do you hear in your head when you're making decisions about your worth or capabilities?

5. What did you learn about your role in the world based on your gender, birth order, or family position?

"Strategies that once protected us can become the very things that limit us."

Identifying Your Ancestral Patterns
6. In what situations do you automatically make yourself smaller, quieter, less visible, defensive, or aggressive?

7. What physical sensations (tension, shrinking, voice changes) signal that your "Survivor" has taken over?

8. How do you respond when someone's tone, posture, or energy triggers your ancient alarm system?

9. Where in your life do you find yourself apologizing for existing, taking up space, or having needs?

10. What inherited ways of being "safe" are actually keeping you invisible and unfulfilled?

"Your voice is your power. How you use it reveals how you value yourself."

Examining Your Voice and Presence

11. In what relationships or situations do you struggle to speak your truth with clarity and strength?

12. How do you dilute your message with excessive politeness, apologies, or softening language?

13. What happens in your body when you need to assert yourself or set a boundary?

14. Where do you find yourself whispering when the situation demands you roar?

15. What would change in your life if you spoke with the same confidence you give to others?

"You get to choose the patterns that create your future."

Breaking the Cycle

16. What generational patterns are you unconsciously transferring to your children, employees, and everyone around you?

17. How might your life look different if you operated from your authentic power instead of inherited limitations?

18. What would you do, say, or create if you truly believed your voice mattered as much as anyone else's?

19. Which relationships in your life would benefit from you showing up more fully and authentically?

20. What limiting beliefs about your worth, capabilities, or role keep you from stepping into your full power?

"The Warrior within you has been waiting for permission to rise."

Embodying Your Warrior

21. What does your inner Warrior want to say that your Survivor has kept silent?

22. How would you carry yourself, speak, and make decisions if you fully embodied your authentic power?

23. What boundaries would you set if you truly believed you deserved respect and consideration?

24. What dreams or goals have you dimmed because they felt "too much" or "too threatening" to others?

25. How can you be both connected to others and authentically self-expressed?

Integration Practice

Choose one pattern you identified and commit to interrupting it this week. Notice when it arises, breathe deeply, and consciously choose a different response. Your Warrior is asking you to be authentic, powerful, and unapologetically yourself.

Remember: Breaking generational patterns is about keeping what serves you and transforming what limits you. You can honor where you came from while refusing to be imprisoned by it.

Affirmations
The Invisible Ancestral Script

Your thoughts, feelings, beliefs, voice, and actions create your reality. Each day, choose three affirmations and speak them out loud. Hearing your own words turns affirmations into living declarations that reshape your mind. Speak with intention and feel the words settle deep within you.

Breaking Generational Patterns
- I live my legacy.
- Possibilities open before me.
- Freedom flows through my lineage.

Resilience & Determination
- Opportunities surround me.
- Solutions appear around me.
- Joy flows through my persistence.

Voice & Leadership
- I command with love.
- I elevate those around me.
- My voice speaks with power.

Vision & Possibility
- I create new realities.
- Miracles manifest in my life.
- My wildest dreams become real.

Inner Strength
- I am unstoppable.
- Strength radiates from my core.
- Courage flows through my veins.

Victory Mindset
- Success flows to me.
- I constantly celebrate my victories.
- My actions result in achievements.

Legacy & Impact
- I plant seeds of possibility.
- Dreams become reality through me.
- Opportunities create themselves around me.

Chapter 11: Children Who Raise Their Parents

"To be that child again who was never loved, and to love that child now — that is the healing."

— John Bradshaw

We are children raising children, raising each other, while also raising our parents. The three oldest of us, barely more than babies ourselves—ages three, four, and five—become the caretakers, the providers, the ones who hold everything together. As we get older, the weight grows heavier. Mother's childish pleas echo, "Don't leave me by myself." We feel tired of tending to her every need, of serving as her crutch, of sacrificing our own childhoods to keep her afloat.

Some mornings we bolt out the door for school, desperate for an escape, fully aware of the price that waits for us later—punished for disobeying, for daring to choose ourselves, even for a moment.

This Is My Everyday Reality

Ever since I can remember, I carry responsibilities far beyond my years. As a young girl, mother sends me to the store more than ¼ mile away to buy her soda. By the time I am eight, my responsibilities grow. She makes me do the family's grocery shopping. At nine years old, I walk to the store and buy 30 pounds of meat, a gallon of milk or juice, and other staples. I carefully pack them into paper bags and begin the walk home, my small arms straining under the weight. No matter how careful I am, the butcher's meat drips through the bags, weakening them until they tear open, spilling everything onto the ground. I scramble to gather the groceries, desperate to make it home—knowing the punishment waiting for me if I fail. It all circles back to the same moment—mother beating me senseless for dropping the groceries.

At five, I carry the responsibility of caring for my newborn baby brother—washing his diapers, doing the family's laundry, and cleaning the house. My own clothes stay separate, treated unworthy. No matter how much I do, mother's hunger for more care grows. She moves through the house like a needy child, always reaching for someone to tend to her.

By twelve, the weight of stress grows heavier. Father wakes us up at midnight to pick onions and jalapeños in the fields so we can make rent. There we are—children—working under the car's headlights, shadows cast over the crops, our small hands pulling vegetables from the dirt. And when the work is done, he drives us straight to school, our clothes and hands still covered in dirt, the stench of onions clinging to us as we sit in our classrooms, pretending to be normal kids. Oldest brother carries the weight of enforcing the law against me and the younger siblings. When father leaves the house, he steps into the role of father figure—at just six years old. A child raising children.

This is our world. A world where childhood is stripped away before we ever have the chance to experience it.

A Life of Instability

Father's impulsive decisions force us into constant relocations, making life temporary and uncertain. Sudden impulsive demands from father to pack up and leave instantaneously. Leaving with a paper bag full of belongings and mother carrying the cast iron tortilla griddle and the family archive in her caboodle.

Growing up with parents who lack direction, stability, or the capacity to nurture us is a reality most can scarcely imagine. Father spends his days working on ranches, welding, harvesting fields, or construction, and when he is home, chaos follows. Dinners shrink to a glass of milk and a single slice of bread.

He lives recklessly, often drinking himself into destruction. I am brutally awakened in the middle of the night by father staggering in drunk, covered with blood. I can see him sitting on the toilet lid, my mother grabbing the alcohol, and him demanding to be cleaned up. Other times, his condition sinks so low that the way we see him involves standing on a milk crate, peering through a hospital window, watching him lie in a bed, lifeless—barely surviving another of his self-destructive drunken episodes.

Mother seeks refuge in sleep and TV, numbing herself to the reality around her. When she finishes beating us or ordering us around, she sinks into the Telenovelas on TV, entranced by the flickering light. The device swallows her whole, providing an escape from the chaos she refuses to confront. She is emotionally checked out, unable—or unwilling—to engage in our lives.

Emergency Mode

When she needs something, she suddenly breaks the trance, sending us into emergency mode—a mode that drives our adulthood. Anytime mother cries wolf, we run. We have been conditioned to react, to drop everything, to believe that if we do not, something terrible will happen to her. Her frequent feigned seizures trap us into caregiver roles far beyond our years. Helplessly, we watch as her body melts into the floor with convulsions. We scramble into emergency mode. One of us keeps her from hitting her head. Another slips a spoon into her mouth to keep her from biting her tongue. Fearing she is dead, we put alcohol under her nose to revive her. We tiptoe around the house as if we cradle a sleeping baby, afraid that any disturbance might set something off.

Even my son takes on parenting grandma. When he is 14, he confronts me with righteous indignation: "If I can't have junk food, then grandma can't have it either. The house rules are the house rules—everyone has to follow them." He is furious that I am unable to control her demands for junk food. Mother, stubborn and defiant, argues fiercely that she has to have the foods she wants. "I'm an adult, and this is what I eat," she declares, her voice rising with each word. She acts like a two-year-old throwing a tantrum, demanding her junk food with the same irrational persistence of a child. I know the truth—her health is deteriorating precisely because of her diet. I know the long-term consequences of her choices, yet I am powerless to make a difference. My son sees it, too, the willful destruction of her health masked as personal freedom. He is determined that our family's health standards must apply to everyone, no exceptions. In many ways, it feels like I have two children.

From my late twenties to my thirties, when father randomly disappears, mother lives with me. She struggles with the idea that no one will support her financially in the future. She often guilt-trips me by saying, "What if something happens to you? What will happen to me? Your son has his father to look after him. Who will look after me?" I struggle to grasp that her focus centers entirely on herself. For years, I am supporting mother and other family members financially. The expectation of sacrificing my life for mother is an overwhelming burden.

This all comes to a head one time when mother needs over $5,000 worth of diabetes medication. She inconveniently notices this around 4:30 PM on a Thursday before Memorial Day weekend. She demands that I get her medication. No prescription. No money. Make it happen. I am calling every doctor I know to get mother out of her predicament. At my wits' end, I call my girlfriend to cancel our planned get-together. She asks, "When are you going to stop going into emergency mode for your mother?"

Her words strike me. I live my life in emergency mode for mother. Every crisis, every demand, every time she needs saving—I am there. In that moment, a realization lands: it is time for her to grow up and take responsibility for herself.

My siblings react to mother from emergency mode. Mother continues to expect them to react from that same emergency mode. Their bodies tense, their voices shift, their decisions orbit around her moods. The same childhood patterns that once entrapped us keep driving their responses—patterns wired for crisis, for appeasing, for bracing. Their nervous systems treat her presence like an alarm, even though the danger belongs to another time. They live in emergency mode, run to her every call, and blame me for refusing to overreact as they do.

I choose a different path. I step back, let go, and stop running to her beck and call.

Father's Responsibilities, Children's Burden

Father's responsibilities become ours long before we understand what responsibility means. When he disappears for days, lost in his drinking, his recklessness, his refusal to face the life he created—we step in to fill the void. We become the ones who figure out how to pay the rent, how to put food on the table, and how to keep the lights on. At eight years old, my older brother is enrolling us in school, forging signatures on permission slips, and navigating bureaucratic systems designed for adults. I calculate how many pounds of onions we must pick to cover the bills, my mind doing math that belongs to a man three times my age. We are children being the grown-ups for him. We carry his shame, his failures, his abdication of fatherhood on our small shoulders. And when he comes home, bloodied and broken from another drunken escapade, we get an ungrateful man who expects us to clean his wounds, to pretend everything is normal, to continue carrying the weight he refuses to bear. This is role reversal at its cruelest—caring for a parent's emotional needs, and assuming their most fundamental responsibilities while they remain a perpetual, destructive child.

The Yearning for Love

At the same time, I am grappling with a deep void: my yearning for mother's love. It is a void that no accomplishment, no degree, no success can fill. I remember driving a student back to campus after a coaching session. She looks at me and says, "You have it all. I wish I had your life. You're on TV, on billboards, in magazines— you're everywhere." All I can think is, I wish I had your life. She has everything I desire: connection, love, and a sense of belonging. For so long, I yearn for mother's love, believing her approval will fill the void inside me. I would have gladly given every accomplishment, every accolade, every dream if someone could have given me mother's love. Through my healing journey, I realize her love never exists as something I can receive from her—her heart simply moves through the world differently.

In the summer of 2015, at a personal development conference, something profound shifted. Standing in the back of the room, I recognized deep gratitude for my life's painful steps. With crystal clarity, I understood my journey. These words came to me:

"Thank you, mother. Thank you for beating the hell out of me. Thank you for pushing me away. Thank you for doing everything you did to me, because that's what it took for you to get me out of your life. Because had you not done that, I would be living your life."

This was my turning point—having gratitude for the life I lived. I began understanding patterns, shifting perspectives, and reconciling my past. I learned to build resilience from chaos, creating a life of intention and love, building from a place of peace.

Reparenting: Reclaiming My Inner Child

When I face a life-threatening brain tumor, I am forced to reckon with buried truths. I step back from coaching to focus on myself, understanding that the person I must help is me. I start applying the tools I have taught others: mirror exercises, daily journaling, and phone reminders with affirmations. I told myself the words missing from mother and father. "I love you, Little Rocío. You are amazing, Little Rocío. You are special, Little Rocío." With each practice, I reclaim parts of myself lost to years of pain and neglect, choosing who I can become.

Reparenting myself meant offering the love, validation, and care that were absent in my formative years. It was about recognizing my worth, stepping into the role of my greatest supporter, and providing myself with the emotional safety and unconditional love I always deserved.

This painful lesson becomes liberating. I understand the love I long for stays absent because she lacks the capacity to give it. In her absence, I rise as my own source of love, strength, and validation.

Reparenting yourself is a profound journey of healing, one that allows you to nurture the parts of yourself that were once overlooked, neglected, or wounded. It is a process of offering yourself the love, validation, and care that may have been absent in your formative years. Through reparenting, you have the power to rewrite the patterns of the past, replacing self-criticism with compassion and self-doubt with confidence.

This journey is about recognizing your own worth and stepping into the role of your greatest supporter and nurturer. It is about learning to provide yourself with the emotional safety, encouragement, and unconditional love that you have always deserved.

Reflections
Children Who Raise Their Parents

We invite you to explore these questions with curiosity and self-compassion. Use them to reframe challenges into opportunities for growth, gratitude, and empowerment. Share your responses with trusted people so you feel heard and understood. Revisit the questions over time to celebrate your growth.

1. How has taking on adult responsibilities as a child shaped the way I see myself and my relationships today?

2. What emotions come up when I think about the responsibilities I carried at such a young age?

3. In what ways have I neglected my own needs while focusing on caring for others?

4. What patterns from my childhood am I carrying into my adult life, and how do they affect my well-being?

5. How do I define boundaries, and where do I struggle to enforce them with family or loved ones?

6. What would I say to my younger self who carried these burdens, and what words of comfort would I offer?

7. Am I allowing myself to fully embrace my own desires and dreams, or do I feel trapped in the caretaker role?

8. How can I begin to release the guilt of believing I fell short of "fixing" things for others?

9. How have my coping strategies from childhood served me, and which ones are no longer necessary in my adult life?

10. What would radical self-compassion look like for the child version of myself who carried so much responsibility and pain?

Affirmations
Children Who Raise Their Parents

Your thoughts, feelings, beliefs, voice, and actions create your reality. Each day, choose three affirmations and speak them out loud. Hearing your own words turns affirmations into living declarations that reshape your mind. Speak with intention and feel the words settle deep within you.

- I create my own path.
- I give my inner child love.
- I embrace my worthiness.
- I have healthy boundaries.
- I am worthy because I exist.
- My healing occurs at its own pace.
- I prioritize myself with compassion.
- I receive support, love, and nurturing.
- I focus on my own healing and growth.
- Caring for myself is an act of love and strength.

Chapter 12: Why Abused Children Stay Loyal

"The capacity for dissociation enables the young child to exercise their innate life-sustaining need for attachment in spite of the fact that principal attachment figures are also principal abusers."

— Warwick Middleton

I can hear mother's voice. I am nine. After another brutal beating, she yells, "I want to hear you scream! I want to hear you cry! I want to hear your pain!" That moment changes me. In that instant, I decide to numb my soul so she would never hear my pain again. She can control every part of my existence—where I go, what I do, even what I eat—*I will control* my suffering, and that angers her even more. She gets joy from hearing me cry and watching me suffer. I shut her out and refuse to give her the satisfaction of my tears. My pain is mine alone to control.

The Truth About Childhood Resilience

One of the biggest misconceptions I hear is that children are resilient. The reality? We are not. Abused children disassociate, compartmentalize, numb ourselves, or escape into imaginary worlds. Some of us create stories in our minds, desperate for a way out.

I do.

I have a recurring daydream that I was switched at birth, that my real parents are out there searching for me, that one day they will realize they had the wrong child, they find me, and take me home. It is a fantasy I cling to. A lifeline in a world that feels unbearable.

Abandonment

Mother and father often pack up my siblings and disappear for the day, leaving me behind—alone. Sometimes, darkness falls before they return. Uncle Sergio stops by to visit the family. When he finds me alone, he asks, "Where are your parents?" How can I answer him? How can a 5-year-old child be left alone?

Sometimes he takes me home with him, knowing he will face consequences for it later. Other times, he simply sits with me, listening for hours. I retreat into my fantasy world to escape my harsh reality. I run around with my tattered books, talking about my dreams, and he listens as if my words are the most important thing in the world. I tell him, "Uncle Sergio, when I grow up, I'll become a teacher." In a life filled with so much pain, he makes me feel important. Uncle Sergio does his best to shield me from mother and father's brutal beatings and neglect. No one can.

The Whip

I am in kindergarten when mother's rage turns into one of the most savage punishments I ever endure. She is furious with me again for breathing, and this time, she reaches for one of her favorite tools—a Mexican short whip made of tough leather.

The sharp crack of it against my skin splits the air like a gunshot echoing through the house as she lashes out uncontrollably. Blow after blow, she unleashes her fury, the sting of the leather burning into my flesh, leaving welts and bruises across my small frame. A raw, piercing scream tears from my throat as searing pain explodes through my body. Every lash feels like fire ripping through my skin; each strike carves fresh agony into my flesh. My muscles lock, paralyzed by the torment, my body instinctively recoils from each inevitable blow. My breath comes in short, ragged gasps, my throat raw and burning, feeling like a noose is tightening around my neck. The more I scream, the more it feels like I am suffocating, as if my own cries are choking the life out of me. My lungs fight for air, each inhale thin and shaky, barely enough to keep me conscious. My body jerks uncontrollably, my skin slick with sweat and stinging from the deep, angry welts that spread like wildfire across my back. The agony is unbearable. My screams fall on deaf ears. The whipping continues until her rage is satisfied. When the crack of the whip ceases, she leans in, her face cold and menacing, her voice filled with venom, delivers the portentous warning, "If you tell anyone what happened, it's going to be worse where they take you."

How can it be worse than it already is? I am scared. I carry her warning, choking me like the extension cord she sometimes wraps around my neck, suffocating, unbreakable. The weight of her words sinks into my bones, deeper than the bruises, deeper than the pain.

That night, the torment continues. Every movement sends waves of pain rippling through my body. Lying down is unbearable, the pressure of even the softest surface pressing against my wounds like knives. The mere touch of my clothes is torture—each fiber scraping against raw, open welts, rubbing against bruises that pulse with pain. I try to lie still, holding my breath, afraid that even breathing too deeply will exacerbate the fire beneath my skin. Sleep is replaced by the long, endless night of throbbing agony and the quiet terror that there is something worse than this.

The Moment I Thought Someone Would Save Me

The next day at kindergarten, I sit quietly at my desk, working on my writing activities, my body aching with every movement. Then suddenly, my teacher pulls me out of class. My stomach knots with panic. I am escorted to the nurse's office, where I stand in front of my teacher, the nurse, and the principal. Their eyes are filled with concern, and they study me carefully. The dreaded request comes.

"Can you take off your shirt, sweetheart?"

I panic. Every part of me silently screams, "No". I do as they ask.

As I lift my shirt, their expressions darken. Their eyes trace the welts—raised, purple-black ridges that stretch across my back and sides. I feel exposed.

Fear grips me so tightly that I can barely breathe. Mother's words ring in my head, a sinister warning looping over and over again. If I tell the truth, it will get worse. I had to come up with something. Anything. "It was the little boy next door!"

The words spill from my mouth before I can think. "He hit me! I wanted to play with him, and he hit me. He hit me!"

Silence.

They exchange worried glances, hesitation flickering between them. I can see the doubt in their faces. Helplessly, they have me put my shirt back on and silently return me to my classroom.

No one ever asks me about it again.

As I walk back to my desk, the weight of the moment settles deep in my bones. This is my reality. No one is coming to save me. So, I swallow the pain, the fear, the hopelessness. I carry my secret alone.

Why Abused Children Stay Loyal

Like most abused children, I was still looking to my abusers for safety. Like an abused dog stays loyal after a beating. Mother and father provided the only food and shelter I knew. When survival depends on the abuser, the attachment doesn't break—it intensifies. Abuse is about control, manipulation, and breaking a child's sense of self until they believe that staying close to their abuser is the safest option.

Children are wired to seek attachment and security from their caregivers, even when those caregivers are the source of the pain. It's a cruel paradox—love and fear become indistinguishable. The responses of the brain to fear are fight, flight, freeze, fawn, and disassociate. To avoid further harm, a person who is fawning complies, becomes submissive, and anticipates every shift in mood to minimize danger.

I learned early that doing as mother and father demanded meant fewer outbursts, fewer punishments, and a slightly safer existence. I watched their tone, their posture, the way their breath shifted before a rage-filled moment. How father's voice dropped, how mother's body language changed. I became an extraordinary observer of people, reading microexpressions, predicting emotions, and sensing tension before it exploded. This hyperawareness was in service of keeping my mind ahead of their anger, my words carefully chosen to keep them calm, my presence molded into whatever would keep me safe in that moment. Children shut down parts of themselves and stay silent to stay safe. To the outside observer, this looks like we are being loyal to our abuser or fawning indifference to the abuse.

Children experiencing abuse develop various coping mechanisms to endure their environment:

- **Fawning (People-Pleasing):** Becoming excessively obedient, agreeable, or overly helpful to avoid conflict.
- **Dissociation:** Mentally escaping from reality, numbing emotions, blacking out, or forgetting their lived experiences.
- **Hypervigilance:** Constantly scanning for danger, reading people's emotions, and anticipating threats.
- **Minimization:** Convincing themselves "it's not that bad" to cope with the pain.
- **Stockholm Syndrome:** Developing a psychological bond with the abuser as a way to feel a sense of control.

The Reality of Abuse in Numbers

The statistics are staggering:

- 1 in 7 children in the U.S. experiences abuse or neglect each year.
- More than 90% of abused children know their abuser personally.
- Many people who have experienced trauma in childhood struggle with Complex Post-Traumatic Stress Disorder, anxiety, depression, and trust issues well into adulthood.

Despite these odds, healing is possible.

When I faced a life-threatening brain tumor, I woke up. That diagnosis, though terrifying, was an unexpected gift wrapped in adversity. It forced me to confront my past, to see how I had been living— numb, disconnected, and detached. Through therapy and healing practices, I began to revisit the memories I had buried so deeply. It was excruciating. I wanted to throw it all into a black box and cast it into a black hole. However, healing demanded that I see it, process it, and reclaim my life. I carried the hyperawareness with me. Now, I see it as a tool to deeply understand people and my surroundings. True healing requires us to expose those wounds, feel the pain, and move forward. Facing the past and recognizing my fawning response, I was able to break free from the patterns that once controlled me. By doing this, I was able to reclaim my voice and create a life of my own making.

Reflections
Why Abused Children Stay Loyal

We invite you to explore these questions with curiosity and self-compassion. Use them to reframe challenges into opportunities for growth, gratitude, and empowerment. Share your responses with trusted people so you feel heard and understood. Revisit the questions over time to celebrate your growth.

1. **Revisiting the Silence:** Write about the times you felt silenced as a child. How did it affect the way you express yourself today? What would you say now if you could go back and speak your truth?

2. **Finding Strength in Pain:** Reflect on a moment of pain from your past and explore how it shaped your inner strength. What parts of yourself did you protect, and how can you now honor them?

3. **Breaking the Cycle of Fear:** What fears from your childhood linger in your life today? How can you begin to release them and replace them with feelings of safety and empowerment?

4. **The Safe Space You Deserve:** Describe a place, real or imagined, where you feel completely safe, seen, and protected. What elements are present, and how can you bring aspects of this space into your daily life?

5. **Giving Your Inner Child a Voice:** Write a letter to your younger self, offering them the compassion and protection that was important for them to hear.

6. **Letting Go of the Secret:** Reflect on the emotional burden of carrying secrets from your childhood. How has keeping them impacted your relationships, and what would it feel like to let go of that weight?

7. **Lessons from Adversity:** Think about the most challenging experiences you've endured. What have they taught you about resilience, and how can you use those lessons to move forward with strength?

8. **The Journey of Healing:** Write about what healing looks like for you today. What steps have you already taken, and what are the next steps for you to take?

9. **Reclaiming Your Dreams:** As a child, you had dreams and aspirations. What were they? How can you reconnect with those dreams and create a life that honors them?

10. **Being Kind to Yourself:** How can you acknowledge the courage that it took to cope with your experience?

Affirmations
Why Abused Children Stay Loyal

Your thoughts, feelings, beliefs, voice, and actions create your reality. Each day, choose three affirmations and speak them out loud. Hearing your own words turns affirmations into living declarations that reshape your mind. Speak with intention and feel the words settle deep within you.

- I am safe.
- I am stronger.
- I nurture myself.
- I am courageous.
- I am my true self.
- My voice matters.
- I feel my emotions.
- I have peace and joy in my life.
- I am creating a future filled with love and strength.
- I honor my inner child with kindness, compassion, and patience.

Chapter 13: Letter to Your Inner Child

"You are never too old to have a happy childhood.
The second one is up to you."

— Tom Robbins

Deep within each of us lives a child who remembers everything—every moment of neglect, every unspoken need, every time they looked around hoping someone would notice their pain. This inner child has been waiting, sometimes for decades, for someone to see them, acknowledge their experience, and offer the love they always needed.

For many of us, that inner child learned to hide, to stay quiet, to make themselves small in hopes of staying safe. They develop incredible coping skills, at the cost of feeling truly seen and deeply loved. The wounds they carry stay present across the years, buried beneath layers of adult responsibilities, achievements, and coping mechanisms.

The healing dialogue letter is one of the most powerful tools for reaching that wounded child within and beginning the process of integration and self-compassion. This is a sacred conversation that can rewire your relationship with yourself and break patterns that have been passed down through generations.

When you write to your inner child, you're offering comfort to a memory and actively healing the parts of yourself that carry those early wounds, the parts that influence how you show up in relationships, how you treat yourself, and how you navigate the world today.

The Power of Direct Dialogue

This healing dialogue has the power to transform your relationship with yourself and break generational patterns that may have shaped your family for decades. This seven-step framework guides you through a direct conversation with your younger self, creating a bridge between the wounded child within and the wise, compassionate adult you've become.

The framework uses specific phrases that address the core needs children have: to be loved unconditionally, to be seen and acknowledged, to receive forgiveness, to offer forgiveness, to be given what they need, to have their experiences understood, and to know they are safe, wanted, and protected. These seven elements—"I love you," "Thank you for making me aware of," "Please forgive me," "I forgive you," "I give you," "What I discovered," and "I commit to"—create a healing conversation.

What makes this process so powerful is that it allows you to become the parent, protector, and advocate your inner child longed for. You reshape your relationship with the past. You offer your younger self the love, understanding, and protection they hold as a birthright, and in doing so, you heal the wounds that have been influencing your adult life.

Many people discover that the voice of their inner critic—that harsh, judgmental voice inside—echoes the adults who withheld protection and nurturing during their childhood. By speaking directly to your inner child with love and compassion, you begin to replace those critical voices with ones of understanding and support.

This process also breaks generational patterns because it interrupts the cycle of unconscious wounding. When you heal your relationship with your own inner child, you become conscious of the patterns that were passed down to you, and you can choose to transform them rather than perpetuate them.

Write by Hand

Write this letter by hand. The physical act of writing creates a deeper mind-body connection and allows emotions to flow more naturally through your pen onto paper. Handwriting gives your heart time to catch up with your thoughts. Trust what wants to emerge and let it flow from your hand as you write.

Preparation

You are prepared to begin this exercise. Entirely fatigued people have produced results as great as those of people who have been well rested. I view this as sacred work. Whenever I do this exercise, I set aside

30-45 minutes and leave myself a buffer to continue calmly. I like the reverence of a quiet, private space, free from distractions and interruptions. I set a glass of water nearby, light a candle, and play soft music.

Set up your environment in any way you feel safe and supported. It is powerful to do this when you believe in your ability to handle whatever emotions or memories arise. If you're feeling particularly vulnerable or unstable, consider having emotional support with you. That may be a picture, a pet, a stuffed animal, or a trusted person.

Open Your Heart

Be prepared to discover things about yourself and your past that may surprise you. This process often reveals memories, feelings, or insights that have been buried for years. Approach this with curiosity. Your inner child has been waiting to be heard, and this conversation may reveal truths you are ready to acknowledge. Remember that whatever emerges is valid and deserving of compassion.

The Seven-Step Framework: A Complete Healing Conversation

Use the seven-step framework as your guide, writing each section as a direct conversation with your younger self. Allow the words to flow from your heart to your hand to the paper. Trust what emerges—your inner wisdom knows what needs to be said.

Step 1: *I love you…*

Begin with unconditional love and acknowledgment. Express genuine appreciation for their strength, courage, or specific qualities you admire about who you were as a child.

Examples:
- *I love you for your incredible creativity and imagination…*
- *I love you for your sensitive heart and how deeply you felt everything…*
- *I love you for your determination to keep going even when…*

Step 2: *Thank you for making me aware that…*

Acknowledge the specific experiences, feelings, or needs that were overlooked or dismissed. Be specific about the situations that caused pain.

Examples:
- *You felt invisible when no one showed up to your soccer games…*
- *You felt scared and confused while the adults around you fought…*
- *You needed someone to look you in the eyes and say, "It's OK, you are OK."…*

Step 3: *Please forgive me...*

As your adult self, take responsibility for how you may have continued to neglect or harm your inner child through self-criticism or ignoring your needs.

Examples:
- *For speaking to you with harshness instead of tenderness, and for measuring you against impossible standards...*
- *For overriding your need for rest and driving you past the limits of your body and heart...*
- *For leaving you unprotected from people who caused harm, instead of standing as your protector and shield...*

Step 4: *I forgive you...*

Forgive your inner child for any ways they coped that you now judge as wrong or embarrassing.

Examples:
- *For feeling anger and acting out when fear flooded your body and needed expression...*
- *For believing you were "bad" when you were a deeply hurt, tender child longing for care...*
- *For striving for perfection to earn love, even though your heart always deserved love as a birthright...*

Step 5: *I give you...*

Offer them love, safety, validation, protection, or guidance.

Examples:
- *The safety to feel all your emotions without judgment...*
- *Permission to play and be silly without having to be responsible for adults...*
- *The protection you needed and the voice to say 'no' when something felt wrong...*

Step 6: *What I discovered…*

Share insights about yourself, your patterns, or your healing that have emerged through this process.

Examples:
- *Is that your sensitivity reflects your brilliance and depth, and the world around you often moved with harshness…*
- *Is that your longing for approval reflects a deep need for love and belonging…*
- *Is that you always deserved celebration, appreciation, and honor…*

Step 7: *I commit to…*

Make specific, actionable promises about how you will treat your inner child going forward.

Examples:
- *Listening to your needs and taking them seriously…*
- *Protecting your energy and saying yes to what is within your abilities…*
- *Celebrating your accomplishments, no matter how small…*

Here's an example of my own healing dialogue letter, written during my journey of breaking free from the patterns that had kept me trapped for so long.

Dear Little Rocío,

1. *I love you...* for your incredible courage, even when the world felt scary and confusing.
2. *Thank you for making me aware that...* I overlooked you and stayed distant from your pain of feeling alone and confused about what was happening around you—especially during the Spelling Bee, honor roll, school plays, and other important events in your life. Thank you for showing me how deeply you longed to feel seen, valued, and cherished when you needed your mother's love and support.
3. *Please forgive me...* for numbing your life experience and delaying the care, presence, and support you needed.
4. *I forgive you...* for showing up like a confused child, hurt and alone, who needed love, attention, and understanding that I can now give you.
5. *I give you...* the love, connection, protection, attention, a sense of belonging, and knowing that someone is here by your side in these very important moments in your life.
6. *What I discovered...* is that I wanted mother by my side at these important events in my life and I longed to feel at home in my own body and in my own environment—and now I give that to myself.
7. *I commit to...* acknowledging your life experiences, being by your side, helping you understand what's going on, guiding and support your humanity, and celebrating your every accomplishment with you.

Reflect on Your Letter

Read It Aloud:
- Read your letter out loud to yourself, ideally looking in a mirror
- Notice what emotions come up—allow them to flow
- If it feels right, hold a childhood photo of yourself while reading

Get into the Right Mindset:
- Take several deep breaths and center yourself
- Imagine yourself as the loving, wise adult you are today
- Picture your younger self—what age feels most significant to address?
- Approach this with compassion and empathy

Create a Ritual:
- Keep the letter somewhere special
- Consider writing a response letter from your inner child to your adult self
- You might want to create a small ceremony to honor this healing work

Follow Through:
- The commitments you made are real—start honoring them immediately
- Check in with your inner child regularly through journaling or meditation
- Notice when old patterns arise and gently redirect with your new awareness

Important Reminders
- *Inner child work unfolds. It lives as an ongoing practice*
- *Be patient with the process. Healing often happens in layers*
- *Seek professional support if this brings up overwhelming feelings*
- *You deserve the love and care you're offering to your inner child*
- *Consistent actions toward your healing matter more than grand gestures*

Your inner child has been waiting for this acknowledgment and love. Trust the process, be gentle with yourself, and remember that you're doing sacred healing work that will ripple out into every area of your life.

An Invitation to Profound Healing

We invite you to pick up your pen and create the healing conversation you've needed your entire life—a dialogue of love, forgiveness, and radical self-compassion. Your inner child has been waiting, silently, patiently, for someone to see them, hear them, and love them exactly as they are.

This letter is about healing your past and reclaiming your future. When you offer your inner child the love and understanding that once stayed out of reach, you free yourself from the patterns that have been unconsciously running your life. You break the chains of generational patterns and create space for authentic joy, connection, and self-acceptance.

Remember that this is sacred work. Treat it—and yourself—with the reverence this healing moment requires. Trust the process, be gentle with whatever emerges, and know that you're doing one of the most important things you can do for yourself and for the generations that come after you.

The Ripple Effect of Self-Compassion

When you complete your healing dialogue letter, you will have done something profound—you will have offered up the loving parent, protector, and advocate that your inner child always needed. This is a real conversation that creates real healing and real change in your nervous system, your relationships, and your daily life.

The ripple effects of this work extend far beyond your own healing. When you learn to speak to yourself with compassion, you naturally begin to extend that same compassion to others. When you heal your own childhood wounds, you become less likely to unconsciously wound others. When you break the patterns that were passed down to you, you create the possibility for healthier relationships and, if you have children, healthier parenting.

People find that after writing their healing dialogue letter, they notice shifts in how they respond to stress, how they treat themselves when they make mistakes, and how they show up in relationships. The harsh inner critic begins to soften, replaced by a voice of understanding and support. Old patterns of self-sabotage or people-pleasing begin to loosen as you start honoring the needs and boundaries your inner child can now express.

This letter is the beginning of an ongoing relationship with the most important person in your life: yourself. You may find yourself repeating this letter writing process multiple times to check in with your inner child as new layers of healing emerge.

Remember that the child within you has incredible gifts to offer—creativity, wonder, spontaneity, and joy. As you heal the wounds they carry, you also reclaim these gifts. You heal your past and you liberate your future.

Your inner child has been waiting for this conversation their entire life. They've been waiting for someone to say, "I see you, I love you, and I will always be with you." Today, you have the power to be that someone. Today, you can give yourself the nurturing withheld from you during childhood.

The pen is in your hand. The healing is waiting. Your inner child is ready to be loved.

Your Turn. Write to Your Inner Child

This letter-writing exercise is a powerful tool for integrating parts of yourself that may have been neglected, overlooked, unheard, ostracized, hurt, or abandoned. Follow these steps to create your own meaningful dialogue with your inner child.

Now it's your turn to begin this transformative dialogue with the most important person in your healing journey—yourself.

Step 1: Express Love and Acknowledgment

Step 2: Thank you for making me aware that…

Step 3: Please forgive me…

Step 4: I forgive you…

Step 5: I give you…

Step 6: What I discovered…

Step 7: I commit to…

Chapter 14: Compartmentalization

"If one tries to segment his or her life into separate compartments, one will never rise to the full stature of one's personal integrity—never to become all that his or her true self could be."

— Russell M. Nelson

Compartmentalization: the internal prison. The tunnel vision of compartmentalization is what I use to endure my life. What once protects me becomes a jail cell that keeps me trapped, locked away from my own life.

I spend most of my life believing that the walls I build are for my protection, my fortress in a world that has proven itself capable of unspeakable cruelty. I believe they keep the pain out, shielding me from disappointment that feels like drowning, rejection that burns like acid, and heartbreak that could shatter me into pieces so small I might never find them all.

Through the fog that once kept me in pure defense mode, I miss a deeper truth: those same walls block everything else, too. Love reaches them and stops. Connection approaches and turns away. The full, rich experience of life waits outside while I sit alone in my self-constructed fortress, starving for the very things I have barricaded myself against.

I keep friends at arm's length like dangerous animals that might bite if I let my guard down. I live in an environment I carefully control, where I am both the prisoner and the guard, unwilling to fully share myself with anyone because sharing means vulnerability, and vulnerability means the possibility of being destroyed all over again. People invite me to their weddings, Quinceañeras, and birthday parties, where joy is the only requirement for admission. Yet, I always find an excuse to stay home, each rejection carefully crafted to sound reasonable, responsible, unavoidable. Each excuse becomes another log in the stockade between me and the world.

The truth is, I am afraid—terrified in ways that make my bones ache and my chest feel hollow. Afraid to let people close enough to see me, really see me, beyond the carefully curated version I present to the world. I feel different from them because I have an untraditional familial upbringing they take for granted. I grow up on my own, a child raising herself in a house full of adults who are too consumed by their desires to notice my pain. I skip childhood to care for family, skip adolescence to raise my son, and spend my young adult years juggling life like a circus performer.

A friend tells me, "Rocío, you're like a beautiful star in the night sky, as I drive towards it I feel like I'm getting closer and closer; yet, no matter how far I go, I can never actually reach you." That statement reverberates through my chest like an earthquake. I see how I have turned myself into emotional unobtanium—always glowing, always distant, forever out of reach, even from myself. I realize I spend my entire life making myself unattainable. I believe I am keeping myself safe, yet in reality, I am keeping myself alone.

Mother and Father: The Masters of Illusion

Mother is the master of illusion, a magician who can make reality disappear and replace it with a carefully crafted narrative of the perfect family. To the outside world, she is a devoted mother, with a pasted-on smile. In her version of reality, there is no abuse, no pain, no betrayal. Only the story she chooses to tell, polished until it gleams like fool's gold.

Her greeting to me is always, "I never did anything to you. And if I did, you deserved it."

We're having lunch at my grandmother's house, the sunlight spilling through the lace curtains. I've brought the usual peace offerings—food and knick-knacks. On weekends, I spend time with mother. I take her shopping to buy the things she needs and wants. Now, I watch her enjoying her lunch, leaning back in the chair, and chatting. Then she turns to my grandmother and, as she points at me, says with venom, "I didn't have any bad children. The only bad one is her."

I freeze. The fork in my hand feels heavy, cold against my fingers. My body stiffens. I swallow the words screaming inside, "What the hell! With all that I do for you and after all the harm you've caused me."

My son is sitting across from me, chewing slowly, eyes widening. Grandma's eyes widen, too. The room is charged. I stand up and quietly tell my son, "Go outside and wait for me." He side-eyes me, sees me uncharacteristically infuriated, nods, and slips out.

Grandma flees to her bedroom to avoid the looming conflict. In an attempt to get away from me, mother escapes to the living room with me in hot pursuit. My chest tightens, my heart hammering. I feel the air between us, thick and charged, tasting it, sharp and bitter. "You know you caused me harm," I say. My voice echoes off the walls, firm, controlled, speaking the truth. I repeat it multiple times.

She looks at me, her eyes flicking away, then back, and after a long pause, she says, "Okay… okay, fine. I'll admit it to you. But I will never admit it to anyone in public." I feel like she stabs me in the heart, because if she denies it to the world, she denies the pain she caused.

Our belief in compartmentalization is that experiences can be contained in black boxes if you simply refuse to open them. She keeps the torture she inflicts on me in a box locked away from the public so they will believe she has the perfect life. The same locked box keeps it away from herself and protects her from acknowledging she is a child abuser. She is then able to shift the blame to me saying that I am the problem. This leaves me carrying the weight of the abuse and the burden of their blame.

Father lives in two separate worlds that stay completely apart. In one world, he is kind, generous, and admired—the man who gives you the shirt off his back. Behind closed doors, he transforms into a monster. He is brutal, unpredictable, and strict with a hot temper. His whispers carry manipulation and control. He walks away from responsibility as if it exists somewhere far from him.

I remember the time he says he is going out to get eggs and then vanishes, fleeing the country and leaving us struggling just to keep going. He lives in fragments that refuse to fuse into a whole person.

Like mother, I learn to compartmentalize. Her prison is perfection, every hair in place, every smile rehearsed. Mine is survival. I build mental jail cells to lock away my pain. Mother's cells hold the burn of her slaps, the sting of the horse whip, the cutting edge of her words that tell me I am not enough. Father's cells are darker. I seal them tightly with chains. I construct a separate cell for each beating, each rage, each violation of my body, and all the fears. Having them in separate cells protects me from drowning in them all at once.

I inherit these strategies—mother's obsessive perfection, father's ability to dissociate from reality while living through hell and magically making necessities appear from nowhere—and create my own fortress of separation. To the outside world, I am the model daughter: Spelling Bee champion, honor roll student, math whiz, theater star. Applause and gold stars become my mask to hide my wounds. Every "A" grade, every ribbon for excellent work, every stage performance is proof I can outshine the darkness—at least in public. Education becomes my bunker, my escape route, my proof that I am more than what happens behind closed doors.

Compartmentalizing My Work: The Illusion of Success

I am trapped in the illusion of success, drowning in accolades that feel hollow. To the outside world, my accomplishments are extraordinary. People applaud my dedication, my relentless drive, my superhuman ability to juggle multiple projects at once. They see passion where there is panic, purpose where there is pain.

At the peak of my numbing, I am volunteering for thirteen nonprofit organizations. Thirteen separate worlds, thirteen different versions of myself, thirteen ways to avoid being alone with my thoughts. I am drowning in obligations that make me feel needed and incomplete. The truth is that I am running from my healing like a fugitive fleeing a crime scene.

Compartmentalizing My Relationships: Endless Forgiveness

For years, I allow people to hurt me repeatedly—always forgiving, always excusing, always compartmentalizing their actions as if they exist in separate realities. I put people into isolated compartments in my mind, separating their worst actions from the parts of them I want to believe in. I tell myself they love me, that if I give more, tolerate more, love more—everything will be okay.

By compartmentalizing my pain, I keep allowing the same cycles to repeat like a broken record. I excuse unexcusable behavior, normalize mistreatment and confuse it for love, and sacrifice my own well-being. This endless forgiveness comes at the cost of giving up my whole life for it. Giving up my vitality, my success, and my mental, emotional, financial, and physical freedoms.

The Jail Cells I Build

Night after night, I lie on cold concrete floors, my skin pressed against the chill until my bones ache. The air is thick with fear, so heavy it feels like choking. My ears catch every sound— the shuffle of footsteps, the whisper of a door, my own ragged breathing—because any noise might mean danger is coming for me again. There is no time to think, no time to breathe, no time to sleep. Existence swallows every thought whole. Then morning comes, and the assault shifts form. Mother's hands beat me with her fists, yet her words are sharper than any weapon. "You're worthless," she hisses, each syllable a blade carving into my skin. The bruises bloom purple and yellow, a garden of violence I must hide beneath long sleeves and rehearsed smiles.

Night returns, and father's shadow fills the doorway. His hands, his rage, his violation of my body—each time stealing another piece of my innocence, my safety, my right to exist without terror. The pain is unspeakable. The threats scar me more than any physical wound. "If you tell anyone," he whispers with cold certainty, "I will kill you. Or worse." I have already lived through hell. So I do as I am told. I keep it locked inside. Relief remains out of reach. The abuse is a thousand cuts, one after another, each one deeper than the last. My mind learns to lock each horror into a box to be buried deep into the unconscious. For if I show it, if I speak it, the punishment will be death—or worse.

Sleep is where people heal, where the brain stitches experience into understanding. Sleep stays absent here. Soft pillows of safety stay absent. Vigilance fills the space. Survival runs the show. I know one thing: I guard my secrets like a soldier guards their last weapon. Speaking equals dying. I choose life. So I lock everything away in its own jail cell. Every beating. Every violation. Every threat.

So, of course I compartmentalize. I build this jail, cell by cell and bury it because I want to stay alive. It works. And I am alive. I bury the jail so deep that it takes decades to unearth it. And when it is safe, I dig deep enough to find I have the keys all along. I unlock the cells that have once protected me one cell at a time allowing me to process one abuse at a time instead of all of them at once.

Breaking Free

When I recognize that I am compartmentalizing my pain, my projects, my life—locking everything into separate, sealed cells—I become an observer of myself. I get curious. What else am I compartmentalizing? How does that serve me? How do I bring myself back together so every part of my life integrates, free from cells and separation?

I do the work to break free. The shift unfolds in layers, through many moments of liberation. It is decision by decision, choice by choice, and action by action. Each time a memory surfaces, each time I feel the familiar urge to lock it away, I make an intentional choice to look at it instead. To sit with it. To feel the weight of it without immediately sealing it behind another steel door. Every compartment I open releases decades of stored pain—the beatings, the violations, the threats, the shame. I allow myself to feel what I have spent a lifetime avoiding.

Intentionally, I begin to break down the walls I have built. The jail cells that once protect me become the very thing keeping me fragmented, keeping me from wholeness. I integrate the pieces—the parts of me that carry unspeakable pain, and the parts that hold unshakable strength. I bring myself back together by allowing all of it to exist in the same space—the abuse and the triumph, the wounds and the wisdom, the pain and the power.

I live as more than a collection of locked cells. I am whole.

Keys no longer exist because the cells have dissolved.

Recognition and Transformation

Once I was free of the cells of my past, I learned to use compartmentalization consciously and strategically as a tool. I have learned to compartmentalize for productivity when I want focused work time, to compartmentalize for emotional regulation when I want to function optimally, and to compartmentalize for healing when I want to process memories in manageable pieces. The key difference is awareness and choice.

Understanding Your Coping Patterns

Often, extraordinary people undergo an extraordinary transformation, and for many of us, that transformation begins with breaking the silence that keeps us trapped and dismantling the compartments that keep us imprisoned. The shame, the fear, the helplessness, the walls between different parts of you—these exist as experiences, a temporary identity. They are layers that can be peeled back, examined, reconciled, and released.

You live in silence and separation, and many people walk this same path. You learned early on that speaking your truth brought punishment. You protected yourself by staying quiet in your family, your relationships, and your workplace. You protected yourself by keeping different parts of your life separate rather than risking the vulnerability of integration. You developed coping mechanisms which became patterns —ways to navigate dangerous emotional terrain without getting hurt.

What starts as protection often becomes a prison. The unspoken truths, the swallowed anger, the suppressed pain, the isolated compartments of your existence—they remain with you. They build up pressure inside you like magma beneath a volcano, waiting for the moment when something will give way.

Recognizing Compartmentalization Patterns

You may have developed coping mechanisms that felt normal. These patterns made sense. They kept you safe in unsafe situations. Now they may be keeping you from living authentically and fully. Common patterns include:

- Keeping different parts of your life completely separate—emotions, relationships, family, work
- Internalizing everything instead of expressing your needs
- Believing that kindness and optimism can fix any situation
- Avoiding conflict even when injustice is happening right in front of you
- Feeling guilty or uncomfortable when you do speak up
- Surprising yourself with unexpected emotional eruptions
- Using busyness and achievement to avoid dealing with inner pain
- Compartmentalizing people's harmful actions from their "good" qualities
- Living as different versions of yourself in different settings

The Cost of Compartmentalized Living

When we compartmentalize our pain, separating our true feelings from our daily lives, we create internal pressure that demands release. Every time you withhold your truth or keep parts of yourself isolated, you create what I call an "internal volcano"—emotions and experiences that pile up until they can no longer be contained. When you feel angry or upset with the person in front of you, it might be unresolved life experiences being triggered in you.

When this volcano erupts, you often struggle to recognize the symptoms within yourself. It is the people around you who start questioning the intensity of your reactions. This is why you might find others saying that you are having emotional reactions that are disproportionate to the situation. You experience physical symptoms of stress and tension and are left feeling disconnected from yourself and others—struggling to form deep, authentic relationships.

Start with Awareness: The First Step to Freedom

Notice when you're compartmentalizing. Pay attention to the physical sensations—the walls going up, the emotional shutdown, the automatic separation of experiences. Awareness is the first step to freedom. Start by acknowledging your truth to yourself. Consider writing in a journal about experiences you have kept to yourself. Practice saying "This hurt me" or "This crossed a line for me" out loud, even when you stand alone in the room.

Creating Safe Spaces for Integration

Healing begins when you create safe spaces—both internal and external—where your truth can be spoken and heard, where all parts of yourself can coexist. Finding the right support means seeking out people who offer empathy instead of sympathy. Look for listeners who can hold space for your pain without making it about themselves. Consider professional support from trauma-informed therapists.

Creating internal safety is equally important. Practice awareness when intense emotions arise. Use journaling to give voice to thoughts you kept to yourself. Allow yourself to feel anger, grief, or fear. Listen to your emotions. What might they be telling you about your unresolved experiences?

The Difference Between Sympathy and Empathy

When you're ready to unpack your story, pay attention to how people respond. Sympathy often leads to someone sharing their own experience, shifting focus away from you. Empathy allows your story to unfold freely. It holds space for your pain, honors your experience, and stays present, allowing your process to unfold in its own way. Seek out empathetic listeners who can witness your truth without needing to make it about themselves.

Practical Steps for Integration

- **Practice Integration:** Dismantle your walls one brick at a time. Choose one area where you can practice being more integrated. Maybe it's sharing one authentic thing about yourself with a trusted friend, or allowing yourself to feel an emotion you've been avoiding.

- **Develop Healthy Boundaries Instead of Walls:** Learn the difference between protective boundaries that serve you and walls that isolate you. Boundaries are permeable and conscious; walls are rigid and unconscious.

- **Identify Your Triggers:** Notice when you automatically shut down or change the subject. Pay attention to physical sensations that signal you're avoiding something, and recognize the difference between healthy boundaries and avoidance.

- **Practice Using Your Voice:** Use your voice in low-stakes situations where you can express preferences or opinions. Work up to more significant conversations about your needs and boundaries. Remember that using your voice is a skill that improves with practice.

- **Use Compartmentalization Consciously:** Instead of eliminating it, learn to use it as a tool. Compartmentalize when you want to focus on work, when you want to function during a crisis, or when you want to process emotions in manageable pieces. The key difference is awareness and choice.

Moving Forward with Intention

Breaking compartmentalized silence and living as an integrated person is about reclaiming your right to exist authentically in the world. It's about recognizing that your experiences matter, your feelings are valid, and your voice deserves to be heard. It's about understanding that all parts of you—the wounded and the healed, the strong and the vulnerable—deserve to coexist in one integrated life.

As you begin this process, remember that you have the right to set boundaries and protect your energy. You deserve to be in relationships where your voice is valued, and your whole self is welcomed. Your truth, even when painful, is worthy of acknowledgment, and speaking up is an act of courage.

Build Your Support System: Surround yourself with people who hold space for your whole story, embracing more than the compartmentalized pieces you share. And to the support people, when someone comes to you ready to unpack their experiences, how do you respond? Do you truly listen with empathy, or do you shift the focus back to yourself?

And to the individuals, when the opportunity arises for you to unpack your own story and integrate the separated parts of yourself, do you have the courage to embrace it? You know what patterns are holding you back. You know which silences no longer serve you. You know which walls have become prisons rather than protection. The question is: Are you ready to break free from the compartments you have created and step into the power of your authentic voice?

The goal is to live as an integrated person who can choose when to compartmentalize rather than being controlled by unconscious patterns. You have the power to transform your coping mechanisms into conscious tools for thriving.

Your compartments once kept you safe. Now they keep you stuck. The walls that shielded you now isolate you from the very life you desire. You can reclaim your voice and your wholeness. The choice is yours.

Reflections
Compartmentalization

We invite you to explore these questions with curiosity and self-compassion. Use them to reframe challenges into opportunities for growth, gratitude, and empowerment. Share your responses with trusted people so you feel heard and understood. Revisit the questions over time to celebrate your growth.

1. What invisible walls have you built between different areas of your life? How do these separations serve or limit you today?

2. When you think about your family's patterns of compartmentalization, what unspoken rules did you learn about keeping secrets, maintaining appearances, or separating public and private selves?

3. How do you recognize when you're automatically compartmentalizing pain, emotions, or impactful experiences? What physical sensations signal this protective response?

4. In what ways do you present different versions of yourself in different settings? What would it feel like to show up as the same authentic person everywhere?

5. What parts of your story have you locked away in separate "jail cells"? What would it mean to safely integrate these experiences into your whole narrative?

6. How do you use busyness, achievement, or helping others as a way to avoid sitting with your own emotions or needs?

7. What patterns do you notice in your relationships where you separate people's harmful actions from their positive qualities? How does this affect your ability to set boundaries?

8. When someone tries to get close to you, what automatic defenses arise? What are you protecting yourself from?

9. How has compartmentalizing different aspects of your life affected your ability to form deep, authentic connections with others?

10. What would your life look like if you could consciously choose when to compartmentalize as a tool rather than being controlled by unconscious patterns of separation?

Journaling Prompts
Compartmentalization

1. Write about a specific moment when you realized you were living as different versions of yourself in different settings. *How did this awareness feel? What would integration look like for you?*

2. Describe the "jail cells" you've created for painful memories, emotions, or experiences. *What would it feel like to safely unlock these doors and allow those parts of your story to be acknowledged and integrated?*

3. Reflect on the family patterns of compartmentalization you witnessed growing up. *How did the adults in your life separate their public and private selves? How has this modeling influenced your own behavior?*

4. Create a detailed inventory of all the commitments, projects, and responsibilities you're currently juggling. *How many truly align with your authentic self versus serving as distractions from inner work or ways to avoid intense emotions?*

5. Write about a relationship where you've repeatedly excused harmful behavior by compartmentalizing the person's actions. *What would true accountability look like in this relationship? What boundaries would serve your well-being?*

6. Compose a letter to the part of yourself that has been working tirelessly to keep everything separate and controlled. *What would you want this protective part to know about safety, healing, and the possibility of integration?*

7. Describe what scares you most about tearing down the walls between different areas of your life. *What do you fear might happen if people saw your complete, unedited story?*

8. Imagine your life as one integrated whole rather than separate compartments. *Write in vivid detail what this would look like and how it would feel to move through the world as your complete, authentic self.*

9. Reflect on a time when someone described you as "unreachable," "hard to get close to," or like "a something they could never reach." *What walls were you protecting yourself with? What were you afraid they might discover?*

10. What actionable steps are you ready to take to integrate the compartmentalized parts of your life? *What one step could you take today toward greater authenticity and wholeness?*

Affirmations
Compartmentalization

Your thoughts, feelings, beliefs, voice, and actions create your reality. Each day, choose three affirmations and speak them out loud. Hearing your own words turns affirmations into living declarations that reshape your mind. Speak with intention and feel the words settle deep within you.

- I am deserving.
- I express what I feel.
- I am my authentic self.
- I have a powerful voice.
- I have healthy boundaries
- I am aware of my thoughts.
- I integrate all parts of myself.
- I compartmentalize consciously.
- I have an empowering support system.
- All parts of me can exist in the same space.

Chapter 15: These Are My Boundaries

"Boundaries are the distance at which I can love you and me simultaneously."

— Prentis Hemphill

There comes a moment in every healing journey when the private work you've been doing suddenly demands to be lived out loud. For me, that moment arrives like a tsunami—sudden, overwhelming, and impossible to ignore. I realize I have spent my entire life giving at the expense of myself.

The Universe comes knocking, leaning in close, and saying, "Hey Rocío, do you see this?" I don't. So it sends another messenger, and another, and another…

Messenger: Girlfriend

I keep showing up for my girlfriend, putting my energy, my care, and my resources into helping her, thinking I am making a difference. I realize the lesson is about me.

Back when she was single, raising four kids on her own, I am the steady hand she can lean on. I can still see myself standing in the aisles of the store, comparing the bright colors of notebooks and backpacks, filling up my cart with school supplies for children who feel like family. I remember the sparkle in their eyes as they decorate the Christmas tree I have purchased—the warm scent of pine needles filling the living room, lights twinkling like tiny promises of a better tomorrow. I pour my heart, my time, and what money I have into helping her create a sense of home, of hope, of magic.

Then everything shifts.

She gets married. Together, she and her husband earn $130,000 a year and own two homes—a fortune compared to what I have at the time. Hope rises in me that she will stand on her own *two feet, that this becomes the moment I exhale and trust her independence.*

Instead, she keeps showing up with the same requests for school supplies, decorations, school clothes, and little extras as if everything is the same. And there I am, unemployed, holding on by a thin thread. My thoughts are screaming, "What the hell? How is this fair?"

I feel the sting—sharp and cold—like a slap that no one else can see. I feel unseen, unappreciated, and used.

Messenger: Quinceañera Dress

I sit in the sterile doctor's office, the white walls glaring back at me like a spotlight. The doctor's words echo in my ears, heavy and sharp: "You can have a stroke and die at any moment." I feel the weight of them pressing on my chest, each breath a reminder of how fragile everything is, how uncertain my future has become.

The world keeps moving forward. As a godmother, I'm expected to keep giving. I hear the excitement in my godchildren's parents' voices, smell the faint perfume of celebration, and see the sparkling dresses and decorations in my mind as they describe what she wants. My body feels torn in two—the urgency of self-care pulsing in every vein, and the pressure to provide for someone else's elaborate party. I am expected to buy the Quinceañera dress. How can I provide for myself and my son's future? I voice my concern to the family. My trembling voice cracking as I tell them my fears about having a place to live if I become so ill that I cannot work.

I hear their response as casual and dismissive, "Don't worry, you can come live with us. Buy the Quinceañera dress." What matters is this extravagant celebration. My heart clenches. My son's security, my stability, my very life—none of it registers to them.

How do I reconcile this? How do I plan for a future that feels uncertain while still embodying the person everyone expects me to be? Beneath these questions lies a quiet, stubborn pulse of determination. Somehow, I must show up—for myself, for my son, and for her—even when the world teeters on the edge of death.

Messenger: Duty!

I sit across the table from another nonprofit leader, their eyes gleaming with that familiar mix of admiration and expectation. The coffee between us has gone cold, untouched, while they lean forward with urgency in their voice.

"Rocío, you're first generation. You've achieved so much. You're the person who can show people it's possible."

I feel the weight of those words settle on my shoulders like stones—heavy, immovable, suffocating.

For years, I have spent countless hours in the nonprofit world helping everyone under the Sun. I show up at community events, my voice hoarse from speaking, my body exhausted from giving. I pour my expertise, my story, my very soul into rooms filled with people who nod and applaud and ask for more.

The leaders smile at me with tight, expectant grins. They shake my hand with both of theirs, holding on a beat too long. "We're so grateful for your contributions," they say, their words dripping with sweetness that tastes bitter on my tongue.

When it comes time to discuss compensation, their faces shift. The warmth drains away, replaced by something colder, sharper.

"Well, you understand—this is for the community."

"You know how important this work is."

"Someone like you, with your platform, your success—you have a duty to give back."

Duty! That word lands like a slap every single time.

I look around the conference room, taking in the expensive suits, the designer handbags casually draped over chairs, and their luxury cars parked outside. These leaders are in a much better place than I am financially and in their careers. They draw salaries from the very organizations that ask me to donate my time. They benefit financially from my contributions and the work that I do for the community.

Meanwhile, I am the one sacrificing. I am barely getting by. For as much as I am giving, you would think I lived a pretty decent life. Instead, I scrape by and give far more than I have. I eat in my car. I take meetings in the heat and the cold to help them out. I stay up late into the night preparing presentations I deliver for free while they collect paychecks.

The shame is a weapon they wield with precision.

"Because of who you are."

"Because of what you've accomplished."

"Because you made it out."

As if my survival, my success, my refusal to let poverty, and abuse define me has somehow made me community property. As if the fact that I climbed out of hell means I now have an obligation to set myself on fire to keep everyone else warm.

I feel the resentment building in my chest—hot, sharp, righteous. I see the pattern clearly now: they continue to deplete me by shaming me, while they are elevating themselves. They build their reputations on my back. They advance their careers with my labor. They fill their bank accounts while mine empties.

And when I dare to ask for compensation, when I say that my time and expertise have value, I am met with disappointment, judgment, and the unspoken accusation that I have somehow betrayed the community by wanting to take care of myself.

Here is what I know now: Giving back means giving from overflow, from a full and nourished place. Service flourishes alongside self-preservation. My success turns me into a model of what becomes possible when I honor my worth and welcome only what aligns with what I deserve.

I am done sacrificing myself on the altar of other people's expectations. I am done allowing guilt and shame to dictate my worth. I am done being the one in the room expected to work for free while everyone else gets paid. The community thrives through my leadership. True allies honor my value and stand beside me in equity; exploiters reveal themselves through demands for my sacrifice while they protect their own comfort, even when they speak the language of social justice.

I have given enough. Now, I choose to give from overflow, from a full and nourished place. I choose to value my work, my time, my expertise—because I see clearly. The greatest service I offer is to model what it looks like to break the cycle of limitations.

I am first-generation. I have achieved success. I have made it through. And that means I get to decide what giving back looks like—on my terms, with my boundaries, and in ways that honor my well-being.

The Illusion of Love Through Sacrifice

The awakening is brutal in its clarity. I watch the very people I love—the ones I am helping financially—live the life I long for. They are enjoying the same things I dream of: traveling to places I would love to visit, indulging in luxuries I desire, and building the future of freedom and ease I have envisioned for myself. I am the one funding their lifestyle while sacrificing my own.

I carry this toxic belief into every relationship—friendships, romantic partnerships, professional connections. I take pride in being the person others can always count on. The cost is that I am running myself into the ground through this relentless giving.

I tell myself that love means sacrifice, that giving without limits is noble, that my needs can always wait. I have created an elaborate mythology around my martyrdom, convincing myself that my pain will somehow unlock the love I crave.

Wake-Up Call

I am drained. Exhausted. Trapped in a cycle of over-giving and depletion has become my normal way of existing. My cup is empty—others have been scraping the bottom, wearing it down until it becomes brittle, ready to shatter completely.

Mother questions my shift in priorities with barely concealed resentment: "Why aren't you here at my beck and call anymore? You used to come running every time I called you."

My brother resents my newfound boundaries: "We used to be so close." What he really means is, "You used to say 'yes' to everything."

My son is shocked when I speak up for myself: "I can't believe you're actually saying something."

My closest friends resist my growth with thinly veiled threats: "Don't change too much. I might not like you."

And then, there is my former boyfriend. Instead of support for my healing journey, I am met with manipulation: "I don't like who you're becoming. Stop working on yourself. I like the old you."

I stand there, stunned by the clarity of that moment. Why would someone who claims to love me want me to stay in pain? Why would anyone who truly cares about me want me to remain depleted and self-abandoning?

The answer is devastating: because my pain serves them. My lack of boundaries makes their lives easier. My self-sacrifice funds their comfort. My silence protects their egos.

I have made a decision that will change everything: "I am ready to heal."

Taking Back My Power

I stand my ground, even when I stand alone. I have spent too much time prioritizing everyone ahead of myself, treating my needs as something to postpone—until I realize my needs always deserved a front-row seat in my life.

I have mistaken my silence for kindness, my flexibility for generosity, and my over-accommodation for love. I understand the truth: silence that enables harm betrays kindness. Flexibility that erodes well-being drains generosity. Self-sacrifice that erases the self masquerades as love while it carves a path of self-destruction.

I am done giving from an empty cup. I am choosing myself, even if it means disappointing the very people whose approval I have spent my life seeking.

Lessons Learned & Where I Am Now

That realization changes everything about how I move through the world. I start making different choices—in what I do and, more importantly, in what I allow.

I stop overcommitting my time and energy to projects and people who fully honor the value I bring to the table. I stop absorbing other people's responsibilities, recognizing that rescuing others hurts them more than helps them. I stop mistaking tolerance for kindness, understanding that the apparent compassion of allowing harmful behavior to continue is enabling. I no longer let people delay payments for my services. I require people to uphold agreements because it is about respect and integrity.

I have stayed silent for years to keep the peace, afraid of losing what little connection I have with mother and family. I discover that silence keeps me struggling in relationships that are killing my spirit.

One of the most profound lessons I learned is this: Setting boundaries where none existed before may be a shock for those who benefited from my lack of them. The people who genuinely care about me will respect and support my growth. The ones who stayed because of what they could take from me, may, in time, fall away. And this is a necessary pruning.

Now, my decisions are clearer because they're filtered through my values rather than my desire for approval. My priorities are aligned with my authentic self rather than other people's expectations. My energy now flows toward love that welcomes me fully and reflects my worth.

Self-Love

For decades, I conduct a private experiment in self-destruction, disguised as selflessness. I convince myself that if I give more, sacrifice enough, bend a little further, I will earn mother's love. I believe that dissolving my boundaries unlocks her approval, that self-sacrifice serves as the price of belonging.

Something inside me snaps into clarity. I am being self-destructive. I have lived for others—financing their dreams while ignoring my own, pouring love into people who give me crumbs, mistaking self-sacrifice for self-worth.

And I am doing it all in pursuit of something that may never arrive— mother's love. Every effort I make leaves that void untouched, because love lives outside of how she shows up in the world.

I honor real love. I honor true belonging. I live my values consciously. My life reflects the values I consciously choose.

I recognize that chasing mother's love is a losing game. The love I have been seeking from her has always been inside of me. So, I give myself the unconditional acceptance, the nurturing presence, the validation I have been searching for outside myself. By breaking this cycle, I free myself and future generations to discover the love we seek has always lived within ourselves.

The private experiment failed. I hear the resistance loud and clear. The people who benefited from my boundaryless existence feel deeply unsettled by my transformation. Today, I move forward without seeking permission from mother, from family, from anyone.

I do something new. I stop. I stop over-giving. I stop over-explaining. I stop justifying my boundaries. I stop abandoning myself to keep others comfortable. And I choose myself. This is my power. This is my freedom.

A Guide to Reclaiming Your Power

If any of this sounds familiar, if you recognize yourself in the pattern of over-giving and under-receiving, know that you have the power to change your life starting now. Setting boundaries is essential for your mental health, your relationships, and your ability to show up authentically in the world.

Start with awareness. Notice where you're over-giving, over-explaining, or abandoning yourself to keep others comfortable. Pay attention to the relationships where you feel drained, resentful, or invisible. Identify what you're really seeking. Are you chasing approval, love, or validation from people who are fundamentally unable to provide it? Recognize that some wells will always be dry, no matter how much you pour into them.

Practice saying "no" as a declaration of self-respect. You honor your well-being with every clear choice you make. "No" stands as a complete sentence, rooted in your power. Your boundaries reflect your worth and create the space where you thrive.

Be aware of resistance and stay strong. The people who benefited from your lack of boundaries may resist your growth, even as your evolution invites you into greater freedom and self-respect. Their resistance confirms how necessary your boundaries are.

Give yourself what you are seeking from others. The love, validation, and acceptance you crave come from within. You hold full permission to value yourself.

Freedom on the Other Side

Today, I live in a world where my boundaries are sacred laws that govern how I allow myself to be treated. I have learned that the people who truly love me will respect my growth, even when it's inconvenient for them. The ones who resist my boundaries were there for what they could take from me.

Setting boundaries makes my love more intentional and sustainable. It makes my generosity a choice rather than a compulsion driven by the desperate desire for approval.

The freedom on the other side of boundaries is unlike anything I have ever experienced. It's the freedom to be yourself without apology, to love without losing yourself, to give without depleting yourself, and to receive without guilt.

Your boundaries are gates with locks, and you hold the key to who gets access to your energy, your love, and your life. Use that key wisely. Your future self is counting on it.

The revolution starts with you. The power has always been yours. It's time to reclaim it.

Types of Boundaries

Boundaries come in different forms, depending on the context in which they are set. Here are the main types:

1. **Physical Boundaries:** Relate to personal space and physical touch. Example: Preferring a certain amount of personal space and choosing touch when it feels right to you.

2. **Emotional Boundaries:** Involve protecting your feelings and energy. Example: Choosing to carry only your own emotional burdens and intentionally limiting discussions about certain personal issues.

3. **Mental/Intellectual Boundaries:** Relate to thoughts, beliefs, and opinions. Example: Being able to disagree with someone without feeling pressured to conform.

4. **Time Boundaries:** Concern how you prioritize your time and commitments. Example: Saying no to overtime at work to maintain a healthy work-life balance.

5. **Material Boundaries:** Involve possessions and finances. Example: Lending personal belongings or money at levels that feel comfortable and aligned for you.

6. **Workplace Boundaries:** Define expectations and professional relationships in the workplace. Example: Keeping work emails within business hours or maintaining professional conduct.

7. **Digital Boundaries:** Involve technology use and online interactions. Example: Limiting social media access and AI, setting "do not disturb" hours, or controlling what personal information is shared online.

8. **Sexual Boundaries:** Relate to physical intimacy and consent. Example: Communicating what is acceptable in a romantic or sexual relationship.

9. **Spiritual/Religious Boundaries:** Concern beliefs and practices. Example: Expecting respect for your spiritual or religious beliefs without being pressured to conform to others' views.

Each type of boundary helps create a sense of safety, self-respect, and mutual understanding in relationships. Which ones are you interested in exploring further?

Reflections
These Are My Boundaries

Discovering and understanding your personal boundaries is key to maintaining healthy, thoughtfully ordered, deeper self-awareness. Use them to guide your written reflections to recognize and strengthen your boundaries. Complete one question every week or at a perfect pace for you.

We invite you to explore these questions with curiosity and self-compassion. Use them to reframe challenges into opportunities for growth, gratitude, and empowerment. Share your responses with trusted people so you feel heard and understood. Revisit the questions over time to celebrate your growth.

1. What physical sensations—such as tension, fatigue, or discomfort—do I experience within my own body when I experience people who cross my boundaries? *Paying attention to these bodily sensations can reveal emotional triggers and areas where boundaries can be strengthened.*

2. What situations or interactions make me feel uncomfortable, drained, or resentful? *Recognizing these feelings can be the first sign that your boundaries need attention.*

3. In what areas of my life do I find it uncomfortable to say 'no,' and why? *Exploring this can reveal where your boundaries can be reinforced.*

4. How can I begin honoring my core values in how I allow others to treat me? *Identifying your values helps you set boundaries that reflect your true self.*

5. How do I currently respond when someone crosses my boundaries? *Understanding your response patterns can highlight areas for improvement.*

6. Which of the boundaries listed above seems most important to you? *Examining these areas helps you identify where it would be most productive to work on right now.*

7. Do I experience guilt or anxiety when I assert my needs or preferences? *Acknowledging these emotions can uncover deeper patterns of people-pleasing or fear of conflict.*

8. How can I recognize when someone respects or disrespects my boundaries? *Awareness of others' responses can help you protect your limits with confidence.*

9. Are my current boundaries supporting or hindering my emotional well-being and personal growth? *Evaluating your boundaries ensures they align with your evolving needs.*

10. What practical steps can I take today to strengthen or adjust my boundaries? *Taking action is an important step in turning awareness into meaningful change.*

Affirmations
These Are My Boundaries

Your thoughts, feelings, beliefs, voice, and actions create your reality. Each day, choose three affirmations and speak them out loud. Hearing your own words turns affirmations into living declarations that reshape your mind. Speak with intention and feel the words settle deep within you.

Boundary
- I choose me.
- I respect myself.
- My boundaries are sacred.

Self-Worth
- I am worthy.
- I am lovable.
- I am valuable.

Empowerment
- I am free.
- I am in my power.
- I create my reality.
- I am my own authority.

Chapter 16: Turning Point

"In every life there is a turning point. A moment so tremendous, so sharp and clear that one feels as if one's been hit in the chest … and one knows … that one's life will never be the same."

— Julia Quinn

As the abuse escalates over time, so does my exhaustion. Waking up without a sense of safety is my normal. The people around me—those who have the best intentions to help—often end up hurting me instead. I am desperate for a break, a moment of rest, a chance to breathe.

It comes one day when I am changing my baby brother's diaper. Mother is infuriated that I haven't washed off all of the feces. She begins brutally hitting me over the head, screaming at me, "You can't do anything right." This is another attempt to tear me down. She belittles me for everything.

I run to the backyard to rewash my baby brother's cloth diapers, tears streaming down my face as I scrub. I stand there holding my head, trying to make the pain stop. Why is life like this? Why does the abuse never end? I am five years old, and already, I am tired of the pain.

At that moment, I know I can end the abuse. I can end the pain. The semi-trucks speed by the house. If I run in front of one of them, it will all stop.

As I stand in that backyard, holding the dirty diapers in my hands, staring at those trucks, contemplating my escape, something shifts inside me. Call it a miracle, call it fate, and in that moment of despair, I remember my desire to become a teacher. I want to teach little children. That thought becomes my guiding light.

Desperation follows me throughout my childhood. I contemplate suicide multiple times. I want everything to stop—the verbal abuse from mother, the relentless beatings, the ridicule from brothers, the burden of caring for my younger siblings…and mother, and the horrific sexual abuse from father. Throughout it all, that guiding light keeps me moving forward.

Today, I dedicate my life to teaching people how to create the life they desire by guiding them to become aware of the choices, actions, and patterns that shape their lives. I have the privilege of witnessing profound transformations—families coming together, husbands and wives saving their marriages, and people preserving their businesses against all odds. I watch children step into their power earlier and overcome their limiting beliefs.

Each turnaround is more than a success story; it is a testament to the power of awareness and intentional action. I cherish those moments of joy, the expressions of relief, the gratitude in their voices when they realize they have achieved what once seemed impossible. Watching people reclaim their lives, fulfill their desires, and create a future filled with hope brings me an immense sense of purpose. It is a calling to empower others to see their potential, embrace change, and build the life they truly want.

Despite my horrific past, I achieve what, according to society, would be considered remarkable. I earn degrees, build businesses, own homes, and continue to create a life that I am proud of. The most significant transformation goes beyond what I have accomplished on paper; it is the internal shift to thriving. That is a major change for me—one that requires deep self-reflection, resilience, and a firm commitment to growth.

The journey to thriving is worth all that it took. It shows me that we have the power to create the life we truly desire. Through the work I did on myself, I realize the deeper reason behind my obsession to teach is the desire to stop the cycle of abuse so people can heal, and the children will be free.

Reflections
Turning Point

Going through extreme adversity can leave deep emotional scars, shaking your sense of self-worth and making life feel overwhelming. It's important to take time to reflect, process, and rebuild your self-worth from a place of strength, resilience, self-compassion, and hope.

We invite you to explore these questions with curiosity and self-compassion. Use them to reframe challenges into opportunities for growth, gratitude, and empowerment. Share your responses with trusted people so you feel heard and understood. Revisit the questions over time to celebrate your growth.

1. What aspects of my identity or self-worth have been most affected by my experiences of adversity? *Understanding how your self-perception has changed can help in reclaiming your confidence.*

2. How have I shown strength and resilience despite the challenges I've faced? *Reflecting on your resilience can help you recognize your inner power.*

3. What limiting beliefs about myself have developed as a result of my struggles, and how can I begin to challenge them? *Identifying negative thought patterns is the first step to transforming them.*

4. In what ways do I minimize my own needs, and how can I start prioritizing myself? *Recognizing where you neglect yourself can help you rebuild self-care habits.*

5. What does self-worth mean to me, and how can I cultivate it in my daily life? *Defining self-worth on your terms can empower you to take meaningful action.*

6. When I feel overwhelmed, what are some small, manageable steps I can take to regain control? *Breaking tasks down into smaller actions helps prevent paralysis.*

7. What boundaries will protect my energy and mental well-being? *Establishing limits can help you create a sense of security and balance.*

8. Who in my life supports and uplifts me? *Acknowledging your support system can reduce feelings of isolation.*

9. What accomplishments, big or small, am I proud of? *Celebrating achievements helps reinforce a positive sense of self.*

10. How can I practice self-compassion when I feel overwhelmed by setbacks or challenges? *Finding ways to be kind to yourself can ease the weight of expectations.*

Affirmations
Turning Point

Your thoughts, feelings, beliefs, voice, and actions create your reality. Each day, choose three affirmations and speak them out loud. Hearing your own words turns affirmations into living declarations that reshape your mind. Speak with intention and feel the words settle deep within you.

- I rise.
- I grow.
- I am worthy.
- I choose me.
- I am enough.
- I am resilient.
- I am present.
- I am powerful.
- I have a purpose.
- I trust my journey.

Chapter 17: The Birth of *The MindShift Experience*©

"The greatest revolution of our generation is the discovery that human beings, by changing the inner attitudes of their minds, can change the outer aspects of their lives."

— William James

After years of my own transformation journey, I became obsessed with one thought: How can I make it easier and more accessible for others to unlock their inner power and step into their greatness? I wanted to develop a mind-shifting tool that would help others strengthen the core characteristics that create extraordinary lives. This experience emerges as an immersive, disruptive, deeply impactful journey. I had discovered through my own experience that transformation was about cultivating the essential qualities that allow us to thrive. I identified eight fundamental characteristics that, when strengthened, create unstoppable momentum in every area of life: Courage, Confidence, Vision, Power, Energy, Wisdom, Creativity, and Strategy.

Most people carry these qualities within them and can learn how to access, develop, and strengthen them consistently. When we lack courage, we shrink our goals. When confidence wavers, we stall our growth. When vision is unclear, we miss opportunities we were born to claim. I had lived this reality, and I refused to let others remain trapped in mediocrity when greatness was within their reach.

The MindShift Ecosystem©: Where Neuroscience Meets Breakthrough

The MindShift Experience© was born from this deep knowing that transformation happens when we systematically strengthen our core characteristics. I envisioned an ecosystem that would blend the science of neuroplasticity with practical application, creating experiences that would make personal mastery both accessible and sustainable.

What emerged was a complete ecosystem of transformation tools, each designed to strengthen the eight essential characteristics:

The MindShift Experience©: The flagship immersive event where minds expand, hearts ignite, and futures feel infinite. This high-energy, interactive journey strengthens your courage to take bold action, builds unshakable confidence, clarifies your vision, amplifies your personal power, elevates your energy, deepens your wisdom, unleashes your creativity, and sharpens your strategy.

The MindShift Game™: Because what if developing these life-changing characteristics could be as engaging as playing a game? This interactive experience helps you strengthen courage, confidence, vision, power, energy, wisdom, creativity, and strategy through fast-paced, transformative play.

The MindShift University©: The school of transformation where you systematically develop mastery in all eight characteristics. A structured curriculum that gives you a clear, step-by-step path to strengthening courage, building confidence, clarifying vision, claiming your power, elevating energy, cultivating wisdom, unleashing creativity, and mastering strategy.

The MindShift Challenge©: For those ready to push past their limits and discover the depth of their courage, confidence, vision, power, energy, wisdom, creativity, and strategy. This guided challenge creates momentum through daily practices that strengthen each characteristic systematically.

The MindShift Mastermind©: Where ambitious individuals come together to strengthen their collective courage, confidence, vision, power, energy, wisdom, creativity, and strategy. This mastermind amplifies your development through the power of community and shared commitment to excellence.

The MindShift Mental Performance©: A science-backed system to optimize your mental capacity for accessing and strengthening courage, confidence, vision, power, energy, wisdom, creativity, and strategy at peak levels, in all areas of life.

The Eight Pillars of Transformation

Each component of *The MindShift Ecosystem©* is designed to systematically strengthen these essential characteristics:

COURAGE: The foundation of all transformation. We help you develop the courage to face your fears, take bold action, speak your truth, and step into opportunities that once felt impossible. Courage is taking action in the presence of fear.

CONFIDENCE: Unshakable belief in your abilities and worth. We guide you in building confidence through competence, celebrating wins, and developing the inner knowing that you can handle whatever comes your way.

VISION: Crystal clear sight of your desired future and the path to get there. We help you clarify what you truly want, see beyond current limitations, and maintain focus on your highest possibilities.

POWER: Your ability to influence, impact, and create change in your life and the lives of others. We teach you to claim your personal power, use it responsibly, and channel it toward meaningful outcomes.

ENERGY: The vital force that fuels all action and achievement. We show you how to elevate, sustain, and direct your energy toward what matters most, creating momentum that compounds over time.

WISDOM: The ability to make sound decisions and learn from every experience. We guide you to cultivate your capacity to see patterns, understand consequences, and choose actions that serve your highest good.

CREATIVITY: Your innate ability to generate new ideas, solutions, and possibilities. We show you how to unlock your creative potential and approach challenges with innovation and a fresh perspective.

STRATEGY: The art of planning and executing effectively toward your goals. We help you to develop your strategic thinking, helping you create clear plans and adapt them as circumstances change.

Proven Results That Speak for Themselves

The impact has been extraordinary. Participants report 40-300% increases in focus, confidence, engagement, and success. As a construction leader shared: "Through *The MindShift Experience©*, I completely transformed my business approach. Our employee engagement increased by 40%, and most incredibly, our sales skyrocketed by 300%."

These results happen because when you strengthen these eight characteristics, everything in your life improves. Your relationships deepen. Your career accelerates. Your health improves. Your impact expands.

Flexible Delivery for Maximum Impact

The MindShift Ecosystem© is delivered through three powerful formats, ensuring that character development is accessible no matter where you are in your journey:

ONLINE EVENTS: Interactive virtual experiences that bring the power of community and real-time coaching directly to you, systematically strengthening each characteristic through engaging, practical exercises.

LIVE EVENTS: In-person immersive experiences where transformation happens in real-time, surrounded by others committed to developing these same essential qualities. The energy of physical presence amplifies development exponentially.

SELF-STUDY: Comprehensive programs that enable you to develop these characteristics at your own pace while benefiting from a structured approach and community support.

Your Breakthrough Here

The MindShift Experience© is a systematic approach to developing the characteristics that create extraordinary lives. It's about strengthening what's already within you.

Picture yourself with unshakable courage to pursue your biggest dreams, rock-solid confidence in your abilities, crystal-clear vision in harmony with your future, authentic personal power that inspires others, boundless energy that sustains you through any challenge, deep wisdom that guides your decisions, unlimited creativity that generates solutions, and strategic thinking that turns vision into reality.

This is character development. It's becoming the person who naturally attracts the life you desire because you've cultivated the internal qualities that create external results.

You hold these characteristics already.

The real question is: Are you ready to strengthen them and step into the extraordinary life that waits for you?

Your breakthrough starts here.

For more information, visit www.TheMindShiftGame.com

Chapter 18: Complex Trauma and Its Impact

"Trauma creates change you don't choose. Healing creates change you do choose."

— Michele Rosenthal

What is complex trauma? It results from prolonged or repeated exposure to painful experiences during childhood that are frequently caused by those meant to provide care and safety. Unlike a single traumatic incident, complex trauma disrupts a person's sense of security, identity, and emotional regulation, shaping thoughts, behaviors, and relationships well into adulthood.

Millions struggle with anxiety, depression, low self-worth, and relationship challenges without realizing that unresolved painful childhood experiences often lie at the root. Its impact alters brain development, nervous system regulation, and even physical health. People often adopt coping mechanisms such as dissociation, hypervigilance, or avoidance—responses that once offered protection and later interfere with connection and healing.

The good news? Reconciling these painful life experiences that are impacting us now is possible. With awareness, support, and compassionate self-work, people living with the psychological impact of wounding childhood experiences can shift to empowered, authentic living.

Childhood Trauma and Its Lasting Effects

Children thrive in stable, nurturing environments, and when those environments become unsafe, the effects can be profound and lifelong. Chronic abuse, neglect, exposure to violence, or emotional rejection can alter physical development, attachment styles, and self-perception.

Examples of Childhood Complex Trauma

- **Emotional Neglect:** Love, validation, or comfort withheld or dismissed
- **Physical or Sexual Abuse:** Repeated harm, violation by trusted adults
- **Psychological Abuse:** Criticism, gaslighting, manipulation, or humiliation
- **Witnessing or Experiencing Domestic Violence:** Growing up in constant fear or chaos
- **Parentification:** Being forced into caregiving roles for parents or siblings
- **Household Substance Abuse:** Living with addiction or emotional unpredictability
- **Abandonment:** Emotional or physical withdrawal by caregivers
- **Unstable Living Conditions:** Frequent moves, foster care, or homelessness
- **Bullying or Peer Rejection:** Chronic mistreatment shaping self-esteem

How This Follows Us Into Adulthood

Children raised in any of these conditions often adapt by becoming hyper-alert to danger or emotionally shutting down to cope. Unresolved trauma echoes through adult life:

- **Emotional Dysregulation:** Flashbacks, anxiety, depression, feeling "numb" to life's joys, mood swings, chronic anxiety, or obsessive-compulsive disorder
- **Relationships:** Fear of abandonment, difficulty trusting, codependency, attachment struggles, toxic dynamics, or pushing people away before they get too close
- **Identity Struggles:** Impostor syndrome, perfectionism, or a deep-seated belief of being unworthy
- **Low Self-Worth:** Perfectionism, shame, or a sense of being "broken"
- **Physical and Cognitive Symptoms:** Chronic pain, digestive issues, migraines, autoimmune conditions, fatigue, memory problems, or difficulty focusing

- **Unhealthy Coping Mechanisms:** Addictions, overworking, people-pleasing, or self-sabotage as ways to avoid pain
- **Unresolved Childhood Roles:** Becoming the overachiever, caregiver, scapegoat, class clown, bully, or "black sheep" well into adulthood

Recognizing these patterns is the first step to breaking free from them.

The Healing Journey

Healing from complex trauma is about reclaiming your power and rewriting your future. While scars may remain, you are the one who defines who you are.

Key Healing Approaches

- **Trauma-Informed Therapy:** EMDR, somatic therapy, or CBT to process and transcend the impact of these experiences
- **Inner Child Work:** Offering love, safety, and validation to the wounded younger self
- **Mindfulness & Somatic Healing:** Meditation, breathwork, and body-based therapies to regulate the nervous system
- **Self-Compassion & Reparenting:** Speaking kindly to yourself, setting healthy boundaries
- **Support Groups:** Healing in community with others who understand

Every step toward self-awareness, self-care, and connection builds resilience and freedom from the past.

Breaking the Cycle

Unaddressed experiences often pass from one generation to the next, shaping parenting patterns and relationships. Awareness can interrupt this cycle. As you heal, you model emotional health for those around you.

You Rise in Powerful Company

If these words resonate, take heart: you are whole, and you walk this path with others beside you. With the right tools, support, and willingness to heal, you can release the weight of the past and step into a life of peace, self-love, and empowerment.

This book is an invitation. As someone who has walked this path, I offer these insights, tools, and stories to invite you to reconcile what needs reconciling, transcend what needs transcending, and heal what needs healing.

You came into this world as a person capable of creating the life you love and desire. The world needs you—your truest, fullest self.

The Impact of Judgment

To the people we meet, I feel the weight of eyes that are unfamiliar with my story. A quiet heaviness presses on my chest, stealing the air before I even open my mouth. Your gaze carries its own story— sometimes curious, sometimes cautious, sometimes kind. Sometimes it's incredulous. Sometimes it's wrapped in your own certainty of what you believe you know. It feels like judgment to me. Instead of judging people because of their life experience, get curious to understand where we came from. What life experiences led us to be where we are today?

What you see stays on the surface. What you miss is everything I live through to stand here now. You miss the nights I spend listening to the silence throb like a heartbeat against the walls, waiting for danger to pass, praying for a moment of safety. You miss the pain of my body slamming against the wall, the excruciating blow of a cast-iron pan crashing into my head. You move through a world where impossible life-or-death choices never land on a child's shoulders.

You smell fresh air when you think of home. I smell the damp, cockroach-filled hallway of the place we live. You rest in beds. I lie on the concrete closet floor, desperation pressed against my skin. Dark, chocolate-brown, lace curtains lie on me, posing as a blanket, thin as a whisper, barely protecting me from the cold. I move through days already heavy with the terror of being beaten by mother and father.

The future stands undefined, a blank horizon in front of me. Each moment centers on staying alive in the present, sprinting straight into the fire of the unknown.

What I hear are judgments—"You were a troubled teen." "Why would you run away?" "How could you leave your family?" You speak from a place outside my experience. You speak with the voice of your own life. I recognize the tone of someone who sees the surface of the water and has never felt what it means to sink toward the bottom, lungs burning, vision fading, fighting for one more breath.

I remember when I am a 15-year-old mother, your eyebrows arch throughout the interrogation. "You have a son?" "I can't believe you had sex at that age!" "Why did you leave your son's father?" Time in a single day holds nowhere near enough space to unwind my knotted story of survival into a tidy explanation—so I pour my energy into moving forward, honoring my healing, and living my truth.

My silence is an act of kindness toward myself, a way of honoring my precious energy.

I feel the sting of those moments—the way your words wrap themselves around me like ropes, trying to tie me to your version of who I should have been. You stand outside the scenes that shape me. You stand outside the horrific abuse I endure. You stand outside the nights when silence becomes my armor, the shield I use to keep myself safe.

Today, when I look at my past, I choose grace over guilt. I choose understanding over explaining. Because every decision I make—even the ones people wonder about—comes from a place of protecting my soul. Every part of my story shapes who I am today. A single choice could send ripples into places none of us can imagine. Those choices, as imperfect as they may seem to others, become the bridge between the pain I endure and the woman I am.

So I breathe. I inhale the scent of this present moment—grounding, steady, real. I let the sound of my own heartbeat remind me: I stand. I lead. And I hold gratitude, even for the people who judge. Because I am the one who defines me. I meet you with quiet grace. We do the hard, messy, and sometimes misunderstood work. In healing ourselves, we make the world better for all those who are in contact with us, and we break the generational patterns. Celebrate the life you lived and the person you have become.

Judgment shrinks us. Gratitude expands us. Empathy is my compass. I choose gratitude over judgment—for myself, for my journey, and for others wherever they are on their journeys. I have gratitude and joy for the life we now live.

And that… that is where true power lives.

Reflections
Complex Trauma and Its Impact

We invite you to explore these questions with curiosity and self-compassion. Use them to reframe challenges into opportunities for growth, gratitude, and empowerment. Share your responses with trusted people so you feel heard and understood. Revisit the questions over time to celebrate your growth.

1. How have the coping mechanisms you developed in childhood continued to show up in your adult life?

2. In what ways have your early experiences shaped your understanding of safety, love, and connection?

3. Can you identify the specific childhood roles or strategies you adopted to protect yourself?

4. How do you recognize the difference between your authentic self and the automatic adaptations you created?

5. What unresolved childhood wounds are influencing your relationships, career, or sense of self?

6. In what areas of your life do you feel the impact of your automatic childhood patterns?

7. How has your understanding of your own experiences changed as you've grown and gained awareness?

8. What would it look like to offer your younger self the love, validation, and support you needed?

9. Where do you see the potential for breaking generational patterns in your own life?

10. What small, compassionate step could you take today to begin healing the wounds of your past?

Affirmations
Complex Trauma and Its Impact

Your thoughts, feelings, beliefs, voice, and actions create your reality. Each day, choose three affirmations and speak them out loud. Hearing your own words turns affirmations into living declarations that reshape your mind. Speak with intention and feel the words settle deep within you.

- I heal.
- I am safe.
- I am loved.
- I am whole.
- I trust myself.
- I honor my truth.
- I express my feelings.
- I am gentle with myself.
- I am my own protector.
- I offer myself compassion.

Chapter 19: Collateral Damage

"Unresolved trauma can create a cycle of re-enactment, where the survivor unconsciously seeks out situations that mirror the original traumatic experience, perpetuating the very pain they wish to escape."

– Dr. Peter Levine, Trauma Healing Specialist

Dangerous dance of trauma transference. It's crucial for us to stay well-grounded because we can unknowingly buy into somebody else's trauma—whether it is real or perceived. This invisible transfer happens more often than we realize, and it can destroy relationships, families, and entire organizations.

Picture this: We dislike Mary because Joe tells us a story about her while he is dysregulated, triggered by unresolved life experiences. In his wounded state, he paints Mary as a villain, and suddenly, everyone believes Mary is a bad person. What if Mary stands blameless in this dynamic? What if Joe's unresolved trauma creates a distorted lens through which he sees every interaction?

This happens inside families, friendships, and organizations—everywhere. When somebody carries unresolved life experiences, triggers reveal them. We recognize this by the emotional charge—the intensity, the rage, the disproportionate reaction compared to the actual situation.

The Moon Theory

Dr. Joe Dispenza shares something profound: we blame others for causing us anguish, yet if we ship that person off to the Moon, someone with unresolved trauma will repeatedly find somebody else to project their pain onto. It centers less on the person and more on the unhealed wound calling for healing.

When Trauma Transference Becomes Dangerous

Trauma transference becomes dangerous because we no longer interact with reality. We interact with someone's perceived trauma layered on top of our own unhealed wounds. This collision magnifies the intensity of our experience and convinces us that this version of reality is the absolute truth. That belief carries the greatest danger, because it can fuel more anger, pain, and resentment—and fracture relationships that might have remained intact with awareness of our own feelings and triggers.

What would happen if we pause long enough to ask, "Is this about them, or is this about me?" Triggers do what triggers do. They react. They protect. They attack. At that moment, clarity disappears. We stare into the past, and the past stares back at us through someone else's face.

A Personal Reckoning

I remember sharing stories of my horrific childhood experiences with a friend who was helping me with an earlier version of my memoir. As I described the abuse—the way mother treated me, the patterns of violence and neglect—my friend, who already disliked mother, became triggered. Her own unresolved experiences reawakened. She relived her unhealed wounds, and it changed how she saw and interacted with mother forever.

The Ripples of Unresolved Trauma

Trauma occurs on many levels. Chronic trauma becomes complex trauma in children or compounded trauma in adults. Beyond the impact on the individual, there is a secondary impact on the people they interact with.

This secondary trauma marks the beginning of trauma transference. When the person who experienced trauma is emotionally dysregulated, the people around them can experience trauma themselves. The original person's dysregulation can trigger your unresolved trauma in a process called trauma resonance. Here is where things escalate quickly. When two people experience trauma resonance, neither responds to what stands in the room with them. They both are responding to traumatic memories from the past.

In a widening circle of trauma transference, those who live or work around people with unresolved trauma can experience tertiary trauma. Like a contagion, the impact spreads through families, communities, organizations, and cultures.

This is why inner work matters—and why the who matters just as much as the how. We thrive with guides who hold space for our life experiences and still remain grounded in themselves, who help us process our pain while keeping clear ownership of their own. When we share our deepest wounds with people who have not tended to their own healing, we risk creating a cascade of transferred trauma that can fracture some of the most precious relationships in our lives.

The Reality Check

Before we accept someone else's version of reality, we ask ourselves:

- What emotional charge lives behind this story?
- Is this person triggered?
- Are they speaking from a wound or from wisdom?

Are we being invited into their healing, or recruited into their trauma? The difference between the two shapes everything—whether we build bridges or burn them, whether we create understanding or extend cycles of pain that belong to someone else.

When we ground ourselves in our own healing, we can hold space for others' pain and remain rooted in our truth. We can offer compassion and still protect our well-being. We can be supportive and still refuse to become casualties of someone else's unresolved trauma.

This is the work—healing our own wounds and recognizing the moment someone else's wounds reach for ours.

When The Radio Station Changes

Picture you and me engaged in a conversation. We are on the same wavelength—speaking the same language, feeling connection and mutual understanding. Suddenly, my tone shifts. My eyes glaze over.

My body language changes—pulling back, stiffening, fidgeting as if trying to escape an invisible threat. I am no longer here with you. I am somewhere else entirely, reliving something beyond your view. I have tuned into a completely different radio station, one outside your range. This is what it looks like when I am triggered.

The Hijacking

When someone enters a triggered state, their nervous system has been hijacked. The protective brain—ancient, primal, and lightning-fast—takes over, shutting down the parts of the brain responsible for logic, memory, and relational connection. Fight, flight, freeze, or fawn—automatic responses to perceived danger. From the outside, you see the signs:

- Their face tightens or goes blank, as if a mask drops over their features.
- Their words turn sharp, rushed, or disconnected—sentences that twist out of rhythm, accusations that seem to appear from nowhere.
- Their body betrays them—hands clenching, shoulders rising, breath quickening, or a sudden stillness that feels like they have left their body entirely.

Inside them, a storm rages. Their heart pounds. Their thoughts race or shut down. The agreements you made, the promises exchanged, the rapport you carefully built—all disappear. Their brain shifts out of relational processing. It protects them from a threat that feels immediate and dangerous, as if their life depends on it.

In that state, they cannot access the calm, connected part of themselves that remembers your shared history. They run old, unresolved, emotional programs instead of being present with you.

You have now entered the zone of collateral damage.

Relationships Are Destabilized

Actions and words feel like betrayals. Sudden outbursts. Withdrawal. Withholding. Backtracking on decisions agreed to when calm. You are left reeling, wondering what happened, questioning whether they can be trusted.

Confusion settles in as the new normal. The person you thought you knew shifts into someone unpredictable, volatile, caught in emotional turmoil they struggle to name or contain. The dysregulated person blames you for everything that goes wrong. That causes you to question yourself and ask, "Did I do something wrong?" You start believing it and start taking the blame for things that are not yours to own.

The ground beneath your feet shifts. You no longer know if you stand on solid ground or quicksand. I thought I knew them, you whisper to yourself in the dark, searching for answers that stay out of reach. Your mind races with questions of: How do I protect myself? How do I make it better? How do I get rid of it? The desperation builds until all you can think is, I've got to get out of here. I want no part of this. Reality blurs. Certainty dissolves. You look around and question what is true.

Trust erodes. With no repair, the pattern repeats. Each time it happens, the foundation cracks a little more. You start walking on eggshells, afraid to say the wrong thing, afraid to trigger the next explosion or shutdown. Everyone feels unsafe. Everyone feels unheard.

The Resolution

When the trigger resolves—through time, self-regulation, or intentional healing—you watch someone come back from a trance. Their eyes soften. Their tone normalizes. Their memory returns, often incomplete, fragmented, or clouded by shame. They might look at you with confusion, guilt, or embarrassment. "What did I say?" they ask. "I don't remember." And they mean it.

In that triggered state, they remained elsewhere—trapped in a memory, a fear, a wound that hijacked their entire system. Their body stayed in the room; their mind and heart traveled to another time.

Until they learn to be present, recognize that they are emotionally charged, and it is their responsibility to self-regulate, they will keep regenerating the same cycle.

The Truth About Triggers

A triggered state reflects who they were when they experienced what they experienced—not the fullness of who they are today. It is a protective reflex.

It is the nervous system doing what it was designed to do—keep them alive. The threat has already passed. The danger lives in memory now. The body still remembers and feels. It reacts as if the experience lives in this very moment. The mind holds the role of recognizing that the event belongs to the past, not the present.

That's why bringing ourselves back into the present when we feel triggered matters so deeply. In the present moment, the mind can recognize, "This belongs to the past," while the body learns, "Right now, I am safe." This awareness explains the reaction; it never justifies the harm. The words spoken, the trust broken, the pain inflicted all remain real and valid.

With no conscious repair and accountability after the trigger passes, the damage remains as real as if they meant every word. The relationship suffers. The trust fractures. The connection weakens.

With awareness, with healing, with the courage to name the trigger and take responsibility for the aftermath—transformation becomes possible. This is the path to thriving, from reaction to response, from pain to gold.

The Unconscious Impact

We all move through life on autopilot—unaware of how our words, tone, or energy ripple into the spaces and people around us. We assume we are clear, reasonable, even kind... until something happens that pulls the curtain back. A conversation explodes into conflict. A relationship fractures over something that seemed small. A colleague withdraws. A child flinches. A partner shuts down. We stand there, bewildered, asking, "What happened?"

Beneath the surface, unseen programs run the show—patterns, beliefs, and emotional imprints quietly shaping how we speak, listen, react, and even breathe. Our eyes miss them. Everyone around us feels them.

The Programs Running In The Background

When we feel calm and grounded, we sometimes sense our impact. We notice the subtle cues—the way someone's face changes, the shift in their energy, the pause before they respond. In that state, we can reflect, adjust, empathize, and repair. When we feel triggered, everything shifts. An old wound or unmet need gets poked. The lights flicker. Awareness narrows. Our body tightens. Our breath shallows. Your voice changes—sharper, louder, colder, or completely flat. The rational mind moves to the back seat, and protective instincts grab the wheel.

We lose clear sight of the present moment. We filter it through the past, reacting to an echo instead of the person in front of us. We relive a moment from childhood, replay an old script, defend against a threat that belongs to another time.

In that state, we miss how destructive our energy feels to others. We miss:

- The subtle flinch in their eyes
- The shift in their posture as they brace for impact
- The pause before they respond, calculating whether it feels safe to speak
- The way they start choosing their words more carefully, walking on eggshells around us
- We stand inside the storm and cannot see the emotional ripple we create

Collateral Damage

Like a volcano, unresolved trauma builds pressure beneath the surface. The more we suppress our pain, the more unpredictable and explosive its release becomes. One moment we present on stage, lead a meeting, or celebrate at a party; the next moment, an old wound erupts and consumes the room. This reflects the impact of unresolved trauma.

It touches everything—the way we lead, love, work, serve, parent, teach, and build. One unhealed wound can shift the trajectory of a life, a family, a community.

Examples

Retreat Confrontation

We hosted a retreat to address a woman's complaint that the community leader had sexually harassed her. The allegation was unfounded. What was revealed was that the intonation of the leader's voice was triggering an unresolved trauma from 20 years prior. It was the ghost of the prior trauma that was running the show. The impact was that the organization spent all of its money on professionals to resolve the issue and had to disband.

Her outburst shattered the peaceful energy in the community and left twenty participants shocked, transforming collective healing into collective trauma. Even though she later recognized that she had been triggered, the damage was already done—the leader lost his marriage, his decades-long career was destroyed, and he was forced to move out of state because of her false accusation, all because her unprocessed trauma projected past abuse onto his innocent guidance.

Anniversary Surprise

A client overheard her husband talking in hushed tones with a florist and became convinced he was having an affair like her father. He was actually arranging a surprise anniversary bouquet for their special day. Her accusations and suspicion poisoned what would have been a beautiful gesture of love, turning his thoughtful surprise into evidence of her inability to trust. The anniversary celebration was ruined before it even began, leaving both partners wounded and confused.

Mother's Day Surprise

My thirteen-year-old son asked to stay home on Mother's Day weekend, and my trauma-conditioned mind immediately assumed he was planning to sneak out and play with friends instead of staying home while I went to the grocery store. I confronted him with accusations and suspicion, projecting my own childhood experiences of deception onto his innocent request. Out of desperation, he revealed his true intention—to surprise me by baking a Mother's Day cake. My distrust had already tainted his beautiful gesture, leaving him hurt and frustrated that he was not able to surprise his own mother.

Marriage and Divorce

They start as a picture-perfect couple: candlelit dinners, whispered promises, and a wedding full of hope. Beneath the smiles live two wounded children in adult bodies. When one strays—seeking validation in someone else's arms—the fragile trust shatters. The divorce turns into a battlefield. Words become weapons, messages are filled with accusations, and courtrooms transform into arenas of revenge. Instead of grieving the loss, they claw at each other's wounds, desperate to inflict pain so they avoid feeling their own. Their unresolved trauma poisons the very air they once breathed together.

Parents Weaponizing Children

Two parents, scarred from childhoods where love means control and silence equals survival, now pull their children into unfinished wars. Instead of protecting them, they use the kids as bargaining chips— "Tell your mom I'm the better parent" or "Don't trust your dad." The children's laughter tightens into stomach knots, and their safe home turns into a chessboard. They walk on eggshells to hide their feelings, to carry secrets too heavy for their small hearts. In the shadows of their parents' unresolved experiences, the children quietly collect scars of their own—scars that echo long after bedtime tears dry.

Leaders With Unresolved Trauma

A leader with unresolved trauma may surround themselves with those who mirror their beliefs, nodding at every word. When someone challenges them, their chest tightens, their voice sharpens, and they dismiss the person as "unsafe" or "untrustworthy." The truth is, the threat is the old memory of being ridiculed, silenced, or abandoned as a child. Yet in their adult role, they confuse past danger with present-day difference. Instead of leading with strength, they build echo chambers where growth dies, and their team tiptoes in silence to avoid awakening the leader's ghosts.

Business & Mispronunciation Triggers

In a boardroom, a colleague accidentally mispronounces someone's name. To most, it's no big deal. To the one experiencing the unresolved trauma, it feels like disrespect, rejection, or erasure. Their chest burns, their tone sharpens, and suddenly, the entire project derails. The team feels the tension ripple, productivity stalls, and a cloud of unease lingers long after the meeting ends. The reaction has little to do with the mispronunciation and everything to do with old wounds of being invisible or disrespected. When no one names the real cause, the trauma spreads quietly, infecting the group with mistrust and hesitation.

Cultural Beliefs

Unresolved trauma often hides inside cultural narratives. A person raised to believe "children must obey without question" or "women must sacrifice for family" enforces these beliefs rigidly, even when they cause harm. They pass these unexamined truths forward, convincing others of ideas that keep cycles of silence, shame, or inequality alive. What looks like tradition is often trauma wearing cultural clothing.

Quitting High-Profile Jobs

A professional in a prestigious career walks away convinced their colleagues are hiding information or plotting against them. In reality, the professional's unresolved trauma creates blind spots in communication. Their inability to fully express their needs or ask clarifying questions leads them to interpret gaps in communication as betrayal. Their past abandonment whispers louder than the present reality. They quit their job because their past experiences make it impossible to trust their coworkers.

Vague Communication & Misunderstanding

A manager says, "I like it when files are organized this way," or "I believe people should lead with love languages," assuming these are clear requests. In their mind, they have communicated. To the team, these are casual statements, not directives. The result is confusion, unmet expectations, and frustration. The unresolved trauma leads to the assumption that people "should know" what they mean—an echo of a childhood where needs were unspoken or disrespected.

The Battle of Being Right

Two people stand toe-to-toe, each insisting they're right, their voices rising, their faces red. No matter how many words are exchanged, neither hears the other. The root of their argument lies in the reliving of childhood fights, where being right meant survival, protection, or being seen. The adult disagreement becomes endless because it really is about proving to the ghost of a parent that their pain is real.

Manipulation

Some, stuck in childlike strategies, manipulate to get their way. One person becomes overly kind, showering others with favors, secretly expecting compliance in return. Another erupts in anger, slamming doors or raising their voice, forcing others to yield. Both are manipulation tactics carried from childhood, when they had no power, no tools, and no other way to get needs met. In adulthood, these patterns corrode relationships and trust, because they replace collaboration with control.

These examples show how unresolved trauma distorts present reality and creates collateral damage in relationships, communities, and organizations. Even when something good arrives, we struggle to recognize it—because inside, we brace for impact, waiting for the other shoe to drop. The smallest trigger catapults our whole being back to the familiar battles of childhood. To the wounded tiger, the person standing before us shape-shifts into the father who raged, the mother who shamed, the perpetrator who violated us. Our senses remember everything—the way a voice drops, the temperature of a room, the angle of a raised hand, the scent of cologne mixed with anger. These sensory memories live in our bodies like landmines.

Relationships

For the people around us, this unpredictability shakes their sense of safety and trust.

In intimate relationships, it feels like walking on shifting ground—uncertain which version of us will appear, which word will trigger an explosion, which moment will turn into a battlefield.

In the workplace, it creates friction that blocks progress. Teams hesitate to share ideas. Colleagues avoid difficult conversations. Creativity shuts down because the environment no longer feels psychologically safe. In families, it creates disconnection and pain. Children learn to read moods before they speak. Partners stop sharing their truth. Everyone starts performing instead of being real.

For the person experiencing it, the whole thing feels confusing and illogical. "Why are they reacting this way? What did I do? I thought we were fine."

The impact of unconscious behavior is cumulative—like drops of dye in clear water. Each reaction slowly colors the relationship, the environment, and the culture. Over time, the water shifts from clear to murky, stained, and unrecognizable.

As this pattern repeats without awareness or repair, people begin to protect themselves. They pull away emotionally, even if they stay physically present. They stop trusting. They stop trying. They stop believing that things can be different.

Cost of Unconsciousness

Here is what we lose when unconscious patterns run the show:

- **Connection.** People struggle to connect with someone unpredictable, who shifts without warning, who says one thing and does another.
- **Trust.** Trust grows through consistency, safety, and repair. When unconscious patterns lead, trust erodes.
- **Intimacy.** True intimacy requires presence, vulnerability, and the ability to see and be seen. Triggers block that doorway.

- **Growth.** We repeat the same cycles, blame others, and wonder why nothing changes.
- **Peace.** Living unconsciously exhausts us. We react, defend, and justify. Rest feels distant. Calm feels rare.

Path To Awareness

Awareness rises as the first key. When we begin to observe ourselves—our tone, our tension, our tendencies—we create space between the trigger and the reaction. In that space, choice is born.

- We can see instead of react.
- We can hear instead of defend.
- We can feel without being swept away.
- We can think clearly again.

Pause and Pay Attention

This work invites us to slow down and pay attention—to notice the sensations in our body before they turn into words or actions. It invites us to ask:

- What am I feeling right now?
- Where is this reaction coming from?
- Does this belong to the present moment, or to something from my past?
- What supports me in feeling safe, grounded, and connected right now?

Even a brief pause—a single breath—creates an opening for a different choice.

Transformation Begins Here

Transformation begins the moment we stop allowing unconscious behaviors to run our lives, our relationships, and our teams. It begins when we take responsibility for our impact, even when we never intended harm. It begins when we recognize that our triggers are ours to tend to, rather than someone else's to tiptoe around.

This is the work of becoming conscious—of waking up to the ways we have been operating on autopilot and choosing, moment by moment, to show up differently. This journey centers on awareness, not perfection. It invites us to catch ourselves sooner, repair faster, and build the capacity to stay present even when it feels hard.

The people around us deserve consistency, safety, and the assurance that when things get hard, we stay in the room with them instead of disappearing into our triggers. We deserve that too—the freedom that comes from no longer living under the control of unconscious patterns, the peace that comes from living with intention, the connection that comes from showing up fully, authentically, and awake.

Awareness stands as the bridge between who we have been and who we are becoming.

Reflections
Collateral Damage

We invite you to explore these questions with curiosity and self-compassion. Use them to reframe challenges into opportunities for growth, gratitude, and empowerment. Share your responses with trusted people so you feel heard and understood. Revisit the questions over time to celebrate your growth.

1. In what relationships have you found yourself unconsciously drawn in by someone else's emotional storm?

2. Describe a time when you made a judgment about a third person based on the triggered perspective that someone shared with you?

3. How do you recognize when you're being invited into someone's healing versus being recruited into their trauma?

4. What unresolved wounds cause you to project your pain onto others or attract similar painful dynamics?

5. In what ways have you experienced trauma transferring between people in your family, community, or workplace?

6. How do your emotional triggers differ from a proportional, grounded response to a situation?

7. When you share your own painful experiences, how do you discern whether the listener is holding space or feeding off of your trauma?

8. What patterns have you noticed in your relationships where unhealed trauma plays a significant role?

9. How is your own unprocessed trauma creating a distorted lens through which you view your interactions?

10. What would it look like for you to be fully grounded in your own healing while offering compassionate support to others?

Affirmations
Collateral Damage

Your thoughts, feelings, beliefs, voice, and actions create your reality. Each day, choose three affirmations and speak them out loud. Hearing your own words turns affirmations into living declarations that reshape your mind. Speak with intention and feel the words settle deep within you.

- I hold space.
- I choose clarity.
- I heal my wounds.
- I protect my energy.
- I recognize patterns.
- I share from strength.
- I see people as they are.
- I discern the truth clearly.
- I respond from groundedness.
- I have compassionate boundaries.

Chapter 20: The Path To Self-Efficacy

"The strongest people are not those who show strength in front of us, but those who win battles we know nothing about."

— Unknown

Even those of us who have built strong armor, who show up as Warriors, who carry the superhero mentality—we struggle throughout our lives when we're lacking self-efficacy. Self-efficacy forms the foundation for success, and when it weakens, undesirable experiences appear in our lives.

What Is Self-Efficacy?

Self-efficacy is your belief in your ability to accomplish tasks and achieve desired outcomes. It's the cornerstone of personal and professional success, determining whether you thrive or struggle when challenges arise. It's the deep, embodied belief that you can handle whatever comes your way. When self-efficacy crumbles, even the strongest Warriors fall. You can carry all the armor, the superhero mentality, the success strategies, and without this foundation, you scan the room looking for support as the seats stay empty and the silence grows louder.

The Seven Pillars of Self-Efficacy

1. **Self-care:** Prioritize well-being to reduce stress and boost resilience
2. **Self-awareness:** Gain insight into your thoughts, emotions, and strengths
3. **Self-reflection:** Analyze experiences to refine strategies
4. **Self-regulation:** Manage your thoughts and behaviors effectively
5. **Self-forgiveness:** Ability to reconcile what happened to us
6. **Self-healing:** Give ourselves what we are lacking so that we can move on
7. **Sense of well-being:** Maintain physical, mental, and emotional health

When Life Hits All at Once: My Story

Recently, I experienced this firsthand during what I can describe as a marathon of life events compressed into two weeks—a relentless chain of circumstances that would systematically strip away my self-efficacy and leave me completely dysregulated.

Travel and Depletion

I had traveled extensively for work for the last six months, dealing with unexpected landmines exploding beneath my carefully laid plans. Unexpected complications kept arising: late-night meetings, disagreement with a friend, having to shift housing arrangements, my learning platform being closed down after a large financial investment, setting up e-commerce, my marketing team out of the office during the launch of an important product, and a computer failure. I was exhausted and depleted by the time I made it home for a few days.

Each problem demanded immediate attention, creative solutions, and energy. I had nothing more to give. By the time I made it home, I was already running on empty—exhausted and depleted, telling myself that a few days of rest would restore me.

Family Crisis

Life moved in a different direction. Days later, I found myself on another airplane, rushing back for a family emergency that demanded my immediate presence. My heart felt heavy as I realized I remained physically distant during some of their most difficult moments. Guilt pressed against my chest as I offered emotional support from afar, feeling helpless and inadequate while the people I loved faced their greatest challenges.

Professional Breakdown

The challenges compounded like dominoes falling in slow motion. Support for my program launch failed to arrive—promises dissolved, deadlines pressed closer, and my reputation felt suspended in the balance. Then I got sick, my body rebelling against the relentless pace I had been forcing upon it. As if the universe was testing my limits, people who were supporting me on the project also got sick, leaving me scrambling to hold everything together with hands that were already shaking from exhaustion.

The Performance Marathon

Then came the four-day marathon that pushed me over the edge. I served as a judge in a pitch competition, my mind wrapped in fog while I insisted on showing up professionally. The next day brought live recordings—cameras rolling, performance expected, authenticity demanded from a well already drained. Immediately after, a live networking event awaited me where I debuted my products while filming live sales videos—every moment fueled by sheer depletion.

When Dysregulation Takes Over

By the time the last day rolled around, I was running on fumes after very little sleep for many days in a row. My carefully constructed Warrior facade was shattered by the dysregulation and subsequent low self-efficacy. I felt like a little child in the middle of the storm, alone, and desperate. The feeling hit me like a physical blow, so visceral and immediate that it took my breath away. I kept wondering, "Why do I feel so alone? This isn't fun—do I have to be here by myself?"

The Childhood Echo

That's when past childhood experiences showed up, uninvited and unrecognized at first. I was feeling the same loneliness I felt as a child, looking around auditoriums to see if mother had shown up when all the other mothers were there as their children received awards. Mother was nowhere in sight. It was like that for the Spelling Bee, for honor roll, for the school play, for the school trip, for student events— all the events that were important for a parent to attend. I was there by myself, longing for someone to take care of my needs.

The Illusion of Support

The support I believed I had evaporated at the most critical moment. I remained bound to the event, trapped in a situation where my basic needs went unmet. I asked a friend for support with my project, requested food, and reached out for help with fundamental necessities—no support arrived. My system spun into full dysregulation, intensity surging through my body.

The self-efficacy erosion that developed before this conference, fueled by inadequate self-care, created a cascading effect—impacting both my mental performance and my capacity to self-regulate. I had fallen into the very trap I help others avoid and get out of—allowing external circumstances to erode my internal foundation until I could barely function, much less thrive.

The Hunger for Support

The taunting began subtly, like salt poured into an open wound. My friend came around at the conference, rubbing his belly with exaggerated satisfaction, announcing how "really full" he was from what he had eaten. The gesture felt deliberate, cruel, as I sat there running on empty, my stomach gnawing at itself while he performed his contentment.

Later that evening, when my other friend showed up—an hour and a half later than promised, no communication, no apology—I was beyond exhausted, waiting, hoping someone would care enough to follow through. He picked me up with casual indifference and immediately launched into his own food saga: "Hey, I've eaten three times today! People are giving me food all over the place."

I told him plainly that I was tired and hungry. Even after we stopped so I could fill up his gas tank, I said it again: "I'm hungry." The words hung in the air like they were invisible. No response. As if my voice dissolved between us. Instead, he continued his monologue: "Oh, I already ate. I ate a lot today."

The Shared Experience of Dysregulation

When I debriefed with a friend, a serial entrepreneur, I understood what had really happened. He called me Monday morning, saying, "I want to share something with you," and when we talked, we discovered we had both experienced the same dysregulation throughout that event.

We both had flashbacks of feelings that other people had head starts, that they had teams, that they were more sophisticated, that people were there to support them. These feelings overshadowed us. Impostor syndrome crept in: we felt insecure, too small, insignificant. Mental fog consumed us and shut us down. We barely got through.

In our reflection, we saw the little child within us who felt alone. Being made to feel insignificant, having no value, being different, less than, invisible. It pulled us away from the top of our game and drained our mojo.

Reclaiming Self-Regulation

My friend and I each found our way to self-regulation by sharing time with friends, eating nurturing food, and feeling a sense of belonging. The greatest realization was about self-efficacy. We had been exhausted, drained, pushed to our limits, and overworked. We were expected to perform in full flow with the world while internally feeling far from our best—worn out and exhausted, with unresolved pressures in the background: stress, anxiety, countless unknowns, livelihoods on the line, a wave of overwhelm moving through every part of us.

Understanding Dysfunction and Dysregulation

When we're operating from a place of compromised self-efficacy, we become vulnerable to both dysfunction and dysregulation. Understanding these patterns can help you recognize when you're entering dangerous territory.

Dysfunction occurs when our patterns of behavior, communication, or relationships harm instead of support us. Sometimes we can appear functionally dysfunctional—seeming to manage on the surface while operating through harmful patterns underneath.

Dysregulation is the temporary breakdown of our ability to manage emotional responses, thoughts, and behaviors. When dysregulated, we lose access to logical thinking and decision-making. You might be functionally dysregulated—appearing to manage responsibilities while internally struggling a significant imbalance.

Dysregulation exists on a spectrum from low-moderate (heightened sensitivity, irritability) to severe (requiring professional intervention). It follows a cycle: the rumbling phase (early warning signs), the dysregulation phase (peak overwhelm), and the recovery phase (gradual return to stability).

The Transformation Process

The transformation we had to undergo required acknowledging the past, processing the experience, reconciling what needed to be reconciled to transcend the experience, and begin anew.

Here's the crucial insight: These realizations rise slowly. They surface when space exists in our lives—when downtime, self-care, and breathing room create openings for reflection. When life fills with too many responsibilities at once, reflection disappears. As reflection fades, awareness dims. As awareness dims, past patterns continue to drive present reactions unchecked.

Your Action Plan

Start building your self-efficacy foundation today by prioritizing self-care and developing deeper self-awareness. Reflect on your experiences, regulate your thoughts and behaviors, practice self-forgiveness for your past, and give yourself the healing important for you to move forward. Maintain your overall well-being as the container for all this growth.

Remember: Healing happens when we make space for reflection, downtime, and self-care. This breaks the patterns that keep us stuck.

The Foundation of Everything

Self-efficacy is the deep, embodied belief that you can handle whatever comes your way. When it's compromised by exhaustion, overwhelm, and lack of support, even the strongest Warriors can find themselves feeling like abandoned children, no matter how successful they are on the outside.

The armor we wear, the superhero mentality we carry in The Warrior mode, often compensate for the lack of self-efficacy. True strength rises through recognizing dysregulation, understanding why it appears, and giving ourselves the time and space to heal and rebuild from the inside out.

The bottom line: Your armor gains power through the inner foundation that supports it. Build your self-efficacy first—everything else follows.

Reflections
The Path To Self-Efficacy

We invite you to explore these questions with curiosity and self-compassion. Use them to reframe challenges into opportunities for growth, gratitude, and empowerment. Share your responses with trusted people so you feel heard and understood. Revisit the questions over time to celebrate your growth.

1. When was the last time you felt completely dysregulated? What triggered you, and how did your body and mind respond?

2. In what areas of your life do you notice a gap between your self-efficacy and your actual capabilities?

3. Describe a moment when you realized your coping mechanisms were no longer serving you. What shifted in your understanding?

4. How do your current coping mechanisms reflect the unresolved wounds from your past?

5. Where in your life are you operating from a place of stress rather than thriving? What would it look like to move into growth mode?

6. Reflect on a time when you felt overwhelmed. What unmet needs were underneath your emotional response?

7. How do your patterns of dysregulation show up in your relationships, work, and personal goals?

8. What would it mean for you to expand your window of tolerance and become more resilient?

9. If your nervous system could speak, what would it tell you about how you've been treating yourself?

10. Imagine yourself fully regulated and embodying complete self-efficacy. What changes in your life, relationships, and sense of self?

Affirmations
The Path To Self-Efficacy

Your thoughts, feelings, beliefs, voice, and actions create your reality. Each day, choose three affirmations and speak them out loud. Hearing your own words turns affirmations into living declarations that reshape your mind. Speak with intention and feel the words settle deep within you.

- I am calm.
- I am strong.
- I am present.
- I am resilient.
- I am centered.
- I am powerful.
- I am grounded.
- I expand into my potential.
- My self-efficacy grows daily.
- Peace flows through me naturally.

Chapter 21: The Peace of My Inner Child

"The child who is not embraced by the village will burn it down to feel its warmth. But the adult who embraces that child can heal both the village and themselves."

— African Proverb

Today, I step into a new journey as a woman who sees herself with the clarity of someone who has walked through fire and emerged forged.

There was a time when the echo of a small voice inside me cried out like a bird with a broken wing, desperate and raw: "Pick me. Love me. Hold me. Connect with me. Hear me. Believe me. See me." The words tumbled from her lips like prayers whispered into an empty cathedral, each syllable heavy with the weight of a thousand unmet needs.

She was tender as new skin, fragile as morning frost, longing like a flower turning its face toward a sun that always seemed just out of reach. A child grasping for something that always felt beyond her fingertips—love offered freely, safety that stayed steady, protection given without a price, connection that welcomed all of her without asking her to shrink to fit into spaces too small for her soul, a sense of belonging that whispered "you are home" instead of "you are too much."

She searched with eyes wide as saucers, pupils dilated with hope and terror in equal measure, hands open like empty cups waiting to be filled. She reached out through her entire being—her little fingers splayed and trembling, every cell in her body vibrating with the frequency of desperate need.

And for a long time, I move through life unaware of the truth that holds my freedom. The longing inside me rises from her—the little girl with tangled curly hair and a heart too big for her tiny chest—aching to be embraced, to feel the warmth of belonging seep into her bones like sunlight after a long winter, to have her voice rise above the noise of a world that treats her as insignificant, to be seen through the fog of invisibility that wraps around her, and to be understood in the language of unconditional love that her soul has yet to learn.

She wanted someone to make her feel safe, like the gentle hum of a lullaby that wraps around your heart and promises, "You are safe here." To feel secure, as if life itself held her small hands in its infinite palms, promising steady support with every step. To be protected like a sacred flame—delicate yet fiercely alive, precious beyond measure, worthy of being shielded from every harsh wind that approached her light.

Today moves differently through me. Today, the air carries a sweetness that all my senses recognize. Today, my feet touch the ground with the certainty of someone who knows where she belongs.

I connect with her. I embrace her. I hear her cries echoing through the corridors of my heart and wipe away her tears. I give her space to speak. I invite her voice forward. I treat her as sacred, as worthy of time, tenderness, and attention. I let her move at her own pace instead of rushing her into adulthood. I lift the burdens from her small shoulders and carry them with the strength of the woman I am today.

I listen. Really listen. I hear her tears—the sound of salt water hitting skin, the silence between the sobs, the way her breath catches in her throat, the ache in her voice that speaks of wounds so deep they have no names. I see her—exactly as she is. I see the way she curls in on herself like a wounded animal, hiding in the darkest corners of my heart where she believes no one will find her. I feel her—the trembling that starts in her belly and spreads through her limbs like electricity, the yearning that lives in her chest like a physical ache, the need that pulses through her veins like a second heartbeat.

I understand her story, her fear, her truth. I trace the map of her wounds with the tenderness of someone discovering sacred ground, honoring every scar, every place where love longs to live and cruelty once took up residence.

And instead of handing her off to someone else—hoping a partner would see her worth, that a title would validate her existence, that a moment of recognition would fill the cavern in her chest, or that a touch would heal decades of untouchable loneliness—I became everything she needed.

I gave her what no one else could, what no one else had ever thought to offer: boundaries that felt like safety instead of prison walls, adventure that sparked aliveness in her eyes instead of terror, love that poured over her like warm honey, presence that said "you matter" in every breath, clarity that helped her understand who she had been, and who she was becoming.

And now… she no longer screams. The sound that used to tear from her throat like a wild animal caught in a trap has quieted to whispers, then to peaceful silence. She no longer reaches with the desperation of someone drowning, fingers clawing at air, grasping for anything that might save her.

Because her tiny heart is full. It overflows like a cup placed under a waterfall of love. Her soul lives whole, complete unto itself, radiant with the light of someone who has come home after a long journey.

Inside me, now, she is at ease, like a child who knows with bone-deep certainty that she is loved, safe, protected, and secure. She knows she belongs here, in this body, in this life, in this moment. The restless searching has ended. The desperate reaching has stilled. She has found what she was looking for all along.

And with her healing, I—the woman—am free. Free like a bird that has remembered how to fly, like a river that has found its way to the sea.

Free to build healthy, vibrant relationships—no longer from a place of lack that gnaws like hunger or need that feels like drowning, and now from a place of overflow, alignment, and truth that rings like a bell in the silence. The small, fragile, dependent child who longs to be held is cradled with love. I choose to connect with the curiosity and confidence of a woman who knows her own worth, who brings her wholeness to the table instead of her wounds.

I walk in the world now with fresh eyes—aware like a woman who has lived, loved, lost, and let go. The sky looks different—more vast, more inviting, painted in colors I never noticed before. The wind brushes past my skin like a new language, whispering secrets in my ear: "You're ready. You're ready for all of it."

The experience of my life feels more vivid. Colors deepen—richer, more saturated. Sounds expand—fuller, more textured. I hear layers in birdsong I never noticed before, melodies in the traffic that rise like music. The touch of life feels intentional now, purposeful, chosen rather than simply endured.

And inside me, there is this resonant knowing—the kind that hums like a sacred truth vibrating in the chambers of my heart: I am whole. I am complete. I am enough.

Today, I embrace this chapter as a woman embodied, empowered, and alive. Every cell in my body pulses with the rhythm of someone who inhabits her own skin proudly. The journey ahead lives as an expansion of who I already am. It invites me to live from my wholeness, to create from overflow, to love from fullness, to lead from grounded truth. It is a journey of expression, alignment, and deep presence—bringing all of me to every room I enter, every relationship I nurture, every dream I bring to life.

It is about exploring a fullness that feels like coming alive. About love chosen with intention rather than chased with desperation. About intimacy that feels sacred and deliberate, rising from healed ground instead of bleeding places where wounds once lived.

I take the little girl with me now as a living part of my wholeness, tucked gently inside the locket I wear close to my heart. She lives there safe and cherished, treasured and protected by the woman she helped me become. She is a quiet reminder that her needs stand fully met, that she receives everything she once searched for, and that together we move through this life grounded, loved, and free.

The little girl in me now smiles in peace. Her hands rest gently in her lap, palms open in gratitude. Her eyes shine with the light of someone who has been seen, really seen. Her breathing flows deeply and evenly. She is safe, present, and at ease inside her own body.

And I… I walk forward with arms open in welcome, heart grounded in love, soul ignited by the flame of purpose. My steps are sure, my gaze is clear, my voice is strong.

This is my new beginning, and it tastes like freedom on my tongue.

And I choose it—intentionally, joyfully, completely—with every fiber of my being, every beat of my heart, every breath that fills my lungs with the sweet air of a life fully lived.

MY CLIENTS'
JOURNEYS

Chapter 22: The Courage To Heal

*"The most beautiful people we have known are those who
have known defeat, known suffering, known struggle,
known loss, and have found their way out of the depths.
These persons have an appreciation, a sensitivity, and
an understanding of life that fills them with compassion,
gentleness, and a deep loving concern. Beautiful people
do not just happen."*

— Elisabeth Kübler-Ross

These are stories of profound courage—of individuals who wanted more. More than their past. More than their pain. More than the patterns that had defined generations before them.

Each person you will read about made a revolutionary choice: to do the work of healing. For themselves, for their families, for their communities, and for those they come in contact with. They understood something profound—that healing is a deeply radical act, one that ripples far beyond the individual.

By choosing to heal, they stopped the transmission of generational patterns. By facing their wounds, they created space for their children to grow differently. By transforming their own pain, they became agents of change in their families, their workplaces, and their communities.

These are stories of people who chose healing over repetition. Who decided that their legacy would be their resilience. Who understood that true healing is an act of collective liberation.

When Healing Becomes a Revolution

I witness miracles every day. The real, raw, beautiful kind that happens when someone decides they're done living in the prison of their past. I walk alongside my clients as they untangle themselves from what I call The Roller Coaster of Great Success and Failures—a vicious cycle where successes get thwarted by limiting beliefs, pain, triggers, and self-sabotage that keeps them trapped in patterns that are running their lives.

This cycle is deceptive. It disguises itself as reality, as fate, as an inescapable truth about who they are. Many of my clients feel trapped, unknowingly reinforcing their own pain through the very thoughts and behaviors they believe are protecting them. Yet they all share one pivotal moment: the awakening—the realization that their triggers are invitations to heal.

These are their stories. These are the moments when everything changes. These are the testimonies that prove healing is possible. Now say yes to your own transformation.

Sarah: The Illusion of Reality, How My Clients Create Their Own Suffering

Sarah sits across from me, frustration radiating from every word. "I don't understand," she says, her voice heavy with exhaustion. "I'm doing everything right, but I keep getting overlooked. No one sees my potential."

She has spent years blaming external circumstances—her boss, her competitors, even luck. As we peel back the layers, something deeper emerges, something that makes her entire body shift when she sees it.

The answer lives inside her—in the way she sees herself.

Sarah holds the skills and values the world seeks. Deep down, she has convinced herself she is unworthy. She expects rejection, so she positions herself to receive it. She speaks quietly in meetings, apologizes before sharing ideas, and shrinks when opportunities arise.

Like many of my clients, she has been speaking the language of limiting beliefs without even realizing it. Her body language, her energy, and her very presence broadcast the message: "I don't belong here." And the world, responding to that energy, gives her exactly what she's unconsciously requesting.

The moment Sarah recognizes this pattern, tears fill her eyes. Tears of recognition. "Oh my God," she whispers. "I've been doing this to myself."

That recognition becomes her liberation.

Ethan: The Trauma Loop, Living in the Past Without Realizing It

Many of my clients live in what I call a mental performance loop— repeating the same patterns while believing they are making progress. They are like actors performing the same play night after night, convinced each performance is different when the script remains the same.

There's the executive who keeps jumping from job to job, feeling undervalued, carrying the wound of a father whose acknowledgment remained absent.

There's the athlete who keeps choking in high-stakes moments, replaying the shame of being humiliated by a coach in front of his teammates when he was twelve.

There's the high-performer who keeps burning out, convinced she has to earn her worth through overwork, trying to prove to a mother who demanded more that she is finally enough.

They assume they are living in reality when, in fact, they are living inside their past experiences, replaying them in different costumes on different stages.

Ethan appears successful, respected, and outwardly confident. He lives in a constant state of stress. He micromanages everything, gripping control tightly, convinced that his constant vigilance holds everything together.

"If I don't stay in control, everything will fall apart," he admits, his jaw tight with the effort of holding his world together.

Through our conversations, we uncover the root—Ethan grew up in a home where unpredictability meant danger. His alcoholic father's moods swung like a pendulum, and young Ethan learned that hypervigilance was survival. His nervous system learned that control equaled safety, that letting go meant catastrophe.

When Ethan sees this connection, he realizes something profound: The life he wants—one of ease, joy, and trust—requires the very thing he fears most: surrender.

For the first time in decades, he lets go, just a little. He delegates a project and steps back. He takes a vacation and stays present. The world continues. It opens up. His team steps up. His business thrives. His relationships deepen.

"I can't believe I've been carrying this weight for so long," he tells me, his shoulders visibly lighter. "I thought I was being responsible, but I was being afraid."

Emma: The Unseen Dance, How Unresolved Experiences Shape Relationships

Every relationship is a dance between two nervous systems, two sets of wounds, two collections of unhealed experiences trying to find safety and connection. Only after healing do we meet each other as we truly are.

Emma comes to me with a heavy heart, always finding herself in relationships where she feels unseen, unheard, and unimportant. No matter how much she tries, she always ends up with emotionally unavailable partners who make her feel like she's asking for too much when she simply asks to be loved.

"Why do I always end up in this same situation?" she asks, her voice breaking. "It's like I'm cursed! Every man I meet turns out to be the same person in a different body."

I ask her to pause and reflect: "Who was the first person who made you feel this way?"

Tears well up in her eyes. "Father," she whispers. "He was always there physically, but never really there. I spent my whole childhood trying to get his attention, trying to make him see me."

Emma realizes she has been unconsciously seeking the same dynamic, trying to heal a wound by recreating it. She gravitates toward emotionally unavailable men because they feel like home—the familiarity her nervous system craves. Her nervous system recognizes the pattern of longing, of trying to earn love, of never quite being enough.

The moment she recognizes this, something shifts. She sees the loop of rejection for what it is—a pattern, and patterns can change. A choice, and choices belong to her.

"I keep choosing men who don't love me the way I want to be loved," she says, the truth settling into her bones. "Because if they could love me easily, I wouldn't know what to do with it."

Noah: Relationship Runaway

Similarly, Noah leaves. Every time. He leaves relationships. He leaves friendships. He leaves opportunities that require vulnerability. The moment something feels too good, too real, too close to his heart, he finds a reason to go.

"I don't think I've met the right person," he tells me, but his eyes don't meet mine when he says it.

When we dig deeper, the truth emerges like a splinter working its way to the surface.

Noah grew up in a home where love was given and taken away like a weapon. His mother's affection was conditional on his behavior, his achievements, and his ability to make her happy. He learned that closeness led to pain, that people who loved you could hurt you the most, that the safest place was always out of reach.

So as an adult, he runs from the possibility of loving relationships. His healing comes when he realizes he fears love and that real love lies outside of his experience. It feels too vulnerable, too risky, and too much like setting himself up for the inevitable disappointment.

Lena: Why We Resist Change (Even When We Want It)

A painful truth settles into Lena's chest during one of our sessions, and I watch her face change as the realization hits her.

"What if I've been addicted to my own suffering?" she asks, her voice barely above a whisper.

It sounds absurd at first. "Why would I keep choosing pain? That doesn't make sense."

Then, the answer becomes clear, and it's more uncomfortable than she expected:

Because pain is familiar. Because suffering has given her an identity. Because if she admits she has the power to change, she can no longer blame the world for her circumstances.

Lena carries her pain like a badge of honor, like proof of what she's experienced, like evidence that she's special in her suffering.

"It's my story," she says, defensively, clutching her pain like a security blanket.

"Does it serve you?" I ask gently.

Silence fills the room, heavy with recognition.

She realizes that holding onto the pain is a choice. She has been addicted to suffering because it gives her a sense of identity, an explanation for the struggles, and a way to avoid the terrifying responsibility of creating something new.

Her pain defines her. Her story gives her something to share. Her struggle creates her connections. Letting go means losing her identity. This terrifies her.

Letting go of the pain means freeing herself from the prison she has built around it. The memories remain. The prison falls away.

Slowly, courageously, she starts rewriting her story—one where she is the conscious creator of her future.

The Trigger Is the Invitation to Heal

One of the biggest mindset shifts I teach in my work is this: What if every time you've been triggered, it was life giving you a chance to heal?

This changes everything. Suddenly, triggers become opportunities. They become invitations. They signal that something is ready to be released.

Triggers mean something needs to be seen, acknowledged, and integrated.

Every challenge becomes an invitation:

A chance to observe yourself with curiosity instead of judgment

A chance to recognize your patterns instead of being controlled by them

A chance to choose something different instead of repeating what's familiar

Because when you are triggered, your subconscious mind is actually saying: "It is safe to heal now. You are strong enough to face this. You are ready to be free."

How My Clients Break Free

Through our work together, my clients learn to transform their relationship with their triggers and their past. They discover that healing is about responding from a place of choice rather than reacting from a place of wounding.

They Become the Observer

Instead of being consumed by their emotions, they learn to step back and watch them with curiosity. They pause when triggered and ask, "What story am I telling myself right now? Is this about what's happening now, or what happened then?"

They Take Radical Responsibility

Self-ownership replaces self-blame. They reclaim their power from circumstances and people. They recognize their role in creating their experiences. They ask, "How am I contributing to this pattern? What am I choosing that keeps this cycle alive?"

They Challenge Core Beliefs

They question the stories they've been telling themselves for years. "Is this actually true, or is this what I've always believed? Where did this belief come from? Does it serve me now?"

They Rewire Their Triggers

Instead of seeing triggers as evidence that they're damaged, they see them as opportunities to reprogram their responses. Each trigger becomes a chance to choose something new, to respond from their healed self rather than their wounded self.

They Choose Something New

Instead of shutting down when things get difficult, they lean in with curiosity. Instead of expecting failure, they create conditions for success. Instead of protecting themselves from love, they practice receiving it.

Your Healing Revolution: Breaking Free from Your Loop

If you recognize yourself in these stories, if you see your own patterns reflected in my clients' journeys, know this: your transformation is possible. It waits for your yes.

Notice Your Patterns: Where do you keep experiencing the same outcomes? What situations trigger the same responses? What stories do you tell yourself about why things fall apart?

Question Your Reality: Ask yourself, "Is this actually happening, or is this my past experience coloring my present perception?" Most of our suffering comes from living in the story of what happened rather than responding to what's actually happening now.

Embrace Your Triggers: The next time you feel triggered, pause and ask, "What is this teaching me? What part of me is asking to be healed?" Your triggers are your teachers, showing you exactly where your freedom lies.

Take Radical Responsibility: The world changes when you change how you show up in it. You hold complete control over how you respond to what happens to you.

Choose Something New: Every moment offers you the opportunity to choose differently. You can choose curiosity over judgment, love over fear, growth over safety, healing over familiarity.

The Truth About Healing

Healing is about recognizing that triggers are invitations. Resistance reveals that something beautiful waits on the other side of your fear.

It's about seeing the loops for what they are: echoes of the past trying to recreate themselves in the present. You are the person who chooses differently. You are the one who breaks the cycle. You are the author of what comes next.

You are the conscious choice to break free.

The moment my clients see this—really see it—they take back their power. They become authors of their new reality. They stop living in reaction to what happened to them and start living in response to what they want to create.

The most beautiful people I know are those who have walked through their own darkness and emerged compassionate, empathetic, and victorious.

They have learned the secret that changes everything: What happened to you is your history. What you choose to become is your destiny.

And so can you. Are you ready to step out of your loop and into your liberation? Your healing revolution starts now. Your transformation is waiting.

Your freedom is calling. The question is, "Will you answer?"

Reflections
The Courage to Heal

We invite you to explore these questions with curiosity and self-compassion. Use them to reframe challenges into opportunities for growth, gratitude, and empowerment. Share your responses with trusted people so you feel heard and understood. Revisit the questions over time to celebrate your growth.

For Sarah's Story

1. Where in your life have you unconsciously positioned yourself to be overlooked?

2. How do your internal beliefs about your worth impact your professional and personal opportunities?

3. What courageous step could you take to start valuing yourself differently?

For Ethan's Story

1. In what areas of your life are you micromanaging out of fear rather than necessity?

2. How has your desire for control been a protective mechanism from past experiences?

3. What would it look like to practice surrender in one area of your life?

For Emma's Story

1. How do your current relationships mirror unresolved childhood experiences?

2. Where are you forcing love in places where it is inappropriate?

3. What would it take for you to recognize and choose healthier connections?

For Noah's Story

1. Where in your life are you running from genuine connection?

2. How has your fear of vulnerability prevented you from experiencing true intimacy?

3. What is the next step for you to take to practice being seen?

For Lena's Story

1. How has your identity been tied to your suffering?

2. What might you lose—or gain—by letting go of your familiar pain?

3. What new story are you ready to write for yourself?

Chapter 23: Frank, Communication in Leadership

"The art of communication is the language of leadership."

— James Humes

Frank was at his breaking point. His frustration had been building for months, and it all came to a head in our session. He sat across from me, arms crossed, tension radiating from his body. "I don't know how much longer I can do this," he admitted. "My sister doesn't get it. She's unreliable, she doesn't follow through, and I feel like I'm carrying this business on my own."

Frank and his sister had started their business together years ago with a shared vision and excitement, and lately, their relationship had become strained. He felt like he was the one invested in the company's success, while she seemed disengaged, failing to meet expectations he assumed were clear.

As he spoke, I could hear the weight of resentment and unspoken expectations in his voice. His frustration came from within—from what he had been withholding.

I leaned forward and asked, "Have you ever told her any of this?"

Frank hesitated. "Not exactly," he admitted. "I mean, she should know, right? We started this together. We both agreed on what needed to be done."

There it was—the silent expectation. Frank had been holding his sister accountable to standards he kept to himself.

The Leadership Shift: From Blame to Ownership

Frank believed his sister was the problem, and the truth was, she had no idea what was going on in his mind. He had made assumptions instead of agreements and had been silently expecting her to meet standards he kept hidden from her. Every time she failed to meet those invisible expectations, his resentment grew.

"Frank," I said gently, "Leadership is more than making decisions or driving results. It's about how we communicate, how we express our needs, and how we foster relationships. If you keep your concerns silent, can you hold her accountable for actions she remains unaware of?"

He sat back, exhaling slowly. The realization hit him. His frustration came from his own lack of communication.

So, we made a plan. Instead of confronting his sister with blame, he would own his part in the miscommunication and have an honest conversation. He would express what he needed with clarity.

The Conversation That Changed Everything

That week, Frank sat down with his sister and opened up about how he had been feeling. He spoke from his heart. He owned his silence. He took responsibility.

"I realized I've been holding in a lot of frustration because I expected you to know what I needed from you and I never actually told you. That wasn't fair to either of us. Can we talk about how we can work better together?"

His sister was shocked—because she had no idea he had been feeling this way. From her perspective, things were fine. She believed she was meeting expectations. Without clear communication, the impact of her actions lived outside her awareness.

That conversation shifted everything. Once they started communicating openly, they were able to redefine roles, set clear expectations, and rebuild trust. The tension that had been weighing them down lifted, and their partnership became stronger than ever.

The Leadership Lesson: Communication is Everything

Frank's breakthrough was a powerful reminder that when tensions arise in any partnership, the first place to look is inward.

- What communications are unexpressed?
- What communications are unreceived?
- What assumptions have we made?

By taking responsibility for our part in the dynamic, we create the possibility for real resolution and growth.

For Frank, that shift saved their business partnership and allowed them to thrive at an even greater level. Instead of allowing unspoken frustration to destroy their relationship, he chose leadership—through self-awareness, communication, and ownership.

What a powerful lesson for all leaders!

Reflections
What Is Your Healing Journey?

We invite you to explore these questions with curiosity and self-compassion. Use them to reframe challenges into opportunities for growth, gratitude, and empowerment. Share your responses with trusted people so you feel heard and understood. Revisit the questions over time to celebrate your growth.

1. What are you seeing in this story that relates to your own experience?

2. How does this story challenge or expand your understanding of healing and transformation?

3. What insights or emotions are stirring within you as you read this narrative?

Chapter 24: Nathan, Liberation from Guilt

"We do not inherit guilt for our ancestors' actions."

— Henry Louis Gates, Jr.

Nathan was a multimillionaire, a self-made man who had built his success through hard work, discipline, and a commitment to excellence. Yet, despite all he had accomplished, he carried an invisible weight—one that no amount of wealth, recognition, or generosity could lift.

No one had ever spoken a harsh word to him about it. No one had ever accused him, yet he felt it everywhere he went.

The judgment. The whispers. The unspoken blame.

Or at least, that's what he *believed.*

Nathan was a descendant of people who had committed genocide—whose crimes left scars on humanity. He chose a different path. He spent his life giving back, supporting causes, lifting others up. He carried their name, their blood—and the weight of their sins. No one knew this history, and still, he walked into rooms wondering what people *really* thought of him.

- Did they see him as an extension of his ancestors?
- Did they believe he carried the same sins?
- Did they resent his success, believing it was somehow tainted?

He told himself that his success left him unchanged, that his wealth failed to absolve him.

So he shrank.

The shrinking lived in how he carried himself. He second-guessed his words, softened his presence, avoided taking up too much space.

Even in boardrooms where he was the most powerful person in the room, he hesitated—because somewhere, deep down, he believed he had to prove that he *deserved* to be there.

And when we talked, I asked him one question:

"Who told you they saw you this way?"

Silence.

He searched his memory, looking for a moment when someone had pointed at him and said, *"You are guilty."*

There was none.

No one had ever said those words. No one had ever accused him.

The person holding the gavel was himself.

Nathan had been living inside a perceived judgment. His mind had created the very rejection he feared, and in doing so, he had been rejecting himself before anyone else ever could.

His ancestors had left a mark on humanity. That was true.

His life, his actions, his choices—those were his alone.

Nathan's healing came when he let go of the weight that was never his to carry.

When he realized that his ancestors' actions belonged to them—and his choices belonged to him. That he held responsibility only for how he chose to live in the present.

For the first time, he walked into a room without questioning how others saw him.

Because he now had seen himself.

Reflections
What Is Your Healing Journey?

We invite you to explore these questions with curiosity and self-compassion. Use them to reframe challenges into opportunities for growth, gratitude, and empowerment. Share your responses with trusted people so you feel heard and understood. Revisit the questions over time to celebrate your growth.

1. What are you seeing in this story that relates to your own experience?

2. How does this story challenge or expand your understanding of healing and transformation?

3. What insights or emotions are stirring within you as you read this narrative?

Chapter 25: Michael, The Gift of Feedback

*"Of all the words of mice and men, the saddest are
— 'It might have been.'"*

— Kurt Vonnegut

Michael had always dreamed of launching his own business, and when he and his partner, David, set out to build their state-of-the-art service, he felt like he was on top of the world. Their energy was electric, their ideas innovative, and their shared passion undeniable. They met regularly—sometimes multiple times a week—discussing strategy, refining their offerings, and telling each other that they had the best service in the market.

As the weeks turned into months, the enthusiasm began to wane. Progress was slower than expected. The grand vision they had so confidently spoken about felt out of reach. Michael, always the peacemaker, found himself struggling with a growing sense of unease. David, eager for feedback, frequently asked Michael for his thoughts on their direction, their decisions, and their challenges. Michael hesitated. He chose peace over conflict, chose to protect the vision they had built together. So he nodded along, offering half-hearted encouragement while his true thoughts remained locked inside.

In truth, Michael was deeply discouraged. The entrepreneurial journey proved harder than he imagined. The long hours, the uncertainty, the constant need to pivot and adjust—it overwhelmed him. Each time he considered voicing his concerns, he silenced himself, convincing himself that things would fall into place. They remained unchanged. The weight of unspoken frustrations built up like bricks on his shoulders, until one day, he collapsed under them.

Without a word of warning, he walked away. He left David, the business, and the dream they had built together. Like that, it was over.

At first, he felt relieved. And as the days passed, reflection set in. He realized that the stress, the frustration, the weight he had carried—it had been of his own making. He had chosen silence over honesty. He had withheld the very feedback that could have helped them navigate their struggles. He had been so afraid of conflict that he had allowed their partnership to crumble.

Michael understood he had the power to shape the relationship, to create solutions. He had chosen fear over trust.

As he sits with his thoughts, he wonders—what if he had spoken up? What if he had trusted open communication and they still stood side by side as business partners today?

Reflections
What Is Your Healing Journey?

We invite you to explore these questions with curiosity and self-compassion. Use them to reframe challenges into opportunities for growth, gratitude, and empowerment. Share your responses with trusted people so you feel heard and understood. Revisit the questions over time to celebrate your growth.

1. What are you seeing in this story that relates to your own experience?

2. How does this story challenge or expand your understanding of healing and transformation?

3. What insights or emotions are stirring within you as you read this narrative?

Chapter 26: Jennifer: The Color of Worth

Representative images ... trigger predictable thoughts, feelings."

— Susan Sontag

Jennifer walks into my office because her business is failing. She believes she has a marketing problem—her brand struggles to gain traction, sales are declining, and every attempt fails. She has exhausted every strategy, hired consultants, tweaked her messaging, and still, the needle remains unmoved.

Though I have transitioned fully into leadership development, she seeks me out anyway. Like many before her, she has heard the stories—how in my past marketing firm, I taught strategy; I developed leaders. Through that experience, I learned something profound: success in business is more than external tactics. It's about how individuals approach the opportunity itself.

The business owners who thrived came to me with optimism, did the work, shared the relevant information, tested the strategies, and evaluated their results. The ones who approached the process with doubt, fear, and resistance—who held back, who refused to believe in themselves or the possibilities before them—almost always failed.

Jennifer falls somewhere in between. She believes in her business. She believes in herself. And yet, something deep inside keeps her stuck, like an invisible hand holding her back from the success she can almost taste but keeps slipping away.

The Breakthrough of Dedication

Jennifer does everything right. She follows every step, listens attentively, implements every strategy we discuss. When it comes to personal transformation work, she is a star—she goes above and beyond, completing exercises with thoughtfulness and care. Yet despite her dedication and relentless effort, her results remain frustratingly limited.

Something is missing. I can feel it, and so can she.

Every client receives a journal at the beginning of our work together—a sacred space for reflection, affirmations, and written exercises. The journal serves as a record of their experience, a mirror they can look into later to see their journey, their healing, their patterns, and the things that were out of their awareness.

The journal is a place to integrate their thoughts, emotion, beliefs, behaviors, actions, life experiences, and ultimately their outcomes. It tells their story.

The Moment Everything Changed

In one of our sessions, Jennifer struggles with a mental block. Each explanation I offer meets a wall. She struggles to self-reflect, to grasp the concept I'm trying to convey through words alone. Sensing that my spoken explanations fail to reach her, I decide to take a different approach.

My inner Picasso comes out.

I reach for her journal to draw a stick figure—something visual to help her see what is going on. The stick figure has a body and a head. I draw two curved arrows: one pointing from the head to the body, the other from the body to the head, creating a continuous loop between mind and body.

I'm excited. This visual will help her understand the mind-body connection we've been discussing. This will be the breakthrough.

What happens next shocks me.

Jennifer's body stiffens instantly. Her breath becomes shallow. The energy in the room shifts like a storm rolling in. She becomes enraged. She looks at the journal as if I have violated something sacred, as if I've crossed a line invisible to me until this moment.

Her reaction is much bigger than the moment warrants.

At first, I struggled to understand why she was so angry. Anyone else would have brushed it off, apologized for the lack of permission, and moved on. I've learned that the biggest reactions often point to the deepest wounds. Instead of ignoring it, I get curious.

I pause and gently ask, "Do you want to explore where this is coming from?"

She hesitates, then nods. And that's when the real work begins.

The Unconscious Root of Unworthiness

Neither of us had any idea of where it was coming from. The process of uncovering this took the time it took.

Her reaction transcends privacy. Transcends control. Transcends the journal itself. As we peel back layer after layer, Jennifer uncovers something she has left unconnected—a meaning her mind stored so deeply that even decades later, something as simple as my writing in her journal triggers an automatic response buried beneath her conscious awareness.

All of a sudden, Jennifer is seven years old again. Her face shifts. Her voice quivers as she recounts the story. Her body tells the story of a little girl who has been scolded. It's as if she's back in that moment, living it all over again.

The story is so vivid as she recounts it that I feel like I'm there with her.

She's lying in bed at her grandmother's home—the person she loves most in the world, the one whose approval means everything. Her grandmother comes into the room, her voice stern and disapproving: "If you don't behave and go to sleep, a black horse is going to come and take you away."

Seven-year-old Jennifer lies there in the dark, terrified. The color black. The threat of being taken away. The disappointment in her grandmother's voice saying that she is bad, that she's misbehaving, that something bad will come for her unless she changes.

The pattern becomes clear to us: the color black, the most precious person in her life expressing disappointment, her feeling guilt. The next 28 years of her life were cursed with a deep, lingering sense of unworthiness.

And I had written in her journal with a black pen.

The Invisible Prison

Black becomes more than a color to Jennifer. It becomes a symbol of failure, rejection, and not being enough. That single subconscious association shapes how she sees herself, how she shows up in the world, how she unknowingly holds herself back, and how she engages with others.

It influences her confidence, her decisions, and even the way she allows herself to be seen and heard. Without realizing it, she judges and rejects others based on the color they wear or the ink they write with, mistaking a harmless detail for a deeper threat. What she believes is instinct is actually an old wound dictating her interactions, keeping her from connections and opportunities she's pushing away.

Rather than marketing, her business is failing because, deep down, she has been showing up as unworthy. She has been hesitating, second-guessing, and unconsciously sabotaging opportunities before they can fully materialize.

The seven-year-old girl lying in the dark, afraid of the black horse, is running her life at 35.

Rewriting the Story of Worth

Jennifer sees it. She sees how this unconscious belief has shaped her entire life—how she has held herself back, how she has made decisions through the lens of unworthiness, how she has been living in a prison she was unaware of.

Now, she has a choice. She can continue living from that seven-year-old's fear, or she can rewrite the story.

Jennifer chooses to rewrite.

Her transformation is extraordinary. She transforms her business, saves her marriage, and pursues the dreams she has put on hold for years. She sets herself up for more success than she ever thought possible. She is able to retire early, living in a reality she never thought was possible. All because of one moment of reflection. All because she was willing to look deeper. All because a black pen unlocked a prison she had been living in for 28 years.

The Truth About Healing

Our deepest triggers may be echoes from the past, waiting to be acknowledged, processed, and released.

Jennifer's transformation is about reclaiming her power through acknowledging her experiences, reconciling the past, and writing a new story from a place of worthiness instead of fear.

Some of us have a Jennifer moment waiting to be discovered. We have unconscious beliefs running our lives, keeping us stuck in patterns beyond our awareness, sabotaging opportunities hidden from view, and holding us back from the life we are meant to live.

The question is: Are you willing to look deeper? Are you willing to explore the triggers that seem too small to matter? Are you willing to discover what's really keeping you stuck?

Because on the other side of that exploration is freedom. On the other side of that awareness is transformation. On the other side of that black pen is the life you've been longing for.

Reflections
What Is Your Healing Journey?

We invite you to explore these questions with curiosity and self-compassion. Use them to reframe challenges into opportunities for growth, gratitude, and empowerment. Share your responses with trusted people so you feel heard and understood. Revisit the questions over time to celebrate your growth.

1. What are you seeing in this story that relates to your own experience?

2. How does this story challenge or expand your understanding of healing and transformation?

3. What insights or emotions are stirring within you as you read this narrative?

Chapter 27: Mari, I'm Ready

"Your life does not get better by chance, it gets better by change."

— Jim Rohn

Mari isn't ready. For years, Mari hears about me. A mutual friend makes the introduction, her voice filled with conviction: "You need to work with this coach. She'll change your life."

Every invitation to connect is met with silence, avoidance, or a polite deflection: "Maybe later." Despite the friend's gentle persistence, Mari keeps her distance, building walls between herself and the possibility of transformation.

And then one day, later arrives.

She reaches out, her voice carrying the weight of exhaustion that comes from years of running. "I can't keep doing this," she admits, and I can hear the surrender in her words—the kind of surrender that opens the door to real change. "I'm tired of running in circles."

"I'm ready."

The Reality No One Saw

Mari is a single mother, barely making ends meet, stuck in an endless cycle of struggle that feels like a treadmill spinning endlessly beneath her feet. What most people miss—what she's been hiding behind a carefully constructed facade of "I'm fine"—is that she's homeless.

She sleeps in her car when she can. She crashes on couches when friends will have her. She stays in temporary shelters when there's space. She does whatever she can to keep her child safe and to maintain some semblance of normalcy in a life defined by chaos.

When we start working together, she has a willingness to show up. She arrives with empty hands. Unstable ground beneath her feet. A safety net that vanished long ago. And a deep, bone-tired readiness to stop running and start facing whatever she's been avoiding.

And that willingness? That's enough. That's where all transformation begins.

Epiphany After Epiphany

Mari started attending our Mental Performance coaching. At first, Mari listens, taking in everything, working on self-reflection despite any discomfort. She does the work. She applies what she learns during each session. With each new session, she comes back with a new realization, her voice growing stronger with each truth she uncovers.

She went from "Why is life so hard?" "Why won't my family help me?" "Why doesn't my daughter's father help out with our daughter?" "Why do I have to do this alone?"

She started generating statements like:

"I've been waiting for someone to save me, but I'm the one I've been waiting for."

"I don't have to prove my worth to anyone—I was born worthy."

"I've been numbing myself for so long that I don't even know what it feels like to be truly alive."

One by one, she dismantles the beliefs that have kept her trapped in cycles of poverty and struggle. She lets go of the external distractions— the things she used to escape feeling, the coping mechanisms that shifted from protection to prison. And in doing so, she makes space for something new: self-trust.

Her confidence grows steadily, like a plant pushing through the cracks of concrete. Every day, she examines the results in her life through the lens of curiosity. "Why is this happening to me?" transforms into "What can I learn from this? What is this showing me about myself?"

The questions change everything. Because when you change the questions, you change the answers. And when you change the answers, you change your life.

Then, in a moment of clarity that takes my breath away, she makes a decision that will change everything.

She's going back to university.

The Audacious Decision

When Mari tells me she's applying to university, I see the fear and determination warring in her eyes. She's a single mother. She's homeless. She has no financial cushion, no family support, no backup plan. By every practical measure, this decision seems impossible.

Mari has learned something profound: impossible is a story we tell ourselves when we're too afraid to try.

She applies. She gets accepted. And she shows up.

Breaking the Cycle

Within months, Mari has a job and stable housing. She has a roof over her head, a routine, and—most importantly—a sense of direction. The chaos that once defined her life begins to settle into stability.

She pours herself into her studies, something she once believed was impossible for someone like her. Every test, every paper, every long night of studying reinforces a new truth: She is capable. She is intelligent. She is enough.

And life responds accordingly.

Scholarships start coming. Her name appears on the Dean's List. Leadership opportunities find her. Mari thrives at university, She excels in ways that surprise her.

She becomes a Phi Beta Kappa student, standing among the top scholars in her field. She earns multiple scholarships, proving to herself that she is worthy of success—she was always meant for it. She's recognized nationally for her academic achievements, her name appearing on lists she once thought were reserved for people who came from different circumstances, different families, different lives.

Mari earns accolades. She receives scholarships. She secures stable housing. The most beautiful part of her transformation runs deeper still.

It's what she does next.

Becoming the Guide She Once Needed

Mari turns around and extends her hand to others.

Today, she leads other non-traditional students through their own university journey. She mentors them, coaches them, shows them what's possible when you stop running and start believing.

She knows the doubts intimately—the voice that says you remain an outsider here, that intelligence eludes you, that people like you fail in places like this. She knows the fears that wake you up in the middle of the night, the impostor syndrome that whispers you're a fraud, the exhaustion that comes from constantly proving yourself in spaces built to keep you out.

And because she knows, she guides with a compassion and understanding that comes from having walked the path yourself.

The woman who once avoided every invitation to change is now the one extending the invitation to others. The woman who once ran from transformation is now creating spaces where transformation can happen for those who come after her.

The Ripple Effect of One Decision

Mari's story is proof that when we heal, we heal for ourselves—we heal for those who come after us. We break cycles that have run through generations. We create new possibilities where none existed before. We become living proof that change is possible, that circumstances and destiny stand apart, that "I'm ready" is the most powerful phrase in the human language.

She broke the cycle of poverty, homelessness, and struggle. And now, she's helping others do the same.

She transformed her pain into purpose, her struggle into strength, her story into a roadmap for others who are finding their way.

The Truth About Readiness

Mari stayed unready for years. That's okay. Readiness follows its own timeline. It arrives when we've finally exhausted every other option, when the pain of staying the same becomes greater than the fear of change.

When readiness arrives, everything shifts. Doors that seemed locked suddenly open. Resources that seemed unavailable suddenly appear. The strength hidden within you suddenly rises to meet the challenge.

Mari transformed with empty pockets, zero connections, and no safety net. She transformed because she finally said, "I'm ready."

And in that readiness, she found everything she needed.

When you ask yourself, "Am I ready?" The answer is, "Yes!"

When you say "I'm ready," the universe responds. Life responds. Your own untapped potential responds.

And everything changes.

Ask Mari.

Reflections
What Is Your Healing Journey?

We invite you to explore these questions with curiosity and self-compassion. Use them to reframe challenges into opportunities for growth, gratitude, and empowerment. Share your responses with trusted people so you feel heard and understood. Revisit the questions over time to celebrate your growth.

1. What are you seeing in this story that relates to your own experience?

2. How does this story challenge or expand your understanding of healing and transformation?

3. What insights or emotions are stirring within you as you read this narrative?

Chapter 28: George, Ghosts of Childhood

"Do not let the memories of your past limit the potential of your future."

— Roy T. Bennett

George stands at the pinnacle of his professional world—high-performing, respected, a leader among his peers. His reputation precedes him, a testament to years of hard work and dedication. When his boss hired me to guide George and his team through a hybrid program of coaching, training, and team development, I knew I was working with someone extraordinary.

At first, George is open to the process. He recognizes patterns in himself, identifies areas for growth, and embraces the opportunities ahead. His curiosity is genuine, his commitment apparent. Then, something shifts. Something fundamental breaks open.

The Trigger That Changes Everything

One day, his boss informs him of a new role—one with greater responsibilities, higher stakes, and more visibility. In this moment of celebration and recognition of his potential, George feels rage.

He is furious. He sees this as punishment instead of opportunity. He is ready to walk away from everything he has built, to throw away a career he has meticulously crafted, all because of this seemingly positive development.

Unraveling the Invisible Wound

In one of our sessions, George sits across from me, arms crossed, voice tight with tension. "I don't understand," he admits. "My boss knows I'm good at what I do. Why can't he just leave me where I am? Why is he pushing me into something I don't want?"

I could have reassured him. I could have reminded him that his boss clearly values him. Something tells me to go deeper.

"Do you want to explore why this is upsetting you so much?" I ask.

He hesitates. The vulnerability in that moment is palpable. Then, slowly, he nods.

What unfolds next is a revelation that will change everything.

The Ghosts of Childhood

As we work through the layers of his resistance, George realizes something profound—this goes beyond his boss. This is about his father.

Growing up, George had felt constantly judged. Instead of encouragement, he was met with criticism. Instead of being celebrated, he was reprimanded. His father's voice echoes through decades: "You could have done better." "This isn't good enough." "Why can't you be more?"

So when his boss presents him with this promotion, his subconscious mind registers judgment. Another chance to be found wanting. Opportunity remains invisible.

To George, his boss fails to see his brilliance. It feels like he's saying, "You're not good enough here. You need to be better."

The resistance is about an old wound that was ready to heal.

Breaking Free from the Pattern

As George connects the dots, he sits in stunned silence.

"So all this time… I've been reacting to my past?"

I nod.

"And I was about to quit over something that has nothing to do with my boss?"

Another nod.

His entire perspective shifts in that moment. He realizes his boss is elevating him. The opportunity proves his value.

Once he sees that, the resistance melts away.

The Transformation

George accepts the role from a place of power. He steps into his new position with confidence, no longer held back by the weight of unresolved childhood wounds.

And his career? It skyrockets.

The Power of Awareness

Most of the time, what we think we're reacting to is a decoy. The frustrations, fears, and resistance we feel in the present are often echoes of the past, playing out in real-time.

Our triggers are invitations to healing.

George's story is proof of what happens when we pause and ask, "Where is this really coming from?"

Because when we do, we stop fighting ghosts.

And we step into the life that's waiting for us.

Reflections
What Is Your Healing Journey?

We invite you to explore these questions with curiosity and self-compassion. Use them to reframe challenges into opportunities for growth, gratitude, and empowerment. Share your responses with trusted people so you feel heard and understood. Revisit the questions over time to celebrate your growth.

1. What are you seeing in this story that relates to your own experience?

2. How does this story challenge or expand your understanding of healing and transformation?

3. What insights or emotions are stirring within you as you read this narrative?

Chapter 29: Michael, Embracing Success

*"Relentless criticism in childhood can internalize a …
scorn that no amount of success will silence."*

— Bruce Watson

Michael is extraordinary—a young doctor at the pinnacle of his profession, respected worldwide. His medical expertise is matched by his potential for leadership. He has built a thriving private practice and dreams of taking his insights to global stages, sharing knowledge that could transform lives.

Yet, despite his brilliance, something holds him back. An invisible weight of limitation—unseen yet deeply felt.

The Invisible Cage

Every time Michael has the chance to step onto a stage and share his insights, he freezes. He possesses the knowledge. He has done the preparation. Something deep inside whispers: "You don't belong here."

He lacks confidence. He lacks the feeling of being a leader. He struggles to believe he truly deserves that platform.

At the same time, he carries another weight—his family. He is the provider, taking care of multiple relatives. He prides himself on feeling responsible for everyone's well-being, often putting his own dreams aside to ensure no one in his family goes without. He is exhausted by this weight.

The Childhood Wound

For a year, we work together, peeling back the layers of his resistance. Every session reveals new insights, each one bringing him closer to understanding the truth of his struggles.

Then, at month nine, we reach the core wound—the moment in his childhood that had shaped his entire belief system about success.

Michael was six years old when a caregiver said something that would alter the trajectory of his life:

He had asked for a toy, and the caregiver responded:

"You can't have that. If you get what you want, no one else can have anything."

That one statement planted a seed in his young mind: If I take too much, others will suffer.

The Subconscious Limitation

Subconsciously, Michael built his entire life around this belief.

He limited his own success because deep down, he feared it would take away from others. He gave endlessly to his family, feeling it was his duty to keep the balance. He held back from the stage—his power felt like theft. If he rose, others would fall.

Logic played no role in this belief. The subconscious operates on emotion and memory alone.

The Moment of Liberation

When Michael sees it—really sees it—everything shifts.

"So I've been afraid of taking up space… because I thought I was stealing from others?"

Yes.

"And I've been playing small… because I thought my success would leave others with nothing?"

For the first time, Michael questions the story he has been living by. He realizes that wealth, success, and leadership grow when shared—his rise creates room for others to rise.

That one realization sets him free.

Stepping Into Power

Within weeks, Michael feels lighter. He starts saying yes to speaking opportunities he once avoided. His next time on stage, he feels powerful, aligned, and at peace.

The transformation came from one action: recognizing and letting go of a belief that no longer served him.

The Truth About Limitation

Most of the time, the things that hold us back live in the past—the invisible decisions we made as children that control us as adults.

Michael's story shows that success is about releasing the stories that forbid us to rise.

Because when we rewrite those stories, we stop surviving—and we start thriving.

Reflections
What Is Your Healing Journey?

We invite you to explore these questions with curiosity and self-compassion. Use them to reframe challenges into opportunities for growth, gratitude, and empowerment. Share your responses with trusted people so you feel heard and understood. Revisit the questions over time to celebrate your growth.

1. What are you seeing in this story that relates to your own experience?

2. How does this story challenge or expand your understanding of healing and transformation?

3. What insights or emotions are stirring within you as you read this narrative?

Chapter 30: Kathy, Unseen Patterns

"Rather than blaming, become curious as to how the two of you ended up in this situation. It has as much to do with you, as with your spouse."

— Esther Perel

Kathy comes to me excited, her eyes bright with possibility. She started her new business, building it from the ground up, pouring her heart and soul into every detail. And in a remarkably short period of time, it begins to flourish.

She has every reason to celebrate. Every metric points to success. Her vision is becoming reality.

Then, something changes.

The Shift No One Expected

Instead of basking in her success, Kathy becomes frustrated, exhausted, and disconnected. Our sessions become tense. We are no longer seeing eye to eye. The ease and flow we once had disappears, replaced by resistance and defensiveness.

She is upset about her relationship. Other people are judging her for it, and that judgment cuts deep. At first, she tries to ignore it.

She tells herself she can handle everything—that as long as she keeps pushing, everything will fall into place. She buries herself in work, using her business as a shield against what she refuses to face.

During one of our coaching sessions, the walls come down. She admits that something feels off. Frustration with other people's opinions masks the real issue—she's angry at herself.

The Unseen Patterns

At first, Kathy had been confident and independent. She loved what she did. She loved how she led her life. She was unapologetically herself.

Slowly, without realizing it, she had started shifting to fit into her boyfriend's world. She began adapting, adjusting, and compromising in ways that felt small at first. A comment here. A preference there. Little by little, she molded herself into someone she thought he wanted, someone she thought would be easier to love.

Over time, she lost pieces of herself. The vibrant, confident woman who started her business began to fade, replaced by someone who second-guessed her decisions, dimmed her light, and apologized for taking up space.

She had convinced herself that it was support, that it was partnership. Deep down, she resented him for it.

She had changed herself. The transformation belonged to her alone.

The Moment of Truth

"I made myself small," she says, her voice breaking. "I chose this. And now I'm blaming him for something I did."

The room fills with the weight of that truth. This is about her changing herself like a chameleon to be with him. She was pretending to like all the things hie liked and hiding her true feelings.

Taking Back Her Power

Kathy stops blaming others—her boyfriend, the people judging her, the circumstances around her—and instead, she takes ownership of her choices.

She stops shrinking herself for someone else's comfort. She speaks up about what she truly wants. She redesigns her life in a way that honors both her business and her relationship, refusing to sacrifice one for the other.

And something incredible happens.

She and her boyfriend grow closer instead of pulling away. She shows up as herself. That changes everything.

When she stops pretending, stops adjusting, and stops resenting, she builds a relationship grounded in connection. Real connection. The kind that can only exist between two whole people who honor themselves.

The Liberation

Kathy's business continues to thrive, and now she thrives alongside it. Exhaustion from the facade falls away. Authenticity energizes her as she shows up fully in every area of her life.

Her relationship transforms. She stops changing herself. That was all it took.

The Truth About Love and Success

Kathy's story is a reminder that when we sacrifice parts of ourselves for the sake of a relationship, we lose ourselves and destroy the very connection we seek to protect.

She changed herself. The transformation belonged to her alone. And when she finally reclaimed her power, she created a thriving business and built an extraordinary relationship. Because true love means expanding together. Two whole people choosing each other because each other..

Reflections
What Is Your Healing Journey?

We invite you to explore these questions with curiosity and self-compassion. Use them to reframe challenges into opportunities for growth, gratitude, and empowerment. Share your responses with trusted people so you feel heard and understood. Revisit the questions over time to celebrate your growth.

1. What are you seeing in this story that relates to your own experience?

2. How does this story challenge or expand your understanding of healing and transformation?

3. What insights or emotions are stirring within you as you read this narrative?

Chapter 31: Living Your Gold

"And the day came when the risk to remain tight in a bud was more painful than the risk it took to blossom."

— Anaïs Nin

You are standing at the threshold between who you were and who you are becoming. When you opened this book, you may have been searching for answers, for validation, for proof that your pain mattered. You may have been looking for permission to tell the truth about what happened to you—or permission to stop carrying what was never yours to carry in the first place. Along the way, you have met the parts of yourself that were hidden, silenced, or waiting to be seen. You have walked through the fire of your own story and emerged transformed. The scars remain, and they no longer define you. They are evidence of your experiences, your strength, and your refusal to be erased.

This is what it means to live your gold.

The Journey You've Traveled

You began this journey perhaps unaware that you were still living in the patterns created by your past. You carried nameless wounds, unexplainable triggers, and a deep, aching sense that something was missing. You learned that trauma is what lives inside you when those experiences go unprocessed, unwitnessed, unhealed. You discovered that your body has been keeping score, that your nervous system has been running programs designed to protect you from dangers that exist only in memory.

You came to understand that the coping mechanisms that once saved your life—compartmentalization, hypervigilance, people-pleasing, emotional shutdown—have become the very things keeping you from living fully. And you made the courageous choice to look at them, to honor them for what they were, and to begin the work of releasing what no longer serves you. You have reparented yourself. You have given Little You the love, safety, and validation that was missing. You have learned to speak to yourself with compassion instead of criticism, to set boundaries instead of abandoning your own needs, to choose healing over familiar pain.

This is profound work. This is the work of a lifetime—and you are doing it.

Healing Takes What It Takes

If you are expecting a neat conclusion, a moment when you can say, "I am healed," and close the door on your past forever, we must tell you the truth: healing works the way it works.

Healing is a rhythm—a conversation between your present self and the one who once had to survive. Healing is cyclical, ongoing, and embodied. There will be days when you feel whole, integrated, and free. And their may be days when old wounds resurface, when triggers catch you off guard, and when you find yourself back in old familiar patterns. This proves you are human. Be graceful with yourself, this is the human experience.

Each time you choose awareness over avoidance, compassion over shame, presence over numbing, you continue the work. Each time you pause before reacting, each time you name your emotions instead of burying them, each time you set a boundary or ask for what you need—you are healing. The goal is integration. The goal is to bring all the parts of yourself—the wounded and the healed, the light and the shadow, the past and the present—into a unified, coherent whole. To live as gold means to honor every part of your journey, to hold it all with tenderness, and to move forward with intention.

You Are the Alchemist

No book, no teacher, no therapist can complete your healing. You are the one who continues the work—the alchemist of your own story. You are the one who decides when to open the jail cells you built for protection. You are the one who chooses to feel instead of numb, to connect instead of isolate, to trust instead of protect. You are the one who rewrites the narrative, who reclaims your voice, who steps into the life you were always meant to live.

This is your power. This is your gold.

Living your gold means:

- **Choosing yourself** without guilt or apology
- **Setting boundaries** that honor your energy and well-being
- **Speaking your truth** even when your voice shakes
- **Feeling your emotions** without being consumed by them
- **Building relationships** based on authenticity
- **Creating a life** that reflects your values
- **Being the person** you needed when you were younger

It means showing up fully—as the person healing has revealed you to be.

The Invitation

As you close this book, we invite you to pause. To breathe. To feel the weight of how far you have come. You are no longer the child who had to hide, to shrink, to protect yourself at any cost. You are no longer defined by what was done to you or what you had to do to make it through. You are whole. You are worthy. You are gold. The work continues in the choices you make every day—in the way you speak to yourself, in the boundaries you set, in the love you allow yourself to receive. It continues in the moments when you choose healing over familiar pain, when you trust yourself enough to step into the unknown, when you refuse to abandon yourself ever again.

This is your life. This is your story. And you get to decide what comes next.

A Final Word

You are not broken. You never were.

You are a person who is learning to thrive. You are a Warrior shedding their armor. You are a human being who is learning to live fully, authentically, and without apology.

The pain you carried has been transformed. The scars you bore are now sources of wisdom, strength, and compassion.

You have **Turned Your Pain Into Gold.**

Welcome home. And now, you get to **Live Your Gold!**

Reflections
Client Stories and Living Your Gold

We invite you to explore these questions with curiosity and self-compassion. Use them to reframe challenges into opportunities for growth, gratitude, and empowerment. Share your responses with trusted people so you feel heard and understood. Revisit the questions over time to celebrate your growth.

1. How are your unresolved experiences currently showing up in your relationships, career, or personal goals?

2. What "mental performance loop" are you stuck in, and how is it preventing you from creating the life you desire?

3. When you think about your triggers, what invitation to heal might they be offering you?

4. What new behaviors and responses will you practice when you encounter your typical triggers?

5. What familiar pain or suffering have you been unconsciously choosing because it feels safer than the unknown?

6. How are you currently showing up through the mask of your past experiences rather than your authentic self?

7. What shifts in your internal world would allow you to break free from your current patterns?

8. How will you know when you're operating from your healed self rather than your wounded self?

9. What specific actions will you take in the next 30 days to begin creating your desired reality instead of repeating your familiar patterns?

10. How might you nurture the parts of you that you once had to hide?

Affirmations
Living Your Gold

Your thoughts, feelings, beliefs, voice, and actions create your reality. Each day, choose three affirmations and speak them out loud. Hearing your own words turns affirmations into living declarations that reshape your mind. Speak with intention and feel the words settle deep within you.

- I feel fully.
- I set boundaries.
- I love the new me.
- I am defined by my own choices.
- I build a life that reflects my truth.
- I am present to my life experiences.
- I honor every step of my healing journey.
- I am whole, worthy, and deserving of love.
- ***I am the alchemist of my own story.***
- ***I am gold.***

IN CLOSING

Chapter 32: Available Therapies

"There is no one-size-fits-all solution. Whether you're working on improving your mental fitness or you are interested in how you can augment your current practices, try taking a completely different approach."

— Dr. Mark Epstein

Here is a list of therapies available for people who have experienced trauma. This is not a complete list and we do not make specific recommendations for any therapy modality. Each individual will decide for themselves what works best for them. As you read this list, check in with yourself and see which of these therapies resonate with you. If there is one that particularly captures your attention, find a skilled practitioner of that modality for you to work with. Any place to start is a good place to start.

Effective Psychological Therapies

Scientifically supported therapies designed to heal trauma, regulate emotions, and reshape thought patterns.

Effective psychological therapies are evidence-based approaches designed to promote healing, emotional regulation, and cognitive transformation. These therapies help individuals process trauma, manage distressing emotions, and develop healthier thought patterns for long-term well-being.

- **Cognitive Behavioral Therapy (CBT):** Reshapes negative thought patterns to improve emotions and behaviors.
- **Trauma-Focused CBT (TF-CBT):** Tailored for people who have experienced trauma, integrating trauma-sensitive interventions.
- **Dialectical Behavior Therapy (DBT):** Balances emotions through mindfulness, distress tolerance, and interpersonal skills.

- **Narrative Therapy:** Empowers individuals to rewrite personal stories and reclaim self-identity.
- **Internal Family Systems (IFS):** Promotes inner healing by addressing different parts of the self.
- **Prolonged Exposure Therapy:** Helps individuals process and confront traumatic memories to reduce avoidance.
- **Group Therapy:** Provides shared support and healing in a community setting.

Cognitive Behavioral Therapy (CBT): Reshaping Thought Patterns

CBT is a structured, evidence-based therapy that helps individuals recognize, challenge, and change negative thought patterns, leading to healthier emotions and behaviors. It is widely used for anxiety, depression, and stress management.

- Identifies and restructures cognitive distortions
- Encourages practical coping strategies and problem-solving
- Provides long-term tools for emotional resilience

Trauma-Focused CBT (TF-CBT): Tailored for Trauma Survivors

TF-CBT is a specialized form of cognitive therapy designed for people who have experienced trauma, particularly children and adolescents. It integrates trauma-sensitive interventions with cognitive restructuring to foster emotional healing and resilience.

- Uses gradual exposure to reduce trauma-related distress
- Helps individuals process and reframe traumatic experiences
- Involves caregivers to enhance support and recovery

Dialectical Behavior Therapy (DBT): Balancing Emotions

DBT combines mindfulness, emotional regulation, and distress tolerance techniques to help individuals manage overwhelming emotions and improve relationships. Originally developed for borderline personality disorder, it is now used for a range of emotional experiences.

- Teaches skills for distress tolerance and emotional balance
- Incorporates mindfulness for self-awareness and acceptance
- Enhances interpersonal effectiveness and relationship stability

Narrative Therapy: Reclaiming Your Story

Narrative therapy empowers individuals to reshape their personal stories, helping them gain control over their experiences and redefine their identity. It separates problems from the person, fostering a sense of empowerment and self-agency.

- Helps individuals reframe life narratives positively
- Encourages self-exploration through storytelling
- Builds resilience by redefining past experiences

Internal Family Systems (IFS): Healing the Inner Self

IFS explores different "parts" of the self, fostering internal harmony by addressing inner conflicts and promoting self-leadership. It is especially effective for trauma, anxiety, and self-compassion work.

- Identifies and integrates internal "parts" for healing
- Strengthens self-awareness and emotional balance
- Encourages self-compassion and inner harmony

Prolonged Exposure Therapy: Facing Fears

Prolonged Exposure Therapy is an evidence-based treatment for PTSD, helping individuals gradually confront and process memories to reduce fear and avoidance. Through repeated exposure, it helps regain control over distressing emotions.

- Uses gradual exposure to reduce anxiety
- Helps reprocess memories in a safe space
- Improves emotional resilience and reduces avoidance behaviors

Group Therapy: Healing Together

Group therapy offers a supportive environment where individuals connect, share experiences, and learn from one another under the guidance of a trained therapist. It fosters emotional support, self-growth, and coping skills.

- Encourages shared healing through peer support
- Provides diverse perspectives and coping strategies
- Enhances social skills and emotional resilience

Somatic and Brain-Based Trauma Healing Therapies

Focused on releasing trauma stored in the body and reprocessing traumatic memories for healing.

Somatic and brain-based trauma therapies use body awareness, breathwork, and neural reprocessing to release stored trauma and restore emotional balance. These approaches engage the mind-body connection to promote deep healing and long-term resilience.

- **Eye Movement Desensitization and Reprocessing (EMDR):** Uses guided eye movements to help reprocess and heal traumatic memories.
- **Neurofeedback:** Monitors and retrains brainwave activity to improve emotional regulation and mental clarity.
- **Somatic Experiencing (SE):** Releases trauma stored in the body by regulating nervous system responses.

- **Feldenkrais:** Uses gentle movement to retrain the brain and improve body awareness.
- **Brainspotting:** Unlocks deep trauma through focused eye positions and brain-body connections.
- **Breathwork Therapy:** Harnesses breath techniques to release emotions and promote relaxation.
- **Yoga Therapy:** Integrates movement, breath, and mindfulness to support emotional and physical healing.

Eye Movement Desensitization and Reprocessing (EMDR): Rewiring the Brain

EMDR is a structured therapy that helps individuals reprocess traumatic memories using guided eye movements. By stimulating the brain's natural healing mechanisms, it reduces emotional distress, shifts negative beliefs, and promotes resilience.

- Uses bilateral stimulation to reprocess trauma
- Reduces PTSD, anxiety, and distressing memories
- Strengthens adaptive coping mechanisms

Neurofeedback: Regulating Brainwave Activity for Emotional Balance

Neurofeedback is a brain-training technique that monitors and retrains brainwave activity to enhance emotional stability. By providing real-time feedback, it helps regulate mood, reduce stress, and improve focus.

- Uses EEG technology to optimize brain function
- Helps with anxiety, PTSD, ADHD, and depression
- Promotes self-regulation and cognitive clarity

Somatic Experiencing (SE): Releasing Trauma from the Body

SE is a body-based therapy that helps individuals release stored trauma by gently renegotiating physical tension and nervous system responses. It restores balance and resilience by completing the body's natural trauma-processing cycle.

- Focuses on bodily sensations and nervous system regulation
- Helps resolve chronic stress and trauma-related tension
- Encourages gradual, safe trauma release

Feldenkrais: Gentle Body Awareness Relearning

Feldenkrais is a movement-based therapy that improves body awareness, flexibility, and coordination. Through gentle, mindful movements, it helps release tension, rewire movement patterns, and enhance overall well-being.

- Encourages neuroplasticity through slow, intentional movement
- Reduces pain and improves posture and mobility
- Supports emotional regulation and mind-body connection

Brainspotting: Unlocking Trauma Through Focus

Brainspotting is a deep healing therapy that identifies trauma-related brain activation points through focused eye positions. It allows the brain to process and release deeply stored emotional pain.

- Uses eye positioning to access unresolved trauma
- Enhances emotional processing and self-awareness
- Effective for PTSD, anxiety, and performance blocks

Breathwork Therapy: Guided Breathing Techniques for Emotional Release and Relaxation

Breathwork therapy uses intentional breathing techniques to release emotional blockages, reduce stress, and enhance mental clarity. It activates the nervous system's healing response, promoting relaxation and emotional resilience.

- Uses breath patterns to regulate emotions and energy
- Helps release stored trauma and suppressed emotions
- Supports mindfulness, relaxation, and inner healing

Yoga Therapy: Using Movement, Breath, and Mindfulness to Regulate Emotions and Heal Trauma

Yoga therapy integrates breath, movement, and meditation to help individuals process trauma, regulate emotions, and restore physical and emotional balance. It strengthens the mind-body connection for holistic healing.

- Combines movement, breathwork, and mindfulness practices
- Helps reduce anxiety, depression, and trauma symptoms
- Enhances self-awareness, flexibility, and emotional resilience

Holistic and Energy-Based Healing Therapies

Alternative approaches addressing trauma, emotional well-being, and energy regulation.

Holistic and energy-based healing therapies focus on restoring balance to the body, mind, and spirit by addressing trauma, emotional well-being, and energy regulation. These alternative approaches promote relaxation, self-healing, and overall vitality by working with the body's natural energy systems and consciousness.

- **Craniosacral Therapy:** Gently balances the nervous system to relieve tension, stress, and trauma responses.
- **Reiki:** Channels universal life force energy to clear blockages and restore harmony.

- **Energy Enhancement System (EESystem):** Uses quantum scalar energy to promote cellular regeneration and deep healing.
- **Sound Healing Therapy:** Uses vibrational frequencies to calm the nervous system and promote relaxation.
- **Himalayan Salt Therapy:** Detoxifies the body, supports respiratory health, and reduces stress.
- **Ho'oponopono:** A Hawaiian practice of forgiveness and emotional cleansing to release negativity and restore inner peace.

Craniosacral Therapy: Nervous System Balance

Craniosacral therapy is a gentle, hands-on technique that releases tension in the craniosacral system, helping to regulate the nervous system, relieve pain, and restore balance. It enhances the body's ability to self-heal.

- Uses light touch to release restrictions in the craniosacral system
- Helps relieve stress and chronic pain
- Supports nervous system regulation and deep relaxation

Reiki: Healing Energy Balance

Reiki is an energy healing practice that channels universal life force energy to restore balance, reduce stress, and promote emotional and physical healing. Practitioners use gentle hand placements to facilitate energy flow.

- Balances energy centers (chakras) to support well-being
- Promotes relaxation, emotional clarity, and healing
- Helps release energetic blockages and stress

Energy Enhancement System (EESystem): Quantum Energy for Healing

The EESystem generates scalar waves and bioactive fields to enhance cellular regeneration, reduce stress, and promote deep healing. This quantum-based technology supports the body's natural ability to repair and rejuvenate.

- Uses scalar energy to balance the body's energy field
- Promotes deep relaxation and cellular repair
- Supports emotional, mental, and physical well-being

Sound Healing Therapy: Using Vibrations to Promote Healing

Sound healing therapy uses frequencies from instruments like singing bowls, tuning forks, and gongs to promote relaxation, reduce stress, and enhance emotional well-being. The vibrations help harmonize the body's energy.

- Uses sound frequencies to balance the body and mind
- Reduces anxiety, emotional tension, and stress
- Enhances deep meditation and relaxation

Himalayan Salt Therapy: Detoxifying the Body and Mind

Himalayan salt therapy, also known as halotherapy, involves breathing in micro-particles of salt to cleanse the respiratory system, boost immunity, and promote relaxation. It is known for its detoxifying and anti-inflammatory effects.

- Supports respiratory health and detoxification
- Helps reduce stress and improve skin conditions
- Enhances lung function and overall well-being

Ho'oponopono: Hawaiian Practice of Forgiveness and Emotional Cleansing

Ho'oponopono is an ancient Hawaiian healing practice that focuses on forgiveness, reconciliation, and emotional cleansing. Through repeated affirmations, it helps release emotional burdens, restore harmony, and promote self-healing.

- Uses the mantra: "I'm sorry, Please forgive me, Thank you, I love you."
- Helps release guilt, resentment, and emotional pain
- Promotes inner peace, healing, and self-awareness

Mindfulness and Expressive Therapies

Integrating mindfulness, creative expression, and movement for emotional healing and self-awareness.

Mindfulness and expressive therapies integrate meditation, creative expression, and movement to foster emotional healing, self-awareness, and resilience. These approaches help individuals process trauma, regulate emotions, and explore their inner world through mindfulness, art, music, movement, and storytelling.

- **Mindfulness-Based Stress Reduction (MBSR):** Uses mindfulness techniques to cultivate present-moment awareness and reduce stress.
- **Art Therapy:** Encourages emotional processing and self-expression through visual arts.
- **Music Therapy:** Utilizes sound, rhythm, and melody to enhance emotional well-being.
- **Dance/Movement Therapy (DMT):** Promotes healing by expressing emotions through body movement.
- **Drama Therapy:** Uses role-playing and storytelling for self-exploration and personal growth.

Mindfulness-Based Stress Reduction (MBSR): Anchoring in the Present

MBSR is a structured program that combines mindfulness meditation and body awareness to reduce stress, anxiety, and emotional distress. By cultivating present-moment awareness, individuals develop greater emotional resilience and self-regulation.

- Uses mindfulness techniques to manage stress and emotions
- Enhances focus, relaxation, and overall well-being
- Supports healing from anxiety, depression, and chronic pain

Art Therapy: Using Visual Arts to Process Emotions and Trauma

Art therapy allows individuals to express emotions, process trauma, and explore self-identity through creative mediums like painting, drawing, and sculpture. It fosters emotional healing without relying solely on verbal communication.

- Encourages self-expression and emotional release through art
- Helps process trauma, grief, and inner conflicts
- Supports self-discovery and emotional resilience

Music Therapy: Healing Through Sound, Rhythm, and Melody

Music therapy uses sound, rhythm, and melody to enhance emotional and psychological well-being. Listening to, creating, or moving to music helps regulate emotions, process trauma, and foster connection.

- Uses music to reduce stress, anxiety, and depression
- Enhances emotional expression and cognitive function
- Supports trauma healing and emotional regulation

Dance/Movement Therapy (DMT): Expressing Emotions Through Movement and Dance

DMT integrates movement and psychotherapy to promote emotional, cognitive, and physical well-being. It encourages self-expression, releases stored trauma, and enhances body awareness.

- Uses movement to process and express emotions
- Helps release stress and trauma stored in the body
- Promotes self-confidence, connection, and emotional healing

Drama Therapy: Role-Playing and Storytelling for Self-Exploration and Healing

Drama therapy uses role-playing, improvisation, and storytelling to help individuals explore emotions, reframe experiences, and develop new perspectives. It is an interactive and creative approach to healing.

- Encourages self-expression and emotional exploration
- Helps process trauma, anxiety, and social challenges
- Builds confidence, communication skills, and self-awareness

Reflections
Available Therapies

We invite you to explore these questions with curiosity and self-compassion. Use them to reframe challenges into opportunities for growth, gratitude, and empowerment. Share your responses with trusted people so you feel heard and understood. Revisit the questions over time to celebrate your growth.

1. Which therapeutic approaches (EMDR, somatic therapy, CBT, inner child work, etc.) feel most compelling to you, and what draws you to them?

2. What specific symptoms or patterns would you most like to address through therapy right now?

3. How do you envision your chosen therapy helping you transform the areas of your life that feel most stuck or painful?

4. What would successful healing look like for you—how would you know that therapy is working?

5. What fears or resistance do you have about beginning or deepening your therapeutic work, and how might you work through them?

6. How ready are you to commit to the time, energy, and resources that healing requires?

7. What support systems do you have in place to help you navigate the challenges that may arise during your healing journey?

8. What would you gain in your relationships, career, and personal life if you fully addressed your unresolved experiences?

9. How might your healing impact you, your family, and your community?

10. What would it cost you—emotionally, relationally, and personally—if you chose not to pursue healing at this time?

Chapter 33: The Final Blessing

"Father, forgive them; for they know not what they do."

— Jesus Christ (Luke 23:34, KJV)

I'm walking out of mother's home, the words falling from my lips like a prayer. I continue saying: "God bless you." The air between us crackles with her rage, electric and dangerous. Her voice cuts through the silence like broken glass: "How dare you say God bless you? Why do you say that to me?"

I continue to repeat it—"God bless you, God bless you, mother"— the words becoming my anchor as I compose myself, gathering every ounce of strength I have left to walk out of her presence. My legs feel unsteady. I keep moving toward the door, each step a small victory over the chaos consuming the space around us.

Hours earlier, mother and I had planned lunch together. For years, I had accommodated her drastic schedule changes, showing up to hear the same refrain: "I don't want to go anymore." I was tired of the game of who has control, tired of being jerked around by her whims.

I left the recording studio, my heart lit with excitement to see her. "Hey, mother, I'll see you soon," I had said, anticipating our time together.

Her voice on the phone was ice-cold venom: "I know you've been talking about me and our family. You need to stop it. It's not true. It's not true. You need to stop it. If you don't stop, I disown you. Forget you ever had a mother. Don't come over."

The words hit me like physical blows. I'm driving down the highway, tears flowing down my face, my heart hurting, my hands gripping the steering wheel so tightly my knuckles are white, composing myself, making sure I can arrive at my next meeting without falling apart completely. I struggle to embrace the reality of what happened—mother's continued denial of the reality I had lived, the reality she had forced upon me.

I stumble through my meeting, my nervous system completely dysregulated, while I try to appear normal, professional, put-together. Inside, I'm screaming.

After I gather myself enough to think clearly, one thought rises above the chaos: "No, mother doesn't get to decide whether I'm her daughter or not. I'm her daughter." And I drive to her apartment down the street, my heart pounding against my ribs like a wild caged bird.

A neighbor lets me into the building. When I reach mother's door, she opens it and confronts me with astonishment, "Who let you in?"

"We need to talk," I say, my voice steadier than I feel.

I look her in the eyes and speak the truth that has been burning in my chest for decades: "I am your daughter, and you will always be mother. I was a child. I was five years old. Father raped me."

I use the word rape deliberately, letting it hang in the air between us like a sword.

She is infuriated, her face contorting with rage: "You did this to me! You and your father did this to me! You were the ones who did this! I was the only victim in this situation!"

The words slam into me with the force of a freight train. These were the words that turned my entire childhood upside down. I look at her—this woman who was supposed to protect me, who is again blaming her child for her and her husband's crimes—and something inside me breaks open.

"Mother, I can't. I can't," I whisper.

I compose myself enough to walk toward the door, ready to leave this toxic space forever. I silently repeat the words, "God bless you, mother. God bless you, mother." These words become my mantra, a shield, the thing standing between me and complete collapse.

As I reach for the handle, I look back at her and say out loud, "God bless you, mother."

She reacts with vicious anger, her voice a snarl, "How dare you say God bless you to me!"

"Those are the only words I can think of," I tell her, my voice barely above a whisper. "I'm walking out."

Her final words follow me like daggers, "I was the only victim in this experience!"

I keep walking on the verge of breaking down completely. I continue to say to myself, through the tears, through the devastation, through the complete shattering of any hope I had left, "God bless you, mother."

What else do you say to a woman who was supposed to protect you and chose to blame you instead? What else do you say to a mother who looks at her raped child and declares herself the victim?

You bless her, because she is so consumed by her own pain that she refuses to see the child standing in front of her, bleeding from wounds she inflicted on me.

You bless her, and then you walk away.

Epilogue

Where there is righteousness in the heart, there is beauty in the character. When there is beauty in the character, there is harmony in the home. When there is harmony in the home, there is order in the nation. When there is order in the nation, there is peace in the world.

— A. P. J. Abdul Kalam

The most profound truths we have learned through decades of healing, transformation, and guiding others to thriving.

The Myth of Universal Understanding

One of the biggest misconceptions people carry is that we're all at the same place in our journey because we are physically together. When you have unresolved complex trauma, you're in a completely different universe where:

- Gravity pulls differently
- The air feels thinner
- Every breath is precious
- Feelings hijack us

This is the reality for those navigating complex trauma.

Beyond the Gratitude Trap

When people casually say, "Just be grateful!" they do not understand our experience. It's about being in a constant state of fear. It's about counting breaths. It's about making it through the next minute, the next hour, the next day, the next inevitable crisis.

What Protective Mode Really Steals

Protective mode impacts your mood and hijacks your entire human experience:

- Clear thinking disappears
- Deep connections become impossible
- Creativity vanishes
- Emotional regulation breaks down
- Present moment awareness dissolves
- Self-care becomes a distant concept
- Future vision feels like a threat

Everyone Understands This: When someone is in protective mode, they may be dysregulated and without the capacity to function. This may last for minutes, days, months, years, or even decades.

The Truth Behind Our Behaviors: These are protective mechanisms: procrastination, impostor syndrome, self-sabotage, and others. They are automatic tools developed in fundamentally unsafe environments.

The Uniqueness of Human Experience: We are unique beings, each with our own world of experience. As my grandmother would say, "Every mind is its own world." Each of us has had different experiences and different reactions to those experiences.

The Journey of Understanding: True empathy comes from walking our own healing path. The more we understand ourselves, the more compassionately we can understand others.

The Hope That Heals: Here's the transformative truth, healing is possible. The heart can open. The nervous system can learn safety. People can move to truly living.

To Those on The Other Side of Healing

It's like watching a butterfly, wings still damp from the cocoon, telling all the untransformed caterpillars to get up and fly. The butterfly forgets what it was like to be a caterpillar. In the miraculous transformation occurring in the cocoon, the memories of the experience of being a caterpillar are erased. The butterfly believes it has always been a butterfly.

We watch it happen often—that profound imperceptible shift in you. In the moment of healing, when you burst forth from the cocoon you made (believing it would keep you safe), you inhale the sweet air of freedom. You forget the weight that once pressed against your chest so heavily that breathing felt like betrayal. You forget when silence screamed louder than sound. You forget what it felt like when the only way to cope with the experience was to become numb to it. You believe you've always been this way. You now become self-righteous, saying to the others: "I've done my work, now do yours. Just heal. The past is in the past. Forgive and move on. Choose happiness."

I invite you to have compassion.

For those of us who have walked through the fire of healing, who have emerged from the cocoon and stepped into the light of transformation, may we always walk with compassion toward others, finding their way. Once upon a time, someone met us there—in our trembling, in our confusion, in our pain—and offered us compassion.

That compassion becomes a bridge.

That bridge becomes a lifeline.

And that lifeline becomes the very reason we can rise.

Authors' Reflection

Rocío and David began this journey as fellow travelers mapping a landscape of healing that has been too often misunderstood, too frequently silenced.

Our collaboration emerged from a profound recognition: trauma is a collective human story. What happens to one of us impacts all of us. The wounds we carry are beyond personal—they are ancestral, systemic, and deeply interconnected.

Through *Identity Alchemy*, we created a living, breathing testament to human resilience—a map for those finding their way through the darkness. A mirror that reflects the pain and the extraordinary capacity for transformation that resides within each of us.

We've shared stories previously hidden—stories of abuse, of reclaiming power, of turning the most profound pain into revolutionary healing. These narratives are invitations. Invitations to see yourself, to recognize your own strength, to understand that your experience is valid, that your healing matters.

Healing is more than a solitary journey. It invites being witnessed. It invites community involvement. It asks for the courage to be seen, to be vulnerable, to admit that we are all—in our own ways—in the process of becoming.

We wrote this book from a place of continuous learning. Every client story, every shared moment of breakthrough, every tear, every revelation has been a teacher. We continue to be students of this profound journey of transformation.

To those reading this, know that your story matters. Your pain is a portal to a fulfilled life. ***No darkness is too great to overcome.***

Healing is a revolutionary act of choosing yourself, over and over again. It is about creating space for all of who you are—the wounded parts and the Warrior parts. The parts that remember and the parts that are ready to be reborn.

We offer *Identity Alchemy* as a beginning. A conversation. A bridge between what was and what could be.

This is the true alchemy—turning pain into gold and using that gold to light the way for others.

May you find the courage to do your inner work, the compassion to hold space for others, and the wisdom to celebrate every healing step.

Writing this book has been a life-changing journey for us. May this book be a companion on your journey. May it remind you that no journey is too dark to overcome. May it reflect back to you the extraordinary light that has always lived within you, waiting to be remembered.

May your healing make the world a safer and kinder place.

With love,

Rocío Pérez, IMBA & Dr. David Wheeler
The Identity Alchemists

Discover more beyond these pages.
Scan the QR codes and extend the experience.

http://bit.ly/4pNgBGd

IDENTITY ALCHEMY

https://bit.ly/4pUO0yX

skool

www.themindshiftgame.com/

THE
MINDSHIFT
GAME.
by Rocío Pérez

NOTES

NOTES

____

____

____

____

____

____

____

____

____

____

____

Rocío Pérez, IMBA & Dr. David Wheeler

**IDENTITY
ALCHEMY**

http://bit.ly/4pNgBGd

Rocío Pérez, IMBA & Dr. David Wheeler

IDENTITY
ALCHEMY

http://bit.ly/4pNgBGd

NOTES

____

____

____

____

____

____

____

____

____

____

____

Rocío Pérez, IMBA & Dr. David Wheeler

**IDENTITY
ALCHEMY**

http://bit.ly/4pNgBGd

NOTES

NOTES

Rocío Pérez, IMBA & Dr. David Wheeler

**IDENTITY
ALCHEMY**

http://bit.ly/4pNgBGd

NOTES

___

NOTES

Rocío Pérez, IMBA & Dr. David Wheeler

**IDENTITY
ALCHEMY**

http://bit.ly/4pNgBGd

NOTES

____

____

____

____

____

____

____

____

____

____

____

____

Rocío Pérez, IMBA & Dr. David Wheeler

IDENTITY
ALCHEMY

http://bit.ly/4pNgBGd